ALSO BY MICHAEL CORCORAN

*The Golf Dictionary*
*Break 100 Now*
*The PGA Tour Complete Book of Golf*
*Never Out of the Hole: How to Win at Match Play*
*How to Break 90*
*The Golfer's Guide to the Meaning of Life* (with Gary Player)

# DUEL
# IN THE
# SUN

### TOM WATSON AND JACK NICKLAUS
### IN THE BATTLE OF TURNBERRY

## Michael Corcoran

SIMON & SCHUSTER

NEW YORK · LONDON · TORONTO · SYDNEY · SINGAPORE

SIMON & SCHUSTER
Rockefeller Center
1230 Avenue of the Americas
New York, NY 10020

SIMON & SCHUSTER and colophon are registered trademarks
of Simon & Schuster Inc.

For information regarding special discounts for bulk purchases,
please contact Simon & Schuster Special Sales at
1-800-456-6798 or business@simonandschuster.com

Manufactured in the United States of America

1   3   5   7   9   10   8   6   4   2

Library of Congress Cataloging-in-Publication Data
Corcoran, Mike.
Duel in the sun : Tom Watson and Jack Nicklaus in the battle of Turnberry / Michael Corcoran.
p.   cm.
1.  British Open (Golf tournament) (1977 : Turnberry, Scotland)
2.  Watson, Tom, 1949–    3.  Nicklaus, Jack.   I.  Title.

GV970.3 C67 2002
796.352'66—dc21                                                    2002025156
ISBN 0-7432-0310-0

FOR BIFF AND MARY
&
BILL AND TERRY

*The coast, the course, and the Turnberry Hotel. (Credit: Courtesy of Leonardo.com)*

*Long live the king: Jack Nicklaus and Arnold Palmer at the U.S. Open at Oakmont in 1962, where Nicklaus defeated Palmer in an eighteen-hole play-off. (Credit: AP/Wide World Photos)*

*Tom and Linda Watson at Carnoustie, 1975. (Credit: AP/Wide World Photos)*

*Nicklaus and Watson make their way through the shirtsleeved (and shirtless) crowd. (Credit: Phil Sheldon)*

*Hubert Green and Roger Maltbie, among the leaders at the start of the third round, wait out Friday's lightning storm. (Credit: AP/Wide World Photos)*

*Nicklaus, Watson, and Alfie Fyles on the rocks during the storm. (Credit: Phil Sheldon)*

Nicklaus and Watson, accompanied by their caddies Angelo Argea and Alfie Fyles (Credit: AP/Wide World Photos)

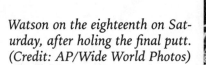

Watson on the eighteenth on Saturday, after holing the final putt. (Credit: AP/Wide World Photos)

Turnberry lighthouse and Ailsa Craig. (Credit: Tony Roberts)

# PROLOGUE

⭐

GOLF AT THE HIGHEST LEVEL OF THE PROFESSIONAL game is a contest spread out over four eighteen-hole rounds, one round per day on four successive days. The winner is the player who records the fewest total strokes for the four rounds. This type of competition is known as stroke play, and it is one of the two basic competitive formats in golf. The other widely used format is match play, and it is the preferred form of competition among amateur enthusiasts of the game because it disregards the total number of strokes taken during a round and instead pits a player against his opponent on a hole-by-hole basis. There is nothing subtle about match play: While the stroke play event unfolds slowly and encourages conservative tactics, match play is a fistfight from the moment the first shot is struck. There is resolution on each hole of match play, and as such it appeals to the basic human desire to prove superiority over others. In short, a golfer engaged in match play feels as though he is fighting for survival on every shot.

As professional golf evolved from the mid-1800s and throughout the twentieth century, players and bureaucrats concurred that the best way to determine the world's champion golfers was stroke play. For the competitors, tournament organizers, and starting in the early 1960s, television networks, this made sense. In regard to the manner in which it challenges competitors, stroke play is more difficult. It means that every single stroke over four days is significant. A single bad hole out of the seventy-two can wreck a player's chances.

The player who wins a professional stroke-play event is unquestionably a superb golfer, but more often than not he secures victory in a manner that lacks a true sense of struggle against anyone other than himself. There is no guarantee that he will be playing in the same group and battling his nearest competitor(s) as the tournament reaches its climax. In fact, golf fans very seldom get to witness two gigantic talents playing side-by-side in a tourna-

1

ment of historic significance where the opponents, quite literally, match each other blow for blow over the length of an entire day. It is for this very reason that golf strikes many people as a dull game. When Tiger Woods won four consecutive major championships in the 2000 and 2001 seasons, the feat was correctly regarded as astounding, and praise, fame, and money rained down upon him as well it should have . . . and yet many golf fans found Woods's run left them feeling numb. Three of his victories were won handily, and the other, the 2000 PGA Championship, was high on drama but came at the expense of a player (Bob May) with whom most fans were completely unfamiliar. For all of Woods's supreme effort and accomplishment, the golf fan was left to marvel strictly at his talent. Left unfulfilled was the yearning on the part of golf fans to see the greatest champion of his day face down, *mano a mano*, another player vying to establish himself as one of history's great players.

The stroke-play format, for all of its fairness, has seldom produced a prolonged man-to-man battle between great players, where every stroke was played with the match-play survival instinct surging through the minds of the two golfers. But in 1977, on the southwest coast of Scotland, such a confrontation took place. During a scorching hot week in July, Jack Nicklaus, by then regarded as the best player the game had ever known, fought furiously with Tom Watson, a talented and cerebral young man bent on joining Nicklaus in the upper echelon of the game. Playing together—just the two of them—over two days and thirty-six holes, they distanced themselves from the rest of the field to such a degree that they were competing solely against each other. At stake was the game's oldest and most sought-after title, the Open Championship, and Nicklaus's position as the world's dominant player. The outcome would be decided in the oldest way known to man: face to face.

# ONE

★

IN THE SUMMER OF 1977, THE EIGHT BEST GOLFERS IN the world were all veteran American players. Jack Nicklaus was the most accomplished player and the biggest star among a murderer's row that included Lee Trevino, Tom Weiskopf, Johnny Miller, Raymond Floyd, Hubert Green, Hale Irwin, and Tom Watson. When these eight players teed it up at the Open Championship at Turnberry in southwest Scotland during the first full week of July that year, they were joined by an emerging threesome of extraordinary talent that would one day rise to eminence: nineteen-year-old Nick Faldo of England, twenty-year-old Severiano Ballesteros of Spain, and twenty-two-year-old Greg Norman of Australia. The scions of America's championship golf tradition, led by twenty-three-year-old Jerry Pate and twenty-five-year-old Ben Crenshaw, were also on hand at the Turnberry Hotel that week to compete in the 106th playing of the Open Championship. It was the first time that Turnberry had hosted the Open.

There were, of course, other big-name golfers at Turnberry, including the biggest name of them all. At age forty-seven, Arnold Palmer's best days as a player were behind him, but he was still the most recognizable golfer in the world. He was alone among the U.S. players in remembering and experiencing a time not even twenty years before when America's best golfers were reluctant to play in the Open. Some were undoubtedly too small-minded to grasp the significance of competing in the Open, a condition that was aggravated by the small amount of prize money available. Others shrunk from the challenge simply because of the arduous journey to Britain and the fact that, having made the journey, they would still have to survive two qualifying rounds before they even got to play in the championship proper. Still another obstacle in the days before widespread and convenient transatlantic air service was the proximity on the calendar of the U.S. PGA Championship to the Open—the two were usually held within a week or two of each other.

Arnold Palmer went to Scotland to compete in the Open for the first time in 1960, and it would be inaccurate to say that America's undivided attention was focused on him when he crossed the Atlantic Ocean in late June. The Cold War, which had shown signs of reduced tension between the U.S. and Soviet Russia early in the year, had turned more bitter than ever in May when CIA-employed Gary Powers was shot down over Russia in his U-2 spy plane. It was also a presidential election year, and in the summertime the campaign of the young Irish Catholic senator from Massachusetts, John F. Kennedy, was gaining momentum. Sports fans in the States, however, had very little to distract their interest in Palmer's trip to the Open; his timing was just right. When the Olympics started in late August, Americans would be enthralled by the triumphs of Al Oerter, Rafer Johnson, and a skinny light-heavyweight boxer from Louisville, Kentucky, named Cassius Clay. When the World Series was played in the fall, it would feature the New York Yankees for the twenty-fifth time since 1920, led by American League MVP Roger Maris and Mickey Mantle. Despite their big name players, the Yankees lost in the seventh game when Pittsburgh's Bill Mazeroski slugged a ninth-inning home run. A few months after that, Philadelphia Eagles linebacker Chuck Bednarik would sit on top of Green Bay running back Jim Taylor as the clock ran out in the NFL Championship Game at the University of Pennsylvania's Franklin Field. In the sports championship void of high summer, however, Palmer was the biggest news in American sports. When he traveled first to Ireland to play in a tournament called the Canada Cup, and then on to St. Andrews for the Open, the sporting public's interest went along with him.

Palmer's professional contemporaries in America at the time certainly took note of his trip, and since he had been beating their brains out all year, were probably glad to hear he wouldn't be around for a few weeks. With the exception of Palmer, top-level American professional golfers in 1960 thought all the talk of the history surrounding the Open Championship and the significance of winning it was just so much flapdoodle when you got right down to it. American players reasoned that a trip to the Open was a money-losing proposition *even if they won top prize* (which in 1960 was £1,250, or $3,500), and cited this as the reason they stayed home instead of trekking to Great Britain to try to win the game's grandest championship. Henry Longhurst, the brilliant English writer, didn't hold it against them. "With so much money at stake at home," wrote Longhurst in 1959, "the leading American professionals no longer venture across the Atlantic as [Walter] Hagen and [Gene] Sarazen did in the golden age of golf. Much as we may regret it in Britain, we can hardly blame them, yet I venture to believe that they lose something by not coming at least once, and that even [Ben] Hogan felt that the British Open added a sense of completeness to his career."

Palmer's bid for the Open title at St. Andrews in 1960 would be only the fourth by a leading American professional at the top of his game since the championship resumed after World War II. Frank Stranahan, an American amateur and heir to the Champion spark plug fortune, finished as the runner-up in the 1947 and 1953 Opens and played in the tournament regularly during the postwar years. Sam Snead, from West Virginia, won the first Open played after the war, in 1946 at St. Andrews, and then not a peep was heard from America's best professionals until 1953, when Texan Ben Hogan arrived to play in his one and only Open at Carnoustie on Scotland's east coast. Hogan won, adding the Open to the Masters and U.S. Open titles he won earlier in the year. He was the only player to win three professional majors in a single season until Tiger Woods matched the feat forty-seven years later. The Scots admired Hogan's single-mindedness, but quickly realized he lacked a warm side in public, dubbing him "the Wee Ice Mon."

During the postwar years, appearances by Americans were so rare that it was news during the 1951 Open that an American caddied in the tournament. His name was Bob Carlsson, and he wore a University of California sweatshirt while working the bag for K.E. Enderby. In 1955, the top American finisher was Ed Furgol, who had won the 1954 U.S. Open. Furgol finished eleven shots behind the winner, Australian Peter Thomson, and was joined in the field by Americans Johnny Bulla and Byron Nelson, who had by then retired from competitive golf. In 1956, the Open was played in England and Snead and Hogan were there just prior to the championship to play in the Canada Cup. Neither bothered to play in the Open. American Cary Middlecoff made the trip in 1957, one year after winning his second U.S. Open, but in 1958 the only recognizable American face at the Open belonged to fifty-six-year-old Gene Sarazen, who won the championship in 1932.

The 1959 Open was played near Edinburgh at a golf course called Muirfield, the home course of the oldest golf club in the world, the Honourable Company of Edinburgh Golfers, established in 1744. (It is worth noting here that a golf *club* is a group of people—members—and the golf *course* is the playing field used by the members of the club.) Despite the venerable site, not a single American professional showed up. The top golfers from the rest of the world were there, however: Fred Daly from Ireland; Bobby Locke and Gary Player from South Africa; Antonio Cerda and Roberto De Vicenzo from Argentina; Dai Rees from Wales; Flory Van Donck from Belgium; Kel Nagle and Peter Thomson from Australia, who found the excuse of inadequate prize money a poor reason for not playing in the Open. "I know I was making money, or I wouldn't have been going," said Thomson. "The first prize I won at the Open was £750. You could buy a reasonable house for that amount in those days. There was plenty of money to be made out of winning the Open Championship, but there wasn't much to be made by coming in second. Anyone who went to the Open worried about not getting their money back was probably better off out of it anyway."

Fifty years after he made his first trip to Britain in 1951, Peter Thomson recalled that "it took three days because a single air crew took the plane the whole way, and they had to rest every night. After leaving Australia, we stopped the first night in Singapore. The next night was spent in Karachi, and on the third night we finally made it to London. That was if the plane didn't break down, of course. In those days there were frequent breakdowns. It was a great adventure for me. I was a young man on a fact-finding mission." Thomson made regular trips to compete in the U.S. Open as well.

The Argentine De Vicenzo on occasion endured even more than Thomson to play in the old championship. "It is not so easy to get there," said De Vicenzo in broken English fifty-two years after he first made the trip. "I play for first time in 1948 and finish pretty good behind Henry Cotton. I keep this in mind and come back next year and I did good again. Then I decide to play every year. One year, I think it was 1949, I think I cannot go because I do not have the money to go on the plane. Some fellow at a boat company give me a free ticket to go, and it took seventeen days to get to England. When I woke up in Liverpool, I walk off the ship looking like a lost golf player."

South African Gary Player won the 1959 Open at Muirfield, but the talk of the town early in the week was "Papwa" Sewsunker Sewgolum, an Indian-born man playing out of Durban, South Africa, who shot a seventy-one in the qualifying rounds using a cross-handed grip. (For a right-handed player, which Sewgolum was, that meant placing his left hand lower on the club, beneath his right hand.) A black South African named Edward Johnson-Sedibe also tried to qualify to play at Muirfield. He borrowed a set of clubs, turned in a score of eighty-eight in the qualifying and told anyone who listened that he liked being there so much that he planned on sticking around, especially if someone would give him a ride to London. The journey from South Africa to Edinburgh was certainly more daunting and expensive than a trip to the same destination from New York, and if Johnson-Sedibe, a player who didn't even have his own clubs, understood what just having a chance to compete in the Open should mean to anyone who loved the game, were America's best players simply myopic in completely dismissing the Open?

The easy answer to that question is yes. The one thing American professionals could see clearly was the dollar sign. Palmer had won $14,400 when he won the U.S. Open in June 1960, roughly four times more than he would get if he won at St. Andrews. The prize money had never been big in the Open, but the lack of it hadn't deterred adventurous American professionals like Walter Hagen and Gene Sarazen from going to Britain in the 1920s and '30s to see how they stacked up against the rest of the world. Compared to the players who came before them, American tour players in 1960 were living large. Writing in the May 2, 1960, issue of *Sports Illustrated*, Herbert Warren Wind noted that the young Americans, led by Palmer, "were fortunate in hitting the pro ranks at the golden moment when purses were reaching new highs, and endorsements and promotions frequently doubled what they earned in prize money." Wind, a keen observer of the game and its trends who also wrote about golf for many years for *The New Yorker*, was dead on the mark. Even players who *completely* lacked Palmer's appeal were making endorsement income. The magazine advertisements of the time support Wind's observation: *Bob Goalby Autographed Clubs by Rawlings. More and more the choice of the young pro; Dow Finsterwald won the Los Angeles Open in Munsingwear. Winners wear Grand Slam Golf Shirts by Munsingwear.* Don January won the Tucson Open wearing Munsingwear, too. A golf ball advertisement for U.S. Royal golf balls summed things up nicely. Beneath photos of Ken Venturi, Fred Hawkins, Al Besselink, Bill Collins, and Howie Johnson, the copy reads: *Major tournament winners say: "You're longer off the tee with U.S. Royal . . . the ball with H.I.V.!"* Several decades before the world was familiar with the AIDS virus, "the ball with H.I.V." was not the shocking thing about the advertisement (it stood for "high initial velocity"). What was astonishing was that as of 1960 none of those five men had won a professional golf championship of historic significance. The money they made from these endorsements certainly paled in comparison to the bounty reaped by current-day professionals, but it was income nonetheless.

America's leading golfers in 1960 were not a destitute lot who couldn't afford a trip to the Open. The median annual family income in America in the mid-1950s was $5,657. From 1949 to 1959 the lowest amount won by the leading money winner on the American golf tour was $26,088.83 by Sam Snead in 1951. By 1954, Bob Toski had more than doubled that total by winning $65,819.81. Palmer led the list in 1958 with $42,607.50. Even considering the expense of traveling to play on the American tour, the top money earners could have gone to the Open with some degree of regularity if they had any desire to prove they were the best in the world, even if it meant stretching the family finances and even if they made the trip only every other year. Where was the desire to prove oneself against the best that all professional athletes claim burns deep within? Moreover, what happened to the sense of adventure that Americans claim is part of their national heritage?

The reasons American players stayed away from the Open had to be deeper than money, and they were. The United States had emerged from World War II as the wealthiest and most advanced nation in the world in terms of technology and creature comforts. It never took much for Americans to assume that anything at home was better than what the rest of the world had, and during the postwar Eisenhower years this feeling ran deeper than ever. (Incidentally, Ike himself took to the links of Scotland. Grateful for his wartime service, the British had given him the run of the joint at Culzean Castle, just down the road from Turnberry. He played more than a few rounds at Turnberry.) "In those days," said Bob Toski nearly fifty years after he led American money winners, "if you were tops in America, you were tops in the world. The strength of the foreign players was nothing like it is today. I didn't have anything to prove by going over there. Even if I won, it wouldn't have covered the expense involved." For Toski and his fellow American professionals, it was easy to feel justified in their belief that professional golf in the U.S. was the game at its highest level. American teams regularly routed those from Great Britain during the biennial Ryder Cup competition, and non-American players rarely won significant tournaments in the U.S.

There were other reasons the Open did not appeal to American players. The golf courses used for the Open were not watered except when it rained, and this meant that the ball could take unpredictable bounces when it landed. At the time, competitive rules set by the Royal and Ancient Golf Club of St. Andrews (the Open's organizing body) dictated the use of a ball that was smaller in circumference than the 1.68-inch one used in America. The 1.62-inch "British" ball required some getting used to on the part of visiting players. As such, the Open Championships of the late 1940s and 1950s were viewed as an aberrant form of the game that favored those who grew up playing it. On the basis of what they knew of foreign golfers, American players could easily convince themselves that the Los Angeles Open had a better field than the so-called world championship played each summer in Great Britain. The great American players of the first half of the twentieth century had looked across the ocean and seen the world's best players embodied by the likes of England's Harry Vardon. An American golfer in the 1950s looked across the sea and saw nothing.

The American distaste for the Open was acquired at the expense of British golf fans, particularly the Scots. The British fans wanted to see *all* of the best players compete in their championship, and that included the Americans. Their love for the game was uncompromising; they were even interested in the week-to-week tournaments in the States, not to mention the three major championships played there. *The Evening Telegraph,* a Scottish newspaper, ran an American comic strip called "MacDivot" and encouraged readers to "sit back and travel the tough American golf circuit. Follow Sandy's adventures on the dollar trail in the exciting MacDivot picture strip."

Essentially, the leading professional golfers in America during the mid- and late 1950s didn't care one wit about the British readers of "MacDivot" or about what Longhurst described as a "sense of completeness" to their careers. The reality was that America's best players had rather lazily turned their backs on the game's oldest championship. The fact that every American player who sought true greatness before them had competed in the Open Championship was lost on all of them but one.


THE GOLF TOURNAMENT that American sports fans routinely refer to as the British Open does not have the word "British" in its name. It is simply the Open Championship. The qualifying "British" is a convenient way of distinguishing between the Open Championship and the U.S. Open Championship and was put into use by writers with an American audience. Over the years, American fans and most American professional golfers have considered their own U.S. Open to be the premier championship in the world and as such attribute to British snobbery any suggestion that the British version is *the* Open. There is, however, no arrogance involved in referring to the world's oldest golf championship as the Open. In fact, aside from the fact that it is sometimes held on golf courses in England and occasionally won by English golfers, the Open is not so much British as it is Scottish. (The current-day Great Britain is composed of England, Scotland, Wales, and Northern Ireland. Each has a very distinct national identity while still acknowledging a single monarchy, the House of Windsor, embodied by Queen Elizabeth.) The championship's roots are in Scotland, and to this day it is conducted by the Royal and Ancient Golf Club of St. Andrews, Scotland (R&A), a body that is the game's primary governing and rule-making body throughout the world with the exceptions of the U.S. and Mexico. For the first thirty-five years of the Open's existence, there were no other meaningful championships that allowed professionals to compete, hence there was no need to call it anything other than the Open Championship. (It is only logical, and the same principle pops up in other places. British golf professionals are members of the Professional Golfers' Association, whereas their American counterparts are members of the Professional Golfers' Association of America. When the British formed their association, no other group of golf professionals existed. Similarly, the amateur championship of Great Britain, first played in 1885, is known as the Amateur Championship.)

When the Open was first played in 1860, it's unlikely that anyone in London or the rest of England even knew it had taken place. Certainly no one in America was aware that it had. The first transatlantic cable between the U.S. and Britain had been completed two years before, but broke after just a few weeks, laying silent until 1866. Even if another method of quickly and effectively transmitting the news had existed (it didn't), most Americans didn't care about anything that was happening elsewhere in the world. The few Americans who had time to pursue leisure activities in 1860 certainly weren't playing golf. In New York, a man might pass some time at Harry Hill's sporting house, watching and wagering on which of two game-cocks with razors affixed to their claws would kill the other. If he grew bored of that, he might go across town to Sportman's Hall to watch a rat-baiting handicap or classic. The hall held 250 spectators who paid up to a $1.50 to watch a handicap, in which a dog was timed to see how long it would take to kill its weight in rats, and $5 to watch a classic, where a specially trained terrier was thrown into an eight-foot-long pit with one hundred rats and timed to see how long it would take him to dispatch of all of them. The best terriers could get the job done in twenty minutes.

Only six million Americans—about one in five—lived in urban environments in 1860, so amusement took on whatever form was handy in rural areas. When they had time for entertainment out on the farms, they turned to things such as cornhusking and country dances. The family might gather in the parlor at night and take turns reading to one another or play Dumb Crambo, a game similar to charades. During the day they *were* playing a game that had British roots, but it wasn't golf. It was baseball, which in rural America at the time was called barn ball, old-cat, or town ball.

Across the Atlantic, after having suppressed the rebellion in India in 1858, Great Britain was at peace. Queen Victoria was one-third of the way through her reign, placing the still vast British Empire in the midst of what history would come to refer to as the Victorian Age. With the empire having set aside war for the moment, its citizens had time to reflect upon more cerebral pursuits. In 1859 they were shoved directly into the deepest intellectual question of them all with the publication of Charles Darwin's *On the Origin of the Species by Means of Natural Selection*. Those who couldn't be bothered with Darwin's evolutionary theories could divert themselves by reading Charles Dickens's newest work, *A Tale of Two Cities*. It would still be a few years before they would see the words of Walt Whitman's "I Hear America Singing," which was written in 1860, but it is probable that the thing of primary interest to them from America was not poetry but whether or not the Union's naval blockade of the Confederacy would affect shipments of cotton to Britain. (It did. By the end of 1862, 458,000 people who worked in Britain's cotton-related industries were out of work and collecting relief administered by the Poor Law Board.) Members of the upper class might have heard news from the continent regarding Claude Monet and a chap named Renoir, two emerging artists, or perhaps of a young man named Paul Morphy, an American from New Orleans who was touring Europe and successfully defeating all comers at the chessboard.

Up in Scotland (up from England, that is), many of Her Majesty's subjects were using their free time to pursue the game of golf. They had been doing so for hundreds of years by the time Victoria ascended to the throne, and certainly during the reign of King James IV of Scotland (1488 to 1513), who has gone down in history as the man who issued the royal order banning "futeball and golfe" because he felt it was interfering with the archery practice of his soldiers. It turned out the king was correct: When he led his army in an invasion of England in 1513, he and his forces met the English at the Battle of Flodden. At day's end, James IV and most of his men lay "cauld in the clay." The surviving Scots presumably retreated to Scotland and resumed playing golf. James IV was the grandfather of Mary Queen of Scots, who herself enjoyed playing golf before being deposed in 1567. Kings and queens continued to pursue the game despite Mary's bad luck (she was eventually beheaded), but job responsibilities kept getting in the way. Charles I of England was playing a round of golf on the course in Leith (near Edinburgh) in 1641 when a rider approached carrying news of the Irish Rebellion. While the rider knelt before his sovereign, his horse munched quietly on the grass.

The round of golf being played by Charles I when he was so rudely interrupted was not all that dissimilar from the modern game. For certain, the clubs and balls were different, as were the rules and the number of holes that were played. Nevertheless, if an observer from the early days of the twenty-first century were spirited back to that day on the Leith links, he would undoubtedly realize that Charles I was playing golf.


FORTY YEARS AFTER he went to St. Andrews in 1960, Arnold Palmer said that he made that trip because he remembered reading about the British Open as a schoolboy and seeing other accounts of players such as "Bob Jones and Walter Hagen, who not only played in the Open, but won it. Ever since I had robbed my wife, Winnie, of a Walker Cup honeymoon by turning pro late in the fall of 1954 after winning the National Amateur, I'd had it in my mind to play in the British Open. [The Walker Cup is a biennial match between amateurs from the U.S. and those from Great Britain and Ireland. The 1955 Walker Cup was played at St. Andrews.] I went in 1960 because it was at St. Andrews, and by then I had done well enough to afford to go. Of course, it turned out to be especially important after I won the Masters and the U.S. Open earlier that year." Palmer was on track to be the first professional golfer to win all four of golf's major professional championships in a single year. After watching Palmer pull off the largest ever final-round comeback to win the U.S. Open in June, Herbert Warren Wind wrote in *Sports Illustrated* that Palmer had "unshakable faith in himself and is wonderfully ambitious. Behind him lie the Masters and the U.S. Open now and before him the Centenary British Open. He will go to St. Andrews with a very good chance to continue his sweep [of all the major titles in a single year], for here is not only a marvelous golfer but, if you will forgive a Victorian phrase, he seems to be destiny's favorite."

Palmer's timing was propitious for the Open Championship as well as himself. The championship was celebrating its one-hundred-year anniversary, but its age was showing in the worst possible way. The championship *was* old, so old in fact that even Palmer probably didn't quite comprehend its true age. The Open predated the sinking of the *Titanic* by fifty-two years, the Wright Brothers' flight at Kitty Hawk by forty-three years ("No Balloon Attached to Aid It!" cried the headline in the *Virginian-Pilot* newspaper), the massacre at Little Bighorn by sixteen years, the Transcontinental Railroad by nine, and the first bank robbery by Frank and Jesse James by six.

It's considerable age, however, wasn't enough to bolster the Open's fading prestige. The failure on the part of the best American players to fully participate had damaged the tournament. America had the most of a lot of things, among them the most recreational golfers (golf fans) and the most top-shelf professional players, and the absence of America's best players and the interest of its fans had pushed the Open to the brink of becoming an anachronism. The thing that had always made the Open stand alone in the world of golf was that it was the de facto world championship played in the land where the game began—a championship that not only was open to all who aspired to play in it (assuming they were good enough), but one that encouraged and nurtured the perception of itself as a true international event. It had been that way almost from the outset in 1860 when the members of the Prestwick Golf Club, on the west coast of Scotland, laid the foundation for the Open. (While even nongolfers are aware of St. Andrews's reputation as the "home of golf," that town is on Scotland's east coast, on the opposite side of the country from Prestwick. St. Andrews is indeed the spiritual home of golf and is today the "home" of the Open insofar that the tournament's organizing body resides there. The Open's "birthplace," however, is Prestwick.)

The need to have a recognized champion in any pursuit of physical and mental skill is as old as man, a requisite for the content existence of both the highly skilled competitors and the not-so-talented who gather around to watch them. Contests of skill exist in every culture for two reasons: They lessen the tedium of life and, more important, they resolve doubt, which is one thing humans have a lower tolerance for than tedium. It was the gnawing of doubt that led to the Open. Throughout the 1850s, everyone in Scotland who knew anything about golf knew that Allan Robertson was the best golfer of them all. Robertson, who is regarded as the first golf professional in history, earned his living crafting golf clubs and balls (by boiling enough goose feathers to fill a top hat, stuffing them into a leather casing, and sewing it shut) at his shop in St. Andrews. On occasion, Robertson would put aside his tools and take to the links, where he had a reputation as a money player. The high-stakes games of the day had more in common with Thoroughbred racing than with today's modern professional golf tournaments. In Robertson's day, individuals would financially "back" players in competition, and during the course of play, spectators would crowd around the players and make countless bets as well. Robertson was considered the top gun in such matches and had been so since 1849 when he teamed with his understudy, Tom Morris, to defeat Willie and Tom Dunn of Musselburgh, with £400 up for grabs. When Robertson died in 1859, it left a void in the minds of the game's enthusiasts—there was no one who could be pointed to as the champion golfer among all others.

At the spring meeting of the members at Prestwick on May 30, 1860, one of Her Majesty's officers proposed a solution to the "problem" facing the golfers of Scotland. He was Major J.O. Fairlie, and his idea was that "a private subscription should be opened with a view to procure a Medal for *professionals* [author's emphasis] to be competed for under regulations submitted to the meeting." The men in the room immediately consented to put five guineas toward the purchase of the medal, with the hope that the other leading clubs in Scotland would contribute funds as well. They did not, and Prestwick was left holding the bag as it were. Undaunted, the men of Prestwick assumed the sole responsibility of creating the championship, and they eventually provided thirty guineas from the club's coffers for the purchase of a red morocco leather belt with silver plates attached to it. It was called the Challenge Belt, and the members of Prestwick declared that any man who won it three years running would take permanent possession of it.

On Wednesday, October 17, 1860, the tournament for the Challenge Belt was played at Prestwick. There were eight players in the field, and in that single day they went around the twelve-hole Prestwick links three times for a total of thirty-six holes. To understand how the Open actually became "open," it is important to review the scores of the eight men: Willie Park (174), Tom Morris (176), Andrew Strath (180), Bob Andrew (191), Daniel Brown (192), Charlie Hunter (195), Alex Smith (196), and William Steel (232). The three leading players, Park, the winner, Morris, and Strath played superb golf by the day's standards, with Park and Morris averaging slightly less than five strokes per hole and Strath averaging precisely five strokes. After those three players, the scoring dropped off significantly, with the last-place finisher Steel taking an average of between six and seven strokes per hole.

When the spring meeting of the Prestwick club took place the following May, some men present, perhaps remembering that not all the professionals had played well in the inaugural tournament, proposed that the competition be expanded to include amateurs. After all, there were plenty of golfers who could go around Prestwick averaging six or seven strokes per hole. Major Fairlie saw merit in this suggestion and on the spot proposed that in addition to professional golfers, "the Challenge Belt be opened to be played for by gentlemen [nonprofessional] players . . . of the following clubs: St. Andrews, Honourable Company of Edinburgh Golfers, North Berwick, Prestwick, Carnoustie, Perth and Leven." By pronouncing this plan, Major Fairlie became the first golf administrator to put his boot in his mouth. His fellow members unanimously carried his suggestion, but in the months between May and September (when the tournament was to be played), there were strong objections voiced by the members of Scotland's clubs who had been excluded from the list of eligible participants. (There was a total of nineteen golf clubs in Scotland in 1857.) The men of Prestwick heard the protests and made a decision that altered the history of golf. At a meeting on

September 25, 1861, one day before the second competition for the Challenge Belt, it was "unanimously resolved that the Challenge Belt to be played for to-morrow and on all future occasions until it be otherwise resolved, shall be open to all the world." It was never "otherwise resolved." From that moment on, any golfer from any land who thought he had enough game could compete for the championship.

In view of the fact that the British home islands were the only places where golf was played to any significant extent in 1861, Major Fairlie and the other men of Prestwick demonstrated either tremendous foresight or dumb luck by using the word "world" in their proclamation; as the game *was* being played to various degrees by a handful of people outside of Great Britain. In the United States, golf had appeared briefly on the town green in Charleston, South Carolina, from 1786 to 1811 and then seems to have vanished until after the War Between the States, whereupon it reemerged in various forms in West Virginia (1884), Vermont (1886), the western part of Pennsylvania (1887), and Yonkers, New York (1888), on the estate of John Reid, a Scottish immigrant. Reid and a few other fellows started the Saint Andrews Golf Club, the first such club in America and one of the founding clubs of the United States Golf Association in 1895. Canada's first golf club wasn't established until 1873 in Montreal. Golf courses appeared in France at Pau (1856) and later in Belgium and South Africa in the 1880s.

As much fun as it is to imagine that in 1862, given a year's notice, golfers from all over the world boarded ships, saddled up horses or camels, or got on trains headed for Prestwick, it didn't happen. The Open remained a rather small and parochial affair in its early days. Scotland was the only place that had golfers in numbers, and those who were up to competing in the Open had to make the journey to Prestwick, which, as the crow flies, is about sixty-five miles from Edinburgh and one hundred miles from St. Andrews, the two east coast strongholds of golf. Few of the men who competed were full-time golf professionals, rather they were plasterers, slaters, or railwaymen who had a knack for the game. A few years after Jack Burns won the Open in 1888, someone spotted him working near the railway sheds in St. Andrews and asked him about the state of his golf game. "Never better!" said Burns. "I haven't been off the [railway] line for years." Like many talented golfers of his day, Burns realized being a golf champion didn't put food on the table. Ample prize money, however, wasn't the only thing the Open was lacking; if it was going to be a worldwide championship, it needed the world to show up.

The trickle of players from around the world to the Open began with the arrival of players from Scotland's natural enemy, England. They hadn't been playing golf in England for as long as they had in Scotland, but the English had two fine links courses early on: Westward Ho! in North Devon (1864) and Hoylake (today more commonly referred to as Royal Liverpool), founded in 1869. (There were other courses, but none that would prepare a player for Scotland's rugged seaside links.) The first English competitor of note was John Ball, an amateur, in 1883. Writing in 1951, Englishman John H. Taylor, who considered Westward Ho! his home course, recalled the early days of England's challenge to Scotland's golf supremacy. "It was a small and solitary force who in 1890 and the years that followed, set out to challenge the might of Scotland—a forlorn hope indeed, when I myself met the Scottish professionals in 1893 at Prestwick my fears were not allayed though subsequently I found that they were but human in the mistakes they often made."

Englishmen bearing arms had entered Scotland an untold number of times before 1890, and the results usually weren't good for the Scots. The only difference this time was the weapons. It may have taken thirty years for them to gain their footing, but starting in 1890 when Ball won the championship seven years after he first played in it, the English rolled through the Open. Late in the day of Ball's victory, Scotsman Willie Campbell seemed like he was going to win only to be denied when his ball found trouble in one of Prestwick's bunkers. An hour after the championship's conclusion, Campbell and his caddie were seen sitting on upturned buckets weeping bitterly, as only a Scotsman who lost to an Englishman could. By the time Taylor won the title in 1894 and '95, the English were in the Open to stay, and the Open was in England to stay. Taylor won his first Open at the Royal St. George's Golf Club in England, the first time the championship had gone south of the Scottish border. (Taylor and fellow Englishman Harry Vardon comprised two-thirds of what golf historians eventually referred to as the Triumvirate or the Great Triumvirate. The third member was Scotsman James Braid, and between 1894 and 1914, Taylor, Vardon, and Braid won a total of sixteen Open Championships, five each for Taylor and Braid, and six for Vardon.) In 1907, a Frenchman named Arnaud Massy won the tournament at Hoylake. Massy had learned the game in Biarritz and then moved to Scotland to learn from the North Berwick professional Ben Sayers.

In 1887, English author Horace Cox met a young man from San Francisco who was visiting England. "Once the [American] public has seen this good old game, it will become immensely popular," said the American traveler. He was correct. The first American golfer to hit British shores in competition was Walter Travis, who went to England in 1904 to play in the Amateur Championship. Travis was born in Australia but had lived in the

U.S. for most of his life when he began playing golf on Long Island in 1896. In 1904 he was forty-four years of age, old by the standards of champion golfers in any era. Travis struck his hosts as a loner, and the incomparable English writer Bernard Darwin (grandson of the evolutionist) described Travis as "the little middle-aged man from America, with the black cigar . . ." going on to write that Travis "had something of a black and Satanic air" about him. (In Darwin's defense, he also wrote he "had an uncomfortable feeling that we ought to have tried harder to penetrate that uninviting reserve, and gave up the effort too readily.") Satanic or not, Travis won the championship and the comfy parochialism of championship golf was ended until America's playing professionals reintroduced it in the 1950s.

No player born in America won the Open until Walter Hagen did so in England in 1922. The previous year, Jock Hutchison, a player who had emigrated to the States from St. Andrews, had won the Open at St. Andrews, but the Scots considered him one of their own despite the fact that the claret jug awarded the winner went back to the U.S. with Hutchison. (Tom Morris's son, Tom Morris, Jr., won the Open in 1868, '69, and '70. He was permanently awarded the Challenge Belt, just as the men of Prestwick had said would happen back in 1860. Since there was no belt, there was no Open in 1871. In 1872, Prestwick was joined in running the Open by the R&A and the Honourable Company of Edinburgh Golfers. The three clubs kicked in together to pay for a silver claret jug that has been the championship trophy ever since.) Hagen, however, was born in Rochester, New York, so there was no confusing the issue. For the rest of the decade, Hagen and amateur Bobby Jones of Georgia dominated the Open Championship, with Hagen winning four and Jones three by 1930. Now the Open was a world championship, and to boot, the Scots and English were fond of Hagen and Jones, particularly the latter. Said Longhurst, "By his superb skill and unfailing charm Bobby Jones probably did as much to draw Britain and America together as all the diplomats combined."

Hagen was admired for other reasons, namely his personal flair and his advocacy that professional golfers be treated like gentlemen. He had burst upon the scene at the 1913 U.S. Open when he approached John McDermott in the changing room and announced, "I'm Walter Hagen, from Rochester, and I've come to help you boys take care of Vardon and Ray." Vardon and Ray were the two great English stars playing in that U.S. Open. They were "taken care of," but not by Hagen. That feat was handled in a playoff by twenty-year-old amateur Francis Ouimet.

During the decade after Jones won the 1930 Open, it evolved as the world championship of golf, and the fields of competitors and champions were more diverse than ever. The championship was won three times by Americans after Jones during the '30s and six times by various Englishmen, and the fields occasionally included players from South America and Japan. In 1939, England's Richard Burton edged out American Johnny Bulla for the title. Two months after Burton won the Open, the Wehrmacht invaded Poland. There were no Open Championships during the next six summers. Amid the devastation of the war, not many people noticed that the two golf courses at Turnberry had been appropriated and covered in part with concrete for use as airfields.

PALMER WAS IN ST. ANDREWS to win the Open, but at the same time he had a chance to rekindle the bond created when the Scots embraced Bobby Jones as one of their own. On both counts, Palmer was practically alone as an American. The only other recognizable Yank was Sarazen, playing in the Open for the fourteenth time. To their eternal credit, the Scots received Palmer as if the Americans had never been away. "We used to watch and caddie in the Open when we were boys," said John Philip, who was a young man living in St. Andrews at the time. "We didn't see many American players, and then came Arnold Palmer. What a sight he was."

Palmer arrived in the small university town a week before the championship—just after winning the Canada Cup with partner Sam Snead at Portmarnock, Ireland—and quickly got to know the people. He practiced during the day, and in the evenings attended social functions. He signed autographs with patience and a smile, and he signed them all. When the Scots watched him play during practice, it was their first glimpse at the fearless, attacking Palmer style of play, and their first look at the crazy helicopter finish to his swing and his body's expostulations toward the ball.

After retiring to his room for the evening, Palmer reviewed and finalized his plan for the competition. Spread before him were maps of the eighteen holes that made up the Old Course in St. Andrews, golf's most famous and idiosyncratic playing ground. Staring at the charts, Palmer decided how he would attack each of the holes based on the weather and the direction of the wind at a given moment. It was critical that he have multiple ideas on how to assault each hole because the direction and strength of the wind could shift countless times during a round at the Old Course, sitting as it does on Scotland's east coast along the North Sea.

Palmer knew that the instant the tiny British ball (1.62 ounces and 1.62 inches in diameter) was airborne its fate would be out of his control and at the mercy of the wind, the unpredictable and most feared enemy of a pro-fessional golfer. To fully understand this, it helps to consider the game from the perspective of a world-class golfer. Simply put, golf is a game of connect-the-dots played in reverse. As he stands on the teeing ground of a given hole, the top-level player first considers where the actual hole in the ground is cut on the putting green several hundred yards distant. He then deter-mines the point that will give him the most advantageous angle of approach to the hole, and draws up in his mind a series of strokes that will safely get his ball to that point, each shot played to a point (or dot) that presents a friendly angle of approach to the subsequent dot. Playing in a vacuum, the expert player would land his ball precisely at the chosen spot nine times out of ten. Playing in the wind, the player must gauge its strength and direction and make an educated guess regarding the effect the wind will have on the length and direction of the ball's flight. A ball played directly into the wind flies shorter than it normally would, and any curve in its flight is exagger-ated. A shot played straight downwind can be difficult to judge because the breeze negates backspin on the ball and renders it unable to stop when it hits the ground. This effect is exponential on the ultrafirm ground of Britain's links courses, and a ball struck downwind can bound along for what seems forever until something (a bunker or patch of rough) gets in its way. If the wind suddenly gusts stronger or dies down or is swirling above the player's head (where the ball will fly) in a manner that cannot be de-tected, the ball will wander off track and the well-made plan is suddenly be-holden to luck.

Had they been aware of this after-hours preparation by Palmer, British golf fans might have thought it overkill. Writing to the editor of the British periodical *Golf Monthly*, a reader from the era noted that the "American view is that a golf course should be an infallible tribunal for skill alone: for 500 years the English and Scottish view has been the element of luck should predominate—and this is true of St. Andrews."

His nighttime cramming aside, Palmer assimilated himself into the sur-roundings as if he'd been there all his life. While defending champion Gary Player looked like a circus escapee cavorting around in trousers with one white leg and one black, Palmer opted for muted colors, mostly dark, in his choice of attire. While many players in the field wore trendier white golf shoes, Palmer chose black. Henry Cotton noticed that nearly every player in the field was wearing an American-style baseball cap (he referred to it as a jockey hat), but not Palmer. For most of the two weeks while he was on the golf course, Palmer wore the same type of traditional wool cap worn by nearly every man in the crowd. "His dress in quiet colors and his friendly,

modest manner delighted the home crowd," said Cotton after the championship was over. The only thing Cotton thought remotely odd about Palmer
was that he not only wore a leather golf glove on his left hand (many players
did the same, but it was just then becoming vogue), but that he changed
gloves several times during a round and wore them without breaking them
in first. The gloves went directly from the package onto Palmer's hand without a thought.

For all his preparation and despite his impressive playing credentials,
Palmer was not yet assured a spot in the championship proper. There were
two qualifying rounds to be survived before entry into the four-round chase
for the claret jug. With more than 380 players vying for spots in the eventual
field of 77 players, these rounds required two days, Monday and Tuesday.
Palmer survived easily, with a round of sixty-seven on the New Course and
seventy-five on the Old Course. During his Tuesday round at the Old
Course, his first competitive test upon it, Palmer found out how fickle the
ancient field could be. It rained for a good part of the round, and on one
hole, his tee shot was blown out of bounds by the wind. On another occasion he required two shots to extricate his ball from a bunker known as the
Principal's Nose.

The championship proper was scheduled for three days, with eighteen
holes played on Wednesday and Thursday and thirty-six holes on Friday.
The three betting favorites, Player, Palmer, and Peter Thomson (who had
won the Open four times during the period of the absent Americans),
played well the first two windless days with aggregate scores of 143 (Player)
and 141 (Palmer and Thomson). They looked in a bad place, however, because the Argentine Roberto De Vicenzo, had scored matching sixty-sevens
the first two days. Two strokes behind De Vicenzo stood Thomson's fellow
Aussie, Kel Nagle, at 136. Nagle had been driving the ball rather poorly for
the better part of the summer, but while in Texas to play in the Colonial Invitational tournament he found an American-made driver that he fancied.
He drove the ball well with it all week at St. Andrews. With one day to go,
Palmer was seven strokes behind the lead.

Friday arrived a gray and misty day, and Palmer looked for all the world
like he had been born for this moment. Out for the morning round wearing
tan trousers and a slightly darker tan shirt covered by a black cardigan
sweater, Palmer stalked the fairways with his local caddie, Tip Anderson,
who matched him stride for stride in shirt and tie and a trench coat. Palmer
was charging now, and everyone knew it: He was on pace to shoot sixty-
eight if he made par fours at the final two holes. And then it began raining.
The seventeenth hole at the Old Course is known as the Road Hole, and it is

the most difficult hole played anywhere in the world of championship golf. With the rain pelting down, Palmer made a five there, something most of the field would do despite its par of four. The eighteenth hole at the Old Course is a fairly simple and straightforward hole for a professional golfer. The setting is magical, but the hole itself has only one truly striking characteristic: a deep hollow in the front portion of the green known as the Valley of Sin. If the approach shot is misjudged on the short side and the ball settles into the Valley of Sin, taking three putts to get down is a very real possibility for even the best player. With the wind blowing hard off the sea and the rain intensifying, Palmer erred on his approach. The ball came to rest in the Valley of Sin, and he took three putts to finish his round. "I let those two get away," he said to Anderson as he walked from the green. Things weren't as bad as they seemed, however. Palmer had nipped five shots off of De Vicenzo's lead, and one off of Nagle's. He had them in his sight now, and the afternoon round lay ahead.

The afternoon round never came. The rain became a downpour the likes that few St. Andreans could remember. Within twenty minutes of Palmer completing his round, two greens and several fairways were completely submerged. Water gushed down the stone steps of the R&A clubhouse like a waterfall. The Valley of Sin became a small lake, and after the rain had died down a bit, spectators still holding umbrellas over their heads admired the reflection of the imposing R&A clubhouse upon it. The fire brigade was summoned to pump the water out of the valley—no one ever remembered *that* happening before. The R&A decided to postpone the final round until the following day.

On Saturday, the rain was gone as a permanent fixture, although it did drizzle at moments. Palmer exploded from the starting blocks with two consecutive birdies, and scored thirty-four on the front nine, and Nagle made it to the halfway point in thirty-four as well. By that time, De Vicenzo had faltered, and it was left to Palmer and Nagle to fight it out. Palmer was playing a group ahead of Nagle, and when Palmer birdied the thirteenth hole, he trailed by only three strokes. When Nagle took three putts for bogey at the fifteenth, Palmer was only two shots back.

Palmer pressed onward, making a brilliant par to save his chances at the seventeenth, one of the holes that had foiled him the previous day. His approach to the green was long and bounded over the extremely narrow green and onto the footpath that gives the hole its name. Palmer displayed superb touch in playing a shot from off the green with his putter, the ball rolling just strong enough to move through a clump of rough on a bank behind the green, but just soft enough as to not run across the green once it reached the shorter grass. It stopped two feet from the hole. "Now," wrote Wind of that moment, "he [Palmer] finally had a lift after surviving for two hours on fight, fight, fight, and he roared on to birdie the final hole after a fine wedge shot that stopped four feet from the cup." As the putt fell, a roar went up into the sky above St. Andrews.

Back on the seventeenth green, about four hundred yards from where Palmer now stood, Nagle heard the crowd's reaction. He needed to make par fours at the final two holes to win. At the moment, things were looking dicey. He needed to make a six-foot putt to secure his four at the seventeenth. It is in such moments that the seemingly simple task of tapping a ball toward a hole in the ground becomes overwhelmingly complex, when in fact the reality of the task hasn't changed at all. The mind begins to race, and suddenly a golfer knows what it feels like to step on the accelerator when the intention was to step on the brake. But Nagle did not step on the gas; he made the putt and subsequently made his four on the final hole. Palmer had come up a single stroke short.

In the moments that followed, Palmer pushed his white cap back slightly on his head and massaged his temples with his thumbs. All around him, people were congratulating him on a job well done. "It wasn't enough," said Palmer over and over again. He had tied the four-round record for an Open at the Old Course, but he was right. It wasn't enough. If placed in his shoes at that moment, most of his American contemporaries would have headed home never to return. Palmer was different, and the Scots knew it. Already they spoke of him as "the great mon."


IN JULY 1961, Palmer was back at the Open, this time at Royal Birkdale in Southport, England. He was again the lone American competitor of consequence, joined only by fifty-two-year-old Paul Runyan. After the first round of the championship proper on Wednesday, he was two strokes behind Dai Rees of Wales and Harold Henning of South Africa. Stiff winds were blowing along the Lancashire coast as Thursday's early starters, Palmer among them, took to the course. Despite the wind, Palmer birdied five of the first six holes, and was off and running for the moment, but as the gusts continued to pick up force, the game became more difficult. Palmer struggled over the closing holes for a round of seventy-three. Nevertheless, it was an outstanding score; only Peter Thomson, also playing early, scored better (by a stroke). Palmer and Thomson had caught a break—after they completed play, the wind was registering at gale force, and the players who went out late turned in scores in the high seventies and low eighties. During the evening, the gusts blew so hard that exhibition tents were ripped from their moorings, their contents—golf equipment, clothing, and refreshments—scattered about the property. The British magazine *Golf Illustrated* reported "that to see some of the faces of spectators as they looked on at the broken bottles of whisky and beer would have brought tears to your eyes." The wind brought rain with it too, and Friday's two rounds were canceled after some of the players had already begun play.

Palmer was playing well overall, but was especially pleased with his tee shots in the windy conditions. He knew he was prone to an occasional sharply hooked tee shot—one with a darting curve from right to left—and that at Birkdale such a shot could prove particularly horrific to his score. To prevent these sudden snap hooks, he had gone into the golf shop at Birkdale earlier in the week and asked if he could use a vise. He then proceeded to place the shaft of the club in the vise and, using his hands, pull the head of the club to a more open position that would allow him to swing away without fear.

On Saturday morning, after the rain had abated, Palmer went out and shot a score of sixty-nine. It was during that round, at the sixteenth hole, that he played one of the most absurdly great shots in the history of the game. A few days after the championship, Cotton reckoned he had never seen a shot like it. "The ball was in a mixture of brambles, wild strawberry bushes, long grass and the local willow scrub. The ball was eight to nine inches down deep in the stuff. I saw the stroke and watched the ball fly dead straight onto the green, almost one-hundred-fifty yards away, into an almost head on wind. I do not know how one measures golfing strength, but Arnold Palmer is certainly a golfing giant." The shot saved a par for Palmer when he might have made a double bogey or worse, and won him the Open. He still had a round to play in the afternoon, and Rees closed in style to get within a stroke of tying Palmer, but when all the shots had been fired, Palmer held the claret jug. He had done it during a week that Cotton described as "the Open at its unfair, uneven best."

Palmer spoke only a few words when he was presented with the trophy and medal awarded to the winner. "I have won a few tournaments," said Palmer, "but this is the one I wanted to win. Nobody can be satisfied until he wins the British Open Championship." As he made his way toward his final destination at Birkdale before departing, he was buttonholed by a British writer who asked him if he still enjoyed the taste of winning. His answer—given honestly at a time long before superstar professional athletes attended seminars on how to answer stupid questions from the media and long before athletes made so much money that such an answer would sound trite and insincere—cleared up any lingering questions regarding the difference between Palmer and other American professionals of the time. "I go into every tournament with the idea of winning it," said Palmer. "That's why I'm there. I never enter any tournament just to win money. When it becomes apparent that I cannot win, I have to settle for making money."

And with that, Palmer left the writer and stopped by the shop of Bob Halsall, the golf professional at Birkdale. Before he left, Palmer, the son of a club professional, wanted to thank Halsall for making him feel welcome.

The following summer at Old Troon on the west coast of Scotland and not far from Prestwick, Palmer won the Open again. He was at the absolute height of his power as a golfer during the championship, leaving runner-up Kel Nagle six strokes behind. The next closest players, thirteen shots back, were Brian Huggett of Wales and a young American professional named Phil Rodgers, of whom great things were expected. Rodgers was one of three promising young American players at Troon. The others were Gene Littler and Jack Nicklaus.

# TWO

BECAUSE PROFESSIONAL GOLFERS SPEND SO MUCH TIME in the sun, most of them wear a hat to protect their skin and reduce glare as they look things over preparing to play a shot. This is a sensible thing, and over the years hats have become so integral a part of the uniform of professional golfers that the headwear goes largely unnoticed, but Jack Nicklaus never had a head for hats. During the prime years of his career he often eschewed wearing one except in the most ungodly heat. The things sat so awkwardly on his head that he looked silly in them, and no one ever looked more ludicrous in a hat than Jack Nicklaus did posing for photographs prior to the 1962 Open Championship at Old Troon. In Scotland as the reigning U.S. Open champion and playing in his first Open Championship, Nicklaus modeled for advertising photos for the Slazenger golf equipment company. The results bring to mind the hokey publicity shots of American football players from the same era. The images of Nicklaus show a young man with a boyish face and a body that can best be described as thick. His trousers are too tight, as is his cardigan sweater, and the long-sleeve polo shirt under the sweater is fastened closely around his bull neck. It is the hat he is wearing, however, that stands out. It's a cap of the style favored by British men of the time (and to some degree to this day) because it keeps the head warm and does not blow off in the gusts of strong wind so often felt in the British Isles; but the hat worn by Nicklaus would not have blown off in a hurricane and fit his head so snugly that it appears a crowbar would be needed to remove it. He could not wear the hat at a jaunty angle, because to do so would have required a bit of room for maneuvering. There was no such room.

As ridiculous as Nicklaus looked, the Scots neither noticed nor cared, and neither did the British press; what they saw was a frighteningly superb player of the game. They had been aware of his awesome potential for a few years by the time he arrived at Troon. Nicklaus played on the 1959 U.S. Walker Cup team that decimated the home squad at Muirfield, and a year later he was one of four players on the U.S. team in the World Amateur, an event between teams from thirty-two nations. It was played at Merion Golf Club's East Course, a demanding test that had hosted a slew of national championships over the years. The club, in the town of Ardmore on Philadelphia's blue-blood-oozing Main Line, had been the site of the U.S. Open ten years earlier. That year a four-round aggregate of 287 put Ben Hogan in an eighteen-hole playoff, which he won over Lloyd Mangrum and George Fazio. (Merion East was also the golf course where, in 1930, Bobby Jones completed the game's only single-season sweep of major championships.) In the 1960 World Amateur, Nicklaus required eighteen fewer shots than Hogan for four rounds in leading the U.S. team to a crushing triumph. He was the first to admit that his rounds of sixty-six, sixty-seven, sixty-eight, and sixty-eight differed from Hogan's performance in that the course was not set up for U.S. Open play, but the reverberations of the performance reached across the Atlantic. British golf observers were astounded that their home team, which they thought would be competitive in the event, had finished a combined forty-seven strokes behind the four Americans. (The three other Americans were Deane Beman, who would later become commissioner of the PGA Tour, Bob Gardner, and Bill Hyndman. The British and Irish team was led by Michael Bonallack, who would later become secretary of the R&A. Bonallack's score was 296.)

In the British newspaper *The Observer,* writer John Stobbs was enthralled by what had taken place at Merion. "There is undeniably something inspiring and impressive about it," wrote Stobbs, "as there is about anything done really well." In trying to explain to his readers the mind-boggling precision of Nicklaus's play, Stobbs launched into a geometry lesson that explained the slim margin of error in hitting consistently accurate golf shots. The column ended with Stobbs averring that executing the golf swing as Nicklaus had done "is really asking rather a lot of the fallible human calculating machine. In fact, looked at reasonably, Nicklaus just ought not be either possible or allowed." The headline that ran with the story read, "Q.E.D., Nicklaus Is Impossible" (*quod erat demonstrandum,* i.e., that which has been proved).

THE WILLINGNESS TO ACCEPT and appreciate Nicklaus based solely on the merit of his game was something that golf fans in his own country found impossible due to the rapture that embraced them in the presence of Palmer. The fact that a golfer had a large group of fans was unusual in 1960, but Palmer was changing everything about the public perception of golf. People flocked to him as if he were going to open their eyes to something they'd been missing out on in life.

Palmer was born on September 10, 1929, in Latrobe, a small town in western Pennsylvania known primarily for its brewery, which produces Rolling Rock beer. Latrobe sits in the foothills of the Allegheny Mountains, and in the 1930s and '40s when Palmer was growing up, it was typical of small-town America. Arnie, as his friends called him, was the son of Deacon and Doris Palmer, and in the little town bisected by tracks of the Pennsylvania Railroad, Deacon Palmer was the golf professional at the country club. As a boy, Arnie was permitted to play the course in the morning before the members arrived, and in the late afternoon after they had finished playing for the day. "Before I was five years old, my father had taught me how to grip the [golf] club properly," said Palmer many years later. More important, as the product of a small town, Palmer learned how to relate to people on a level that put them at ease.

By the time Arnold Palmer finished a three-year stint in the U.S. Coast Guard in the early 1950s, he was a man's man. A lean five-feet-ten, Palmer's body rippled with muscle. When he won the 1954 U.S. Amateur Championship and subsequently headed out on the professional golf tour in America, he did so with biceps that were bulging beneath the short sleeves of his sports shirts. He was a perfect fit for a time in America when the number of white-collar workers was on the rise and men needed reminders that their manliness was intact even if they didn't get dirty at work. Flipping through a magazine, a reader might come across an advertisement for Sheaffer's PFM (Pen For Men), which touted its "new man-styled heft" and its "broad-shouldered, solid, comfortable" fit in the hand. A few pages later, one of the great taste-bud mysteries of all time was solved with the revelation that the fellow who "does like the Guinness taste . . . is the man who is male, masculine and mighty." The muddy, brown beer from Ireland was a "full-bodied brew for able-bodied men."

Palmer didn't just look like a he-man, he played golf like one. When Deacon Palmer taught his son how to hold a golf club, the result was a grip that was perfect and sure. The son's hands molded to the club as if there was no other purpose for them. With the grip learned as a child and the strength of a man, Palmer could swing the golf club as hard and fast as anyone who had ever played the game. The violence of the slash he made at the ball turned his body toward his target with such force that his metal cleats could barely keep his feet rooted to the ground, and his arms moved at such great speed that in order to avoid whacking himself in the noggin with his hands during his follow-through he had to thrust them above his head at the last second. The finished pose, with his hands above his head rather than next to it in the textbook manner, left the club in a position so that it looked like a blade on a helicopter. This helicopter finish became a Palmer trademark, recognizable to an observer even from a distance. But when Palmer reached that point in his swing, the show wasn't over. As the ball took flight, Palmer would quickly lower his hands in front of his chest, with the club now pointing toward the target. His face screwed into a grimace, his body tilting this way and that, Palmer tried to exert an influence over the ball with body language. Sports fans—and it's important to make the distinction between golf fans and fans of sport in general at this point—had never seen a golfer with so much emotion invested in what he was doing. Here was a man they could empathize with and cheer for with the throaty roar usually reserved for a goal-line stand in football or a critical at-bat in baseball. Palmer not only won over existing golf fans, he converted fans of other sports into golf fans as well. "It is very true that Arnold took golf to the people," said writer Dan Jenkins, who watched it all happen. "He sweated, he chain-smoked, his shirttail came out, he wasn't tidy. He was a man of the people. He was a guy off the street, a coal miner who came out and conquered the country club sport."

As more and more people turned out to see Palmer play golf, his wife, Winnie, mentioned to him that while she understood the game was serious business to Arnie, it also struck her as a game where, according to writer Herbert Warren Wind, "extreme grimness was out of place." Palmer agreed with his wife and remembered to smile at the people and make direct eye contact with as many fans as possible while walking between shots and while waiting to play his next shot. The eye contact was something he remembered from his tenth grade public-speaking class at Latrobe High School. What had started out as an initial popular attraction toward Palmer's take-no-prisoners swing and postshot gesticulations was now consummated by his looking the fans straight in the eye. The people, in turn, went home to tell their neighbors, bridge partners, and people they met at cocktail parties that they had gone out to a tournament where Palmer was playing and "Arnold looked right at me on the thirteenth hole." As curiosity about Palmer grew, sports fans tuned their black-and-white televisions into golf tournaments, and the conversion became complete. American sports fans had not merely become fans of golf, they were fans of Arnold Palmer. They even gave themselves a name: Arnie's Army.

The Army began forming ranks in 1955 when the Palmers hit the American professional golf tour in their two-door Ford. Along the way they picked up a small trailer in Phoenix that served as their home. When they returned home to Latrobe at the end of the season, Palmer had played in thirty-one tournaments, won the Canadian Open and pulled in $7,958 in prize money. The following season he won twice and more than doubled his earnings to $16,145. In 1957, he won four tournaments and $27,803, which placed him fifth on the list of earnings for players on the American tour. Palmer was a rising star, with a chance to become the sport's most prominent player. His breakout came in April 1958, when he won his first major championship as a professional, the Masters Tournament in Augusta, Georgia.

Played annually each April since 1934, excepting three years during World War II, the Masters is the first of golf's four major championships each year. (The only exception was 1971, when the PGA Championship was played in February in Palm Beach, Florida.) Before his prime years as a player ended, Palmer would win the Masters four times. In the spring of 1960 he won it for the second time and did so in a charging, come-from-behind style that electrified his followers and became standard operating procedure for Palmer.

Palmer clung to the lead heading into the fourth round and immediately relinquished it by bogeying two of the first five holes. Playing four holes ahead of him, Dow Finsterwald and twenty-eight-year-old Californian Ken Venturi had grabbed the joint lead by shooting front-nine scores of thirty-three and thirty-four respectively. When Finsterwald barely missed a par putt on the final green, Venturi stood alone in the lead, his prospects for being champion looking very good. By the time Palmer reached the last three holes of the round, Venturi and Finsterwald had finished play. In order to tie Venturi, Palmer would need to play the remaining three holes in one under par, or a total of ten strokes. At the par-three sixteenth hole, Palmer played an indifferent shot from the tee and his ball sat thirty-five feet from the hole. In 1960, it was within the rules to play a putt on the green with the flagstick remaining in the hole. Palmer chose to leave the flagstick in the hole so that if he stroked his ball solidly it might hit the center of the stick and fall in. Even with the aid of the flagstick, he struck the ball too firm. The ball ricocheted off the flagstick and settled next to the hole. When he tapped in, he still trailed Venturi by one stroke.

At the seventeenth tee, Palmer reared back and slashed one of his formidable drives and was left with just an eight-iron shot to the green. The approach shot had too much spin on it and grabbed the green as soon as it landed, stopping twenty-seven feet from the hole. Twice Palmer prepared to play the putt and twice he backed off, distracted by spectators jostling for position to see what he would do. Backing away from a shot is seldom a good signal from a professional golfer, backing off twice even less so.

Palmer, however, simply hunkered down even more. As the ball reached the hole it appeared to be running out of gas—had he hit it hard enough?—and with the last bit of turn the ball came in contact with the edge of the hole and gravity took over. It was in—a birdie three. Palmer broke into a jig.

Palmer stood on the tee 420 yards from the hole cut on the eighteenth green. Nearly every one of those yards climbs up a steep hill toward the clubhouse, and the wind was blowing in his face. Giant pine trees line the right side of the fairway, so a wild drive to the right meant trouble. The mission, as Palmer later remembered it, was to secure a par and tie Venturi, taking his chances in a playoff the following day. He drove solidly down the fairway and played a semi-punch shot with a six-iron into the green. In executing a punch shot, the player chokes down a bit on the shaft of the club and plays the ball slightly closer to his right foot than normal. By adjusting his ball position, the player hits the ball a microsecond sooner in his swing, creating a lower trajectory on the ball. In the follow-through, the player hangs on tightly with his left hand to prevent the clubhead from turning over. In effect, the ball is given a powerful shove. Palmer pulled off the shot to perfection. The ball landed two feet from the hole and, after it had stopped spinning, rested five feet away from victory. Spectators ringed the green, most of the men wearing ties and fedoras and the women sporting bonnets and the conspicuous sunglasses of the times. Palmer did not linger over the putt. "I just tried to remember what my old friend George Low [a renowned putting virtuoso] always said, 'Keep your head down and stay still,'" said Palmer. The putt dropped into the hole. Palmer was Masters champion and for the second time he donned the green sports jacket traditionally presented to winners by the club. His Army was delirious with joy, but Palmer had only begun to get them revved up.

The coming of June brought with it the U.S. Open Championship, to be played at Cherry Hills Country Club in suburban Denver. Cherry Hills had hosted the U.S. Open twenty-two years earlier, but in 1960 it was best known as the golf course that President Dwight Eisenhower had played just hours before having a heart attack in 1955. By the end of U.S. Open week in 1960, Eisenhower's fellow Republicans probably wished they could nominate Palmer to run against Kennedy in November rather than Richard Nixon. Palmer was certainly more popular.

With the warm Rocky Mountain sunlight reflecting off snow-covered peaks, spectator marshals wandered the Cherry Hills course in bright red slacks, and women tournament volunteers wore bright red skirts and red-checked gondolier hats. Along the property lines of the course, children sold lemonade for a nickel a glass. Everything about the scene was wonderful with the exception of Palmer's play in the first three rounds. In 1960, the final two rounds of the U.S. Open were still played on a single day, Saturday. After eighteen holes in the morning, the players would grab a quick bite to eat and head back out for the final round. Palmer's morning round on Saturday was completed in seventy-two strokes, leaving him at two over par and seven shots behind the leader, American tour player Mike Souchak. A seven-stroke deficit is enormous in golf, and very difficult to fully reduce under normal circumstances. At the U.S. Open, with its long grass and difficult greens, closing a seven-stroke gap borders on the impossible.

The opening hole at Cherry Hills was measuring 346 yards from the tee to the green, and when Palmer stepped onto its tee to begin his final round, he was determined to reach the green with a single shot. It was not unfeasible—at an altitude of 5,280 feet, the thin air would allow the ball to fly farther, but Palmer had attempted the feat in the three previous rounds and failed each time. This time he did not. Palmer crushed the ball long and straight, and it skipped through a patch of rough fronting the green and stopped twenty feet from the hole. He took two putts for an easy birdie three. After that came a furious rush of birdies, and he finished the first nine holes in just thirty strokes. Almost every spectator on the course had joined the Palmer gallery by the time he began play on the final nine holes.

The last few hours of the 1960 U.S. Open exemplified that championship's torturous nature. With six birdies on the first seven holes, Palmer had for the most part exhausted his heroics and still did not have a share of the lead. During most of those final agonizing hours, in fact, it was difficult to pinpoint just who *was* in the lead. It is possible, however, to be clear about one thing: Sometime shortly after 4:00 PM, Souchak bogeyed the ninth hole and fell out of the lead. The new leader, at five under par, was a twenty-year-old amateur from Columbus, Ohio, named Jack Nicklaus.

What happened next was something that Nicklaus would remember for the rest of his life. After making a birdie at the twelfth hole, he decided to take a peek at an on-course leaderboard while walking to the thirteenth tee. It's not uncommon for professionals to avoid looking at scoreboards during the first three rounds of a tournament; it can take a player's focus away from his own game and place it upon someone else's game. On the final nine holes of a championship, however, it's essential for a player to know where he stands if he is intent upon winning. The glance Nicklaus took was the first such look he had taken all week. What he saw unnerved him—he knew he was near the lead after scoring thirty-two on the first nine holes, but he did not realize he *was* the leader. The effect of that revelation was not immediate, but almost so. He played a solid drive with a three-wood at the thirteenth, and an easy nine-iron toward the hole that left him in perfect position. He had just twelve feet to the hole and was putting uphill, the favorite putt of all golfers because it allows for a firm stroke and negates worries that the ball will go racing past the hole. Nicklaus played an aggressive first putt, and if it had gone in his lead would have been two shots. Instead, the ball slid by the hole, leaving him a downhill putt of eighteen inches back to the hole. A putt of eighteen inches—even downhill on the slickest green—typically presents little obstacle to a world-class golfer. Nicklaus was unafraid of the length or speed of the putt but was in awe of his playing companion, Ben Hogan, a man whose concentration was so intense that the thought of interrupting it scared even seasoned professionals. So when Nicklaus examined the ground between his ball and the hole and noticed a slight depression in the putting surface left by an incoming ball when it thudded onto the green earlier in the day or week, he was afraid to ask Hogan if the rules permitted him to fix it. (They did.) Flustered, Nicklaus stroked the ball toward the hole, and it did exactly what he thought it would do—it struck the blemish on the ground and was deflected off-line. The instant that ball was redirected four men were tied for the lead at four under par. For the first time all week one of the leaders was Arnold Palmer. A few moments later, Nicklaus fell a shot adrift of the lead with another bogey at the fourteenth hole.

It is the cruelest truth in golf that while a great player can strike the ball fully and expertly well into his later years as a competitor, his aging nerves betray him with the least complicated of all shots in the game, the putt. The putt seems so simple, and indeed it is, but it is enormously different from every other shot in one way: It is played with the expectation that it will complete the work on a given hole. When it does not, it tortures the mind of a player, and after years of such torture, the man who putted so fearlessly as a youth is reduced to mush, psychologically speaking. Despite the youthful trepidation with which Nicklaus viewed Hogan, putting woes had reduced the forty-seven-year-old Texan to so much mush. At an age when most professional golfers are long finished as serious contenders for major titles, Hogan was not only still hanging tough, he was still *the* most consistently superb striker of the golf ball on the planet. In spite of his balky putting nerves, that Saturday afternoon at Cherry Hills found Hogan in position to win an unprecedented fifth U.S. Open Championship. With just two holes to play, Hogan was tied with Jack Fleck and Palmer. (Hogan had reason to fear Fleck. A relatively unknown pro, he had come out of nowhere to force a playoff with Hogan in the 1955 U.S. Open at Olympic when everyone was certain Hogan had won. Fleck won the playoff.) The seventeenth hole at Cherry Hills measured 548 yards, and the realistic chance of a powerful ball-striker reaching the green in two shots was greatly reduced by the fact that the green sat in a lake, surrounded on all sides by water. Hogan played two solid shots to a point where he could safely play a short third over the lake and onto the green. The moment belonged to Hogan, and he made his decision to play a risky shot based on his feeling that Palmer and Fleck would probably birdie this very hole. Palmer, in fact, was standing on the seventeenth tee watching the scene. If Hogan was going to make a birdie he had to hit the ball so close to the hole that even with his nerve-besotted putting stroke he could not possibly miss the putt. The outcome rested squarely on Hogan's ability to hit the perfect shot under pressure, something he had done countless times in earlier days. Hogan struck the ball cleanly, and in doing so imparted a severe amount of backspin on it. The ball landed short of the hole, where the ground rose up from the lake to the green, and skidded backward down the slope and into the water. Refusing to quit, Hogan took of his shoes and socks and plopped the ball out of the water and onto the green. He missed the putt, however, and was now a stroke behind Palmer, who had witnessed the entire thing, and Fleck.

Aware that Fleck, too, was faltering behind him, Palmer played the final two holes safely and wisely in level par five and four. He had shot a round of sixty-five, and when the final putt dropped he knew he had won the U.S. Open. In a single fluid motion as the ball dropped, Palmer reached for the visor on his head and flung it into the sky. He wasn't the first golfer ever to do so, but it became his victory trademark. Arnie had once again justified the faith of his Army.

In the locker room, Hogan endured the questioning of magazine writers and newspapermen. "I guess they'll say I lost it," said Hogan. "Well, one more foot and the wedge on seventeen would have been perfect. But I'll tell you something. I played thirty-six holes today with a kid who should have won this Open by ten shots." The kid, of course, was Nicklaus, who had recovered from his back-to-back bogeys with four consecutive pars to finish alone in second place, two shots behind Palmer. Awash in delirium, Palmer's fans almost completely overlooked Nicklaus's strong showing at Cherry Hills. After the tournament, Palmer mentioned to Pittsburgh sportswriter Bob Drum that he now had a chance to win all four major championships in a single year. It would be, thought Palmer, a modern professional version of the Grand Slam Bobby Jones had won in 1930. By all accounts, it was the first time anyone had mentioned a modern Grand Slam. Palmer went off to St. Andrews in pursuit of it and came up a single stroke shy of grabbing the third part of the Slam.


THE FIRST HEAD-ON COLLISION between Palmer and Nicklaus as professionals produced the greatest jolt Arnie's Army ever felt. It occurred at the 1962 U.S. Open at Oakmont Country Club, a club just to the north of Pittsburgh and within easy driving distance of Latrobe, just forty-two miles away. A Palmer victory in the Masters that April had the Army frothing with anticipation for another Palmer run at sweeping the four major championships in a single season. Now, in what was virtually a home game for Palmer, their man could get the second notch in his belt surrounded by his most fervent supporters. For any young man other than Jack Nicklaus the experience at Oakmont would have been the sporting equivalent of being drawn and quartered. As it turned out, it was the first glimpse for most golf fans of a level of concentration and self-confidence that would forever alter the competitive landscape of the game.

Palmer and Nicklaus were paired together for the first two rounds of the tournament, and Nicklaus's score of seventy in the second round was sensational in view of the scene on the course that day. The American weekly *Golf World* noted that Palmer's "ardent admirers are about as timid as their idol on the course . . . observing play from inside the ropes, writers were berated at every turn, 'Down in front' . . . Nicklaus was playing in adverse conditions, as, when Palmer made a shot, the gallery moved on, leaving Jack with a shot amidst a milling mob. This happened on the greens frequently."

Years afterward Nicklaus said of that week at Oakmont that it wasn't until after the tournament that "I learned many in the crowd rooted loudly against me, but nobody talked to me about that at the time and it did not penetrate my intense concentration during play. So far as I was concerned, the noise was just that—noise."

After completion of the double rounds on Saturday, Palmer and Nicklaus stood tied atop the leaderboard, which meant an eighteen-hole playoff the following day. Despite a poor putting performance all week long, Palmer managed to make a four-foot putt on the final hole of regulation after powering his birdie try for the outright win that far beyond the hole. The two golfers met briefly with the assembled writers in the press tent, and Palmer jokingly said to Nicklaus, "I thought I had gotten rid of you. I would rather be playing someone else."

"You don't really mean that," said Nicklaus.

"Oh, yes I do, you great big strong dude, you," said Palmer.

When Palmer said "strong," he meant it. Renowned as a powerful player himself, he had seen that Nicklaus generated power in his golf swing that was unthinkable at the time. Nicklaus did not just strike the golf ball, he pulverized it, launching it higher and longer and straighter than any player ever had. The fairway bunkers at Oakmont are among the most feared sand pits in the game, but they presented little problem for Nicklaus, who could fly his ball beyond them off the tee. In his final year as an amateur, Nicklaus had *nine* times reduced to smithereens the fiber face insert in the center of his driver's clubface. In the '61 U.S. Amateur at Pebble Beach, he routinely hit shots with his driver that traveled up to 300 yards, and the spectators on hand began calling him the Brute.

The spectators at Oakmont had a few nicknames for Nicklaus as well, two favorites being Fat Jack and Ohio Fats, the latter an allusion to his home state. These were cheap shots aimed at a twenty-two-year-old by people who simply could not help themselves. In their frenzy of adoration for Palmer his fans fell back on the most contemptible default setting of the American character: the belief that physical appearance trumps all in considering a person as a whole. When the small mind wishes to be derisive it looks for the most obvious target, and Nicklaus's appearance was a bull's-eye even the dimmest of minds couldn't miss. (In later years Nicklaus was always careful to point out that Palmer treated him with the utmost respect at Oakmont. Palmer told writers at Oakmont that he was "unhappy" with the way the crowd treated Nicklaus.)

*Golf World*'s writer on the scene suggested that Palmer was the John Barrymore of professional golf. If that was the case, Nicklaus, as he stood on the tee with Palmer, was the John Belushi of the game. Even though he was average height (about five-feet-ten) and had the wide frame of a classic endomorph, Nicklaus was overweight. At somewhere around 215 pounds, he was hardly a slob, but he wasn't physically fit, either. He was wearing the same pair of baggy olive-colored trousers he had worn during the first three hot and humid days of competition, and despite his wife Barbara's valiant efforts to the contrary, they were creased beyond the point of salvaging. He wore a white shirt and a white baseball-style cap over his closely trimmed blond hair. The full effect of the ensemble was that Nicklaus looked like the kid whose mother assures him that he is not fat but rather big-boned.

From his opening howitzered drive in the playoff, Nicklaus never opened the door for Palmer. By the time the two finished play on the sixth hole, Nicklaus was leading by four strokes. The Army waited breathlessly for their man's charge. It came in the middle of the round, and with consecutive birdies at the eleventh and twelfth holes, Palmer pulled to within one of Nicklaus. That was as close as he got. When Palmer took three putts for a bogey on the thirteenth hole, the outcome was merely a matter of Nicklaus hanging on without making any huge gaffes. In time, Nicklaus would become legendary for being unassailable when he had the lead in the clutch, and the closing holes in the playoff at Oakmont marked his first such methodical protection of a lead. By securing the U.S. Open title, Nicklaus became the first player since Bobby Jones to simultaneously hold the national Amateur and Open titles.

In the aftermath of the U.S. Open at Oakmont, Nicklaus was considered a killjoy in the States. Over in Scotland, however, the people were not only anxious to see Nicklaus play, but Slazenger found him appealing enough to endorse their products. The advertisement that ran in British periodicals prior to the Open at Troon featured Nicklaus, sans the goofy cap, and announced, "When Nicklaus tees off in the Open at Troon, he will be playing Slazenger British-made Clubs and the 279 golf ball." Readers were encouraged to "look for the new 279 with jet black numbers and new polyurethane paint and see how it lasts for round after round!" So many Scots turned out to catch a glimpse of the jet black numbers on Nicklaus's ball during practice rounds that police had to be called in to control the galleries that wandered around with him. Palmer had the same thing happen to him.

But Nicklaus's Open Championship debut was a nightmare. Unaccustomed to using the irons required by his agreement with Slazenger and the smaller 1.62-inch-diameter golf ball then mandated by R&A rules, he shot an eighty in the first round. Just as Palmer had tweaked his driver in the pro shop at Birkdale the year before, Nicklaus spent time in the pro shop at Troon trying to grind his new irons until they looked good to him. It's possible he wanted to reduce them to splinters after making a ten at the par-five eleventh hole. *Golf World* let its American readers know his score for the day was "a big, fat eighty." Internally, Nicklaus fretted over the rock-hard ground at Troon—he had never played under such conditions—but he never let on to the fact. "Nicklaus," wrote Tom Scott in *Golf Illustrated*, "despite his failure, had no complaint against the course. He blamed himself."

Nicklaus managed to sneak under the thirty-six-hole cut with a second round of seventy-two. In Friday's double rounds, he scored seventy-four and seventy-nine. It was a horror show for such a talented player, and he finished twenty-nine shots behind the champion Palmer. What mattered most, however, was that he was the best young American player in years—perhaps ever—and he had gone to play in the Open Championship.

IF ARNOLD PALMER HAD STAYED HOME rather than going to Britain to play in the Open Championships of 1960, '61, and '62, it would not have affected Jack Nicklaus's decision to play in the old championship once he turned professional. Palmer had given the Open a sorely needed injection of public interest and certainly changed how American fans and professionals would view the Open moving forward. In short, if Palmer hadn't gone to the Open, American golf fans would have had little interest in future trips made by American players, particularly a player viewed in the villainous light that shone on young Nicklaus.

Unlike the majority of his contemporaries, however, Nicklaus did not need to be led through history. Rather than being a follower, Nicklaus was determined to take his own path, and it would take him directly through the game's four major championships in the same manner as his golf hero, Bobby Jones. (The modern major professional championships differ from what were considered the major titles in Jones's competitive prime. Jones did not found the Masters until after he retired from competition. It is difficult to pinpoint exactly when the Amateur Championships of the U.S. and Britain ceded there position among the big four to the PGA Championship and the Masters, but by the time Nicklaus turned professional, there were clearly four major championships, just as there had been in Jones's time.)

Nicklaus said years later that "almost from the moment I began playing golf I had heard a message, first from history-conscious Scioto members, then from my dad and Jack Grout, then from Bob Jones . . . it was that, if you want to be remembered as a complete champion, you must win all of the great championships. That meant there would always be a question mark against your name unless you crossed the water and added the British Open to your record." (Scioto, a golf club in Columbus, Ohio, is where Nicklaus first started playing. Jack Grout was his first and primary golf teacher until Grout died in 1989.)

From his boyhood years in Columbus, Ohio, Nicklaus was influenced by Bobby Jones. Nicklaus's father, Charlie, frequently talked about Jones to his son, and when Nicklaus was invited to the Masters in 1959, a result of his selection for the Walker Cup team, the bond between father, son, and Jones became a personal one. In 1960, Jones sent a copy of his book, *Golf Is My Game*, to the Nicklauses. The gift prompted a letter from Charlie Nicklaus to

Jones, dated October 31, 1960. Written on the stationery of the Nicklaus Prescription Center (1761 W. Lane Ave., Columbus 21, Ohio), the letter, addressed "Dear Bob," reads in part:

> We have read Mr. O.B. Keeler's book of your life (which Mrs. Keeler sent Jack a personal noted copy [of] when Jack was 14) . . . our respect and admiration has grown in the greatest proportions . . .
>
> I know of no other personage which I could wish that my son follow his splendid example in life, that of being most of all a fine gentleman . . . and also the greatest golfer the world has ever known . . .
>
> Sincerely,
> Charlie

As prophetic as those words seem today, there is no question that Charlie Nicklaus was too humble a man to be suggesting anything other than Jones was the "greatest golfer the world had ever known." That his son might one day ascend to that station in his sport could not have crossed Charlie Nicklaus's mind when Jack, aged ten, regularly accompanied his father for a few holes of golf at Scioto while Charlie recuperated from ankle surgery in late 1949 and early 1950.

The young Jack Nicklaus was interested in all sports, but when school let out in the summer of 1950, he began taking golf lessons—first group, then one-on-one—from Grout. By the following summer, Nicklaus had scored a personal best eighty-one from the men's tees at Scioto, and golf became *the* game for him. Years later he recalled how on a typical summer day he would arrive at Scioto early in the morning, hit practice balls for a few hours, play eighteen holes, eat lunch, practice some more, play eighteen holes in the afternoon, and then practice even more until the sun went down and his mother "hauled me home for supper by the ear." Charlie Nicklaus and Grout eventually installed part of a Quonset hut, equipped with a small heater, on the Scioto practice range so Jack could practice during the long Ohio winters. Many years later Jack Nicklaus said of those winter practice sessions that "I'm sure some of the older members thought I was mentally impaired." One of the primary things Grout taught Nicklaus early on was to hit the ball as hard as he could. To prevent Nicklaus from coming out of his swing while doing so, Grout would stand opposite the ball and firmly place his hand on Nicklaus's head while the boy swung the club. The ability to keep his head perfectly still while creating and unleashing phenomenal torque with his body stayed with Nicklaus all through his competitive career. (That Nicklaus grew up in a country club environment was frequently pointed to as proof that he grew up a "rich kid" and was somehow less deserving of greatness than the hardscrabble professionals who preceded him. Such suggestions are utter nonsense—his family was typical of the burgeoning upper middle class at the time.)

In 1954, the same year Arnold Palmer won the U.S. Amateur, fourteen-year-old Jack Nicklaus entered the Ohio Amateur at Sylvania Country Club in Toledo. Palmer was the defending champion, and walking off the course one day in the pouring rain, Nicklaus noticed a lone figure on the practice tee hitting balls. It was Palmer. Nicklaus watched spellbound for an hour, listening, as he later recalled, as the balls "cracked off the clubface like thunderclaps." By the following summer, Nicklaus was playing in his first national championship, the U.S. Amateur at the Country Club of Virginia. He was eliminated in the first round of match play, but it marked his first appearance at the game's highest levels of competition, a place he would remain for the next thirty years. He steadily improved his performances in the U.S. Amateur until he won it in 1959, at the Broadmoor Golf Club in Colorado Springs, Colorado. In 1960, Nicklaus was knocked out in the fourth round of the Amateur at St. Louis Country Club, but he grabbed the title again in 1961 at Pebble Beach in California. His competition was not limited to amateurs during those years. Starting in 1956, his name started to appear in U.S. Open competitions. That year he was second alternate for the championship at Oak Hill in Rochester, New York, but did not make it into the championship proper. In 1957, at age seventeen, he did, at Inverness in Toledo. He missed the thirty-six hole cut but made it the following year at Southern Hills in Tulsa, Oklahoma. That same year he played in his first PGA Tour event, the Rubber City Open in Akron, Ohio. He finished twelfth, the low amateur in an almost exclusively professional field.

Before winning the U.S. Amateur at Pebble Beach, Nicklaus competed in the Walker Cup in Seattle. He closed out an undefeated Walker Cup career by beating Joe Carr, an Irishman and an outstanding career amateur who had won the 1959 British Amateur. Many years later, Carr recalled seeing Nicklaus for the first time at the '59 Walker Cup at Muirfield. In that competition, Nicklaus defeated Dickson Smith. "I remember some fellow saying, 'I think Dick Smith will be great in a tight finish with the American,' " said Carr. "And someone looked at the fellow and said, 'There's only one problem about that. He'll never get into a tight finish.' " After being beaten by Nicklaus in Seattle, Carr returned home and told the press, "I think I've seen the best player the world is ever going to see."

At Pebble Beach, Nicklaus slaughtered his semifinal opponent, Marion Methvin, by closing him out nine and eight, just halfway through the second eighteen of the thirty-six-hole match. In its account of the championship, *Golf World* described Methvin as "trembling" during the match. In the thirty-six-hole final, Nicklaus won going away, closing out Dudley Wysong by going eight holes ahead with only six to play. *Golf World*'s correspondent could barely contain himself describing Nicklaus. "Having attained man's estate, the world's greatest amateur golfer won the National Amateur championship for the second time . . . he has been low amateur in the National Open twice . . . [and] his score for 144 consecutive holes in two National Opens is lower than that of anybody else, pro or amateur. Various experts have called him the greatest, and he has proved it in the world amateur and otherwise." A few months earlier, the magazine had picked him as a favorite, along with Palmer, to *win* the U.S. Open.

THERE IS A PHOTOGRAPH of Jack Nicklaus as a young man standing behind the counter with his father at the family's Lane Avenue pharmacy in Columbus. It's similar in feeling to countless father-and-son photos pasted in family albums or sitting in shoe boxes in attics around the world; Charlie Nicklaus is wearing a white pharmacist's smock, and his son is wearing one, too. The photo is evocative of the great pride sons take in their hard-working fathers, and it projects the aura of the timeless hope that the son will follow in the father's footsteps. There is, however, one dramatic difference between the photo of Charlie and Jack Nicklaus and the like photos in the collections of other families: In the foreground, sitting on the pharmacy counter and looking twice as large as the two men combined, is the Walker Cup. Jack Nicklaus is nineteen years old in the photo and recently returned from Scotland where he helped win the cup. Meanwhile, the two forces that would pull at Nicklaus from opposite directions after he won his second U.S. Amateur title, just two years after that frozen moment in time, are plainly visible in the photo.

Considering the money that even modestly successful professional golfers could pile up in the later years of the twentieth century and on into the current millennium, it is remarkable to think that Jack Nicklaus struggled with the choice between remaining an amateur and turning professional. (To pick a year at random, consider that in 1996 American professional Steve Stricker ranked fifth in the world in prize money with $1,383,739. On the same list, ranked forty-ninth, was Japan's Nobuo Serizawa, with $599,349. Both Stricker and Serizawa had fine years, but both are historically insignificant golfers.) Yet Nicklaus did indeed wrestle with his conscience over the matter, and there was much to consider. His father had idolized Bob Jones and, stopping somewhere short of burdening his son with a demand, held out hope that Jack would stay an amateur golfer as Jones had done. In addition, his parents had provided huge amounts of emotional support and nearly all the money required to fund Nicklaus's amateur career, by Jack's own reckoning every nickel of it until he got married shortly after the 1960 U.S. Open. Charlie and Helen Nicklaus had been able to do so because their pharmacy business was thriving and growing, but they had built the store from the ground up, and there was every reason on their part to hope that Jack and his sister, Marilyn, would eventually take over the family business. Jones even wrote to Nicklaus encouraging him to remain an amateur (also saying that he would understand if Nicklaus chose not to).

Against all of this, Nicklaus had to weigh his own desires. He was newly married to Barbara Bash, a girl from his hometown, and she had given birth to their first child, Jackie, one week after her husband won the 1961 U.S. Amateur at Pebble Beach. There was also the notion that, aside from the British Amateur title, Nicklaus had achieved almost everything an amateur could possibly hope to do with the exception of matching Jones's total number of major victories while remaining an amateur. In the first days of November 1961, Nicklaus made his decision: He would forsake unknown glory and cash to remain an amateur, but a few days later, the need to see just how good he could be tugged hard on his mind, and Nicklaus reversed course. On November 8, he called two local newspapermen to his home. Aside from the two writers, only Barbara and baby Jackie were on hand for the announcement that Jack Nicklaus was declaring himself a professional golfer. (One side effect of his decision was that he would have to drop out of Ohio State University to pursue his new career.)

In making the final decision, the rookie professional had more than just talent going for him. In order to play on the PGA Tour, all aspiring professionals had to be able to prove they had adequate financial means to make it through a year on tour even if they were a complete flop. In 1962, the required sum was $12,000. For nearly every first year player this meant getting an individual or syndicate to bankroll them for the year. The result was an added burden for new pros, who had to play well not just for their own survival but in order to repay their backers. Here Nicklaus had an ace in the hole in the person of Mark McCormack, who was certainly not the first sports agent but was the first to recognize the enormous financial potential available to superstar athletes at the dawn of the age of televised sports. As a young lawyer in Cleveland, McCormack began his career as an agent with a dream client in Arnold Palmer and then added Gary Player, the 1959 Open Champion, to his stable. In his first meeting with Nicklaus while he was still an amateur, McCormack told Nicklaus that he could secure approximately $100,000 of income for Nicklaus in his first year as a professional, exclusive of prize money. In an era when only a handful of the biggest stars in professional sports earned anything even sniffing six figures, $100,000 meant two things to Nicklaus: He could easily last a year without going broke, and he could play without the pressure of having to repay backers who had a stake in his performance. The latter point was crucial to a rookie pro since there were no paychecks if a player missed the thirty-six-hole cut in a tournament and only small ones to those who finished back in the pack. (In theory, professional golf remains the same today, but the amount of endorsement income available makes Nicklaus's $100,000 seem almost laughable.) In his first five tournaments as a professional in 1962, Nicklaus won checks for $33.33 (last place); $550 (fifteenth place); $450 (twenty-third place); $62.86 (forty-seventh place); and $164.44 (thirty-second place). Such play raised few eyebrows, particularly since Palmer was scorching the tour with six wins, including the Masters, prior to the U.S. Open at Oakmont.

During one of those early-season Palmer victories, the Phoenix Open, Nicklaus finally got his game on track. If no one noticed but his wife and family it is understandable, because Nicklaus finished tied for second with three other players thirteen shots behind Palmer. Nevertheless, something significant happened that week. After struggling with his putting as a professional, Nicklaus concluded the putter he was using—a Ben Sayers model he had picked up in Scotland during the 1959 Walker Cup—was too light. In a chance meeting with legendary putting genius George Low, the subject of trying a new putter came up. Low had a brand-new line of putters on the market under the name of Sportsman, and Nicklaus took a liking to the model known as the Wizard 600, a basic blade-style putter with a slight flange and silver-gray finish. Suddenly the putts began to fall. The Wizard 600 would become something of a celebrity in its own right because it stayed in Nicklaus's bag for the bulk of his major championship career, and no other club in history struck as much fear into the hearts of professional golfers. On the huge and superfast greens at Oakmont during the U.S. Open, Nicklaus putted superbly with the Wizard 600; only once in ninety holes did he require three putts on a single hole. As Arnie's Army filed to their cars, they could only shake their heads at the thought that the fat kid from Ohio had won his first tournament as a professional at the U.S. Open. It would only have added to their chagrin if they knew that Nicklaus would win three more tournaments before the end of the season and finish third in earnings with $61,869.

THE SAME SUMMER that Nicklaus and Palmer had their playoff for the U.S. Open Championship, another golf championship required a playoff to determine its winner. Just north of Traverse City, on Michigan's lower peninsula, the club championship final at Wallon Lake Country Club was thrown into sudden death. Ray Watson came from two down with three holes to play in the match-play final to tie his not quite thirteen-year-old son, Tom. Even though the family was vacationing at Wallon Lake, as they had done for a few years, the match bore no resemblance to the leisurely strolls over a few holes that Charlie and Jack Nicklaus had enjoyed at Scioto. Ray Watson could play, having made it to the fourth round of the 1950 U.S. Amateur. "My father was competitive on the golf course," said Tom Watson as he recalled the match nearly forty years after it had taken place. "He was as tough as you want. He never, ever gave up and I loved playing with him because he was that way. He loved the game and every shot—there was never a throwaway shot in my dad's game.

"On the first extra hole [of the playoff] I hit a beautiful drive and then knocked a shot up there about fifteen feet from the hole. My dad hit it in the trees on the right off the tee, had to pitch out to the fairway, and then he pitched his third shot onto the green about twenty-five feet from the hole. He made his putt and I two-putted. Next hole, I hit it on the green about forty feet from the hole. Dad missed the green and chipped up for a gimme. I rolled my first putt about two and a half feet past the hole, but he didn't concede the short putt coming back. I missed it.

"The next year I got him though."

ANGELO ARGEA ALWAYS SAID HE WAS LUCKY, just as any good poker player should. He might not have been so lucky to get shipped to Asia as an infantryman during the Korean War, but he was once he got there. Nearly fifty years after returning to his hometown of Canton, Ohio, Argea recalled his time in the mud during the war. "We used to take ammo up to the line companies," said Argea. "My first two weeks there, George Company got nearly wiped out, so they sent a bunch of us up to take their place at the front. I was up there for about three weeks sitting in a foxhole. A *deep* foxhole with a Mexican kid named Vince from Fort Worth, Texas. Everything turned out okay."

Argea had been in the United States Army for a few years before the night in 1950 when North Korean and Chinese soldiers crossed the thirty-eighth parallel into South Korea. When he got back to Canton, Argea decided he'd had enough of the army and that it was high time he see more of the world than he could from that hole in Korea. "I wanted to go out and see the country," Argea said. "And I love to gamble, so I ended up going to Las Vegas in 1954, when I was twenty-five or so.

"Not long after I got to Vegas, I was broke. I was living with some friends, which helped, but I needed a job. One day I saw a guy I knew named Terry from the Desert Inn and we got to talking and I told him I needed some work. He asked me if I knew how to caddie, and I said I did because I had caddied as a kid in Ohio. It turned out they needed some good caddies at the DI [shorthand for Desert Inn], so I went out there and caddied there for about seven years. Every year I'd go to the tournament in Palm Springs with the owner of the DI and some of his buddies. I'd drive his Cadillac down to Palm Springs, he would use it all week, and then I'd drive it back to Vegas."

Argea made that drive in 1963 to caddie for his guys from Vegas in the Palm Springs Golf Classic, a tournament where amateurs played side by side with the professionals. (In 1964, this tournament became the Bob Hope Classic, a name it carries to this day.) "For some reason there was a shortage of caddies at the Hope that year, and they didn't have enough for the pros," said Argea. "The caddiemaster told me he needed me to take a pro bag even though I'd gone there with my guys from Vegas. At the time I'd heard about this bad boy from Ohio, so I said, 'Put me down with Nicklaus.' He told me he didn't think Nicklaus was going to play because he'd heard Nicklaus had bursitis in his hip. I said, 'Put me down anyway.'

"Next day comes and Nicklaus shows up. I went to the caddiemaster and said, 'That's my man, right?' So I ended up caddying for Jack that week. We ended up in an eighteen-hole playoff with Gary Player, and it was no contest. I mean Jack just annihilated him. He shot sixty-five and was hitting eight-irons and nine-irons into all of the greens while Player was hitting four-irons and five-irons.

"After we won and he paid me, I asked him about caddying for him in the Tournament of Champions at the DI, which was just a few weeks after the Masters. I told Jack it was my home course and he said that would be great. I said, 'I'll see you there.'"

Nicklaus won the Tournament of Champions at the Desert Inn with Argea on the bag. They agreed to hook up again when the tour returned to Vegas for one of the final tournaments of the year, the Sahara Invitational.

Nicklaus sandwiched twin rounds of sixty-six between rounds of seventy-five and sixty-nine, and the duo ran their record to three for three. Recalling that year, Argea smiles and says, "I was just lucky." Since caddies did not routinely follow players around the tour in that era, Argea would not see Nicklaus again until the following year.

THE SHOWDOWN BETWEEN Palmer and Nicklaus at the '62 U.S. Open was the first time Nicklaus beat Palmer, but it was at the Masters the following year that Nicklaus entrenched himself at the top of the game. The early season win in Palm Springs jump-started Nicklaus's 1963 season, and the Masters lay just ahead. In the six previous Masters, Palmer had finished seventh, first, third, first, second, and first. The Masters had been played for nearly thirty years by 1963, but it was Palmer's dominance of it and the accompanying public interest that pushed the tournament toward its standing as *the* springtime rite that golf fans around the world now look forward to each year. The U.S. Open at Oakmont the prior summer may have been in Palmer's backyard, but Augusta National Golf Club represented the throne of Palmer's kingdom. A victory for Nicklaus at the Masters would mean even more enmity directed toward him by the fans, but he was unafraid of that prospect. "I liked Arnold a lot," said Nicklaus, "and I had an appropriate amount of respect for him. Beyond that, however, I guess the best I can say for myself is that I looked on Arnold just the same way you would expect a blinkered youth fixated on bullheading his way to the top of the mountain. Once the whistle had blown, Arnold Palmer was just another player, another guy trying to go my way on a track only wide enough for one. I wanted to *win,* and then win again and again, every time I teed it up. If that meant not simply beating Arnold Palmer, but also toppling a legend and throwing half the population into deep depression, so long as it was done fairly and squarely, that was fine and dandy with me."

A good bit of the 1963 Masters was a slog through poor weather. Gusting wind on the first day and heavy rain—an inch on the day—in the third round made most of the players wish they were somewhere else. In the third round, Nicklaus was paired with Mike Souchak, who held the thirty-six-hole lead. Souchak was a beefy man and a long hitter, but he grew dispirited in the rain, actually mentioning to Nicklaus that he felt the round would be canceled any minute. A cancellation, in contrast to a postponement, would have wiped out the entire round, even the scores of players who had completed play for the day. Souchak's sentiment was shared by almost every player in the field with the exception of Nicklaus, who said he "preferred to save my energy for solutions to problematic conditions, rather than waste it on whining." As the soaked Nicklaus trudged his way up the steep hill that leads from the tee to the green at the eighteenth hole, he was on his way to a score of seventy-four. Souchak would score seventy-nine. Approaching the green, Nicklaus glanced at the leaderboard and saw a numeral two next to his name, followed by a bunch of other names listed beside the numeral one. This presented a problem for Nicklaus, who is red-green color-blind, because red numbers meant under par and green numbers meant over par. He called to his caddie, Willie Peterson, "Willie, are we leading by three strokes or one?"

"Them others is all green numbers," said Peterson. "You're leading by three, boss."

With a three-shot cushion heading into the final round, Nicklaus was able to withstand late-in-the-day rushes by Gary Player, Julius Boros, Tony Lema, and, most unexpected of all, Sam Snead, who would turn fifty-one the following month. In the history of golf, Sam Snead is the only player who could realistically have been considered capable of winning a championship beyond the age of fifty. Snead was the Ted Williams of golf, a man whose natural athletic skills and flexibility were unparalleled—into his sixties he could kick the top of a door frame from a standing start—and whose swing was so effortless and powerful that even other tour players envied it. This was a last hurrah of sorts for Snead, who had won the Masters in 1949 and 1952, and the crowd not only got behind Snead but was once again openly hostile toward Nicklaus. If Nicklaus hadn't noticed the loutish behavior of the fans at Oakmont, he did so this time. He later said he was surprised and unnerved by people unabashedly rooting against him. Snead actually pulled ahead by two shots after making a birdie at the par-five fifteenth hole, but he faltered down the stretch. Nicklaus caught and passed Snead to win the tournament.

In a moment that must have galled Palmer's fans to no end, their hero presented the winner's green jacket to Nicklaus, as is customarily done by the defending Masters champion. Bob Jones, Nicklaus's boyhood idol and the founder of both the Augusta National club and the Masters, watched the proceedings; Nicklaus gave him the ball he had played on the final hole. Years later Nicklaus would say the look in Jones's eyes was one of the most emotional memories of his life. Nicklaus and Palmer would help each other into jackets over the next two springs, Palmer winning the 1964 Masters and Nicklaus winning in 1965. When Nicklaus won the Masters again in 1966, he simply had to put the jacket on by himself. Two months later, Arnold Palmer suffered the most astonishing collapse of his playing career, blowing a seven-stroke lead on the back nine on the final day at the U.S. Open. Palmer went down in flames because with such a commanding lead he felt it sensible to go for the tournament scoring record. It was a mistake that Nicklaus never would have made, and Billy Casper eventually won the title in a playoff. On the clock of Arnold Palmer's days as a winner of major championships, it was nearing midnight.

ONE OF THE MANY STATISTICS that prove the high caliber of Jack Nicklaus's game and mind during his prime years is that he rarely failed to make it beyond the thirty-six-hole cutoff in major championships. From 1962 through 1980, there were only four occasions when Nicklaus did not play all seventy-two holes in a major championship. The first of those came in 1963 at the U.S. Open, when after working so hard to learn the right-to-left ball flight he felt was necessary to win the Masters, Nicklaus was unable to recapture his dependable and more accurate left-to-right ball flight in time to defend his U.S. Open title at The Country Club, in Brookline, Massachusetts. Professional golfers are often spurred to new heights by near misses in big championships, as Palmer had been during his first three Open Championships, but in another marked difference between Nicklaus and other players, he was equally reinvigorated by near misses and colossal ones. As he prepared for the 1963 Open Championship at Royal Lytham and St. Annes in England, he not only felt good about his chances, but, in his words, "secretly believed there was no way I could lose." This is a remarkable mind-set considering that professional golfers nearly always lose—a handful of wins in a year filled with tournaments is considered a good showing—and furthermore he had stumbled horribly the year before in his only Open appearance. Nevertheless, inspired by his lousy play at The Country Club in June and at Troon the previous July, Nicklaus played his way into contention at Lytham.

Over the closing holes of the final round, Nicklaus held a two-shot lead over a buddy from his amateur days, Phil Rodgers, and New Zealand's Bob Charles, a left-handed player. By his own admission, Nicklaus got cockier than was typical for him and that led to sloppy play, notably a missed two-foot par putt at the fifteenth that he considered "no more than a tap-in." After another bogey at the seventeenth, Nicklaus paused for a moment to consider where he stood in relation to Rodgers and Charles. He didn't trust the small scoreboards scattered about the course, and felt sure that he would get unreliable information if he asked a spectator or steward, so with the wind gusting in his face he listened for crowd reaction back at the sixteenth green, where Rodgers and Charles were playing. When he heard no loud cheers by the time he was ready to play away, Nicklaus assumed neither Rodgers nor Charles had made a birdie. He felt confident that even if he bogeyed the final hole, he would win the Open as long as Rodgers and Charles didn't make any birdies on the two brutal finishing holes.

In retrospect, it's too easy to view Jack Nicklaus standing on that tee as the wily golfer of later years. In those midcareer seasons, Nicklaus would leave no mental stone unturned in making critical on-course decisions, but in the 1963 Open Championship he was competing in only his seventh major championship as a professional. Despite having won two of those seven, Nicklaus's experience was still minimal, and now he made a mistake that just wasn't possible in the other three major championships: It did not occur to him that he *wouldn't* hear any applause behind him on the course because of the white noise of the seaside wind whipping past his ears. Rodgers and Charles had, in fact, both birdied the sixteenth hole. With a closing bogey, Nicklaus finished one shot behind Rodgers and Charles. The New Zealander won a thirty-six-hole playoff the following day, and Nicklaus had his first big taste of just how quirky links golf was compared to the American game.

Whatever internal anger Nicklaus had as a result of his miscalculations at Lytham, he had little time to chew on it. By the next day he was in Dallas for the PGA Championship, the final major championship of the year. The absurd proximity of the Open and the tournament in Dallas left many players emotionally and physically drained. Rodgers failed to make the thirty-six-hole cut, and Charles, the freshly crowned Open Champion, did not play well either. The championship was played in the insane heat of a Texas summer, and in later years Nicklaus's recollections of the week were scant, other than the fact that he won his third major championship—and that the gargantuan Wanamaker Trophy, which had been sitting in the sun during the entire final round, was so blistering hot that he had to use a towel in hoisting it.

With the major championship season over for 1963, the twenty-three-year-old Nicklaus had won every major championship played in the United States. The Open Championship, and all that it represented to him and the people he most admired, was still out there and still not won. In the years to come he would consider his failure to consider *everything* on that final tee at Lytham to be the biggest mental blunder of his career.

# THREE

★

JACK NICKLAUS'S FIRST TWO YEARS OF MAJOR CHAMPI-
onship play as a professional were extraordinary. At Lytham, he had come
within a breath of winning half of the major championships over two
seasons—a beginning to a career that remains unmatched to this day. That
he did not win the Open Championship in his first two tries is not at all surprising because it stands alone as a test of a golfer's complete game. Equally
unsurprising is that right from the start of his professional career he began
gobbling up the major championships played in the United States. They
suited his game and mind-set, and more important, having grown up playing in America in a time when the notion of golf as a precision target game
was evolving, they were comfortable competitions for him.

To suggest that Nicklaus could not have won the Open Championship in
the first or second year of his career would be inane, but the fact that it was
the last of the four big championships he conquered—and the one he had
the most difficult time winning throughout his career—does offer some indication of the unique place the Open occupies in worldwide competitive
golf.

The Masters Tournament is the youngest of the four professional majors. First played in 1934 at the Augusta National Golf Club in Augusta,
Georgia, it has marked the beginning of golf's championship season each
competitive year since then. The Masters has the fewest players of the major
championships, and while the other majors are administered by golf's
governing bodies and associations, the Masters is run by the Augusta National Golf Club, which invites the players. A golfer cannot play his way into
the field via local qualifying tournaments as he might at the U.S. Open or
the Open. The criteria for getting an "automatic" invitation from the club
are well known to professional golfers, but even these are dispensed at the
club's discretion. The club also invites several amateur champions to com-

pete each year, a tradition it holds dear because of the incomparable amateur career of the club's founder, Bob Jones.

There are plenty of professional golf events played each year prior to the Masters, but none is so cathartic for fans of the sport. Having suffered through winter in the northern hemisphere and, regardless of geography, awakened from the emotional hibernation caused by a seven-month absence of true blue championship golf, fans and tournament players await the approach of the Masters as they would an impending birth. Flipping on their television sets, they are usually rewarded with the sight of sunshine, Georgia pines, blooming azaleas, and most heartwarming of all, the vast and impeccably groomed expanses of green grass.

With its rolling hills and firm, closely cropped greens that require a mere tap to send the ball thirty feet or so, the Augusta National course almost invariably provides viewers with a roller-coaster ride of birdies, eagles, and water-splashed bogeys (or worse). The Masters is the only major played on the same course each year, and over time, fans become familiar with the holes and know where the best opportunities are for a player to make up ground and where he might meet his doom. There is little or no long grass bordering the fairways at Augusta National, a quality that allows for aggressive play from the tee without worries that a ball might end up buried in deep rough and subsequently leave the player unable to play the desired approach shot. That approach shot, incidentally, represents the strategic core of the Masters. The wickedly fast and wildly undulating putting surfaces of the Augusta National necessitate that players know the precise spot—sometimes within a foot—where they want to land their ball on the green, lest it catch a knob or slope and slither away from the hole.

As spring turns to summer, the championship season in golf gathers momentum. In the middle of June, the world's best players gather to battle for the U.S. Open Championship, a tournament that is the Bataan Death March of golf. As the name indicates, it's open to any nonexempt player who can survive a series of qualifying tournaments; though most of the spots in the field are awarded to the best professionals in the world based on criteria established by the United States Golf Association (USGA), which is the rule-making body of golf in the United States and Mexico. Similar to the Masters, the USGA also invites a handful of top amateurs to compete, such as the current holders of the Amateur Championships of the U.S. and Great Britain.

More than anything else, the U.S. Open is a survival contest and has been from its beginning in 1895. It's played on golf courses invariably considered among the best in the land and usually located in the northern half of the country in an attempt to avoid oppressive heat; nevertheless, it is often quite hot during the U.S. Open. The USGA prepares these courses in the most severe manner possible, with extremely narrow fairways bordered by moderate rough which, in turn, gives way to taller rough. U.S. Open greens are always hard, and the ball moves along them at a speed that unnerves even the world's best players. The greens, too, are typically ringed by tall grass. (In recent years, the USGA has, depending on the golf course, provided some low cut areas around the greens in situations where they felt it was warranted.) A ball landing just slightly off target in the four- to five-inch tall rough is in no small amount of trouble. After a few visits to the tall grass, the level of frustration within the competitor begins to rise, because from such heavy rough it is very difficult to advance the ball any great distance or to have a comfortable amount of control on what the ball does once it begins moving. A player off his game even the slightest bit has very little chance of contending at the U.S. Open. The one saving element for the strong of mind is that the tournament is predictable. "If you land your tee shot in the fairway at the U.S. Open, it will probably stay in the fairway," said Tom Weiskopf, a contemporary of Nicklaus and the 1973 Open Championship winner. "And if you land the ball on the green, it will probably stay there, too." The winner, figuratively speaking, is the last man standing, and in the early years of the U.S. Open, from 1895 to 1910, the winners were all native Scots. However, once Philadelphia's John McDermott won in 1911, the championship became (and remains) almost the exclusive domain of American players. Since 1911, only ten players born outside the U.S. have won the U.S. Open.

Played in August, the PGA Championship (first held in 1916) is the final major championship on the calendar each year and is somewhat of a "U.S. Open in miniature" in terms of course preparation. Unlike the USGA, however, the PGA of America has over the years frequently chosen golf courses of dubious quality for its championship. This didn't matter much the first thirty-nine years of the championship since it was a match-play event during those years. When the PGA Championship switched to stroke play, however, the often questionable difficulty of the courses used took some shine off the event. The other differences between the U.S. Open and the PGA Championship are these: The PGA Championship is not the national championship; it's usually played in ungodly heat during the middle of August and often on courses geographically located to enhance this cauldron-like effect; and finally, its field is weakened by the presence of numerous PGA of America professionals who are not regular touring players. The latter earn their living giving golf lessons and servicing customers in the shops at the golf establishments where they work, not by playing for cash. The PGA of America is essentially a trade union for these men and as such thinks it's a good idea to let some of its dues-paying members tee it up in its biggest championship. No amateurs are permitted to compete.

Of the four major championships, the Open Championship is the best measuring stick for identifying the best golfer in a given tournament season. "When you factor in everything, the British Open is probably the biggest championship," said Johnny Miller nearly twenty-five years after he won it in 1976. "In my prime years [the early to mid-'70s], the British [Open] was the most consistent in terms of producing quality champions. The guys who won it were at the top of their games. Usually, the guy who is playing best in the world seems to win it."

The factors that Miller refers to are the things that set the Open apart from the other majors. The Open is the only major championship that reveals a player's *complete* game: Power, finesse, imagination, resiliency, patience, intensity, competitive ferocity, experience (acquired knowledge), and physical talent are required to some degree in all of the major championships, but none demands those things of its champions in such equal measure as the Open. The golf courses used for the Open are largely responsible for this balance. Whether played in Scotland or England, the Open is always played on a links course. In American lexicon the term links is used in a random manner to describe any golf course; a links course, however, is a specific type of golf course. Foremost, a links course is situated near the sea. That is not to say that waves are crashing just a few feet away, but they are often close enough to be seen and heard. These bits of coastal land on the island that England and Scotland share are known as linksland, and in his short story "The Pavilion on the Links" (which has nothing to do with a golf course), Robert Louis Stevenson, writing in 1880, tells us that "links is a Scottish name for sand which has ceased drifting and become more or less solidly covered with turf." The Scots long ago discovered that this type of spongy turf is wonderful as a platform for striking golf balls.

The impact of the geographic setting of links courses goes beyond good turf. The wind and constantly changing weather along the island's coast affect play much more so than at most American championship courses. As they say in Britain, "If you don't like the weather, wait five minutes." This creates the need for near constant adjustments to strategy during a round at a links course. The wind not only buffets the ball, but takes a physical toll on players, sapping their strength and creating white noise as it whips past their ears. As Nicklaus learned at Lytham in 1963, this latter effect creates a sense of isolation even when others are present. The full effect of the weather on a player's psyche, however, is that he must play the course as he finds it when it's his time to play. This is true of all championship golf, but at the Open there is the ever-present sense that things could change in a matter of seconds. A player on the course at a certain time of day may find the weather conditions gentle, while a player a few hours before or behind him may find them diabolical. Nature doesn't play favorites, and it tests the player's capacity to accept what happens to him without reducing his will. His fate is his alone.

The holes of a typical links course are laid out over the ground as it naturally exists. Most significantly, the terrain is not flattened to create smooth fairways as it is on American courses. The fairways on a links course are filled with little bumps and humps that can redirect a ball in a manner not always hoped for by the player. Champion golfers spend their lives seeking absolute control over their games and emotions, and the Open Championship is the greatest affront to their control-oriented minds.

The bunkers on the links courses used for the Open are more consistently terrifying than those on any championship course in the United States. Their most distinctive feature is that for the most part they are simply chasms in the turf, with the opening of the hole at ground level. The bottom of a typical bunker in the U.S. is at ground level, and the ground and sand are gradually raised up along the line to the target creating what is known as the "face" of the bunker. For the top-level player, such a bunker rarely offers any impediment to advancing the ball toward the target. The sand hazards on links courses are known as "pot" bunkers, and the effect of being in one is very similar to dropping a golf ball into a large cooking pot. Since the bunker is created by going down into the earth, there is nothing gradual about its perimeter. Typically several feet deep—and often high enough that a man cannot see over its "wall"—a pot bunker is devilish in a number of ways. The sand rests flat on the bottom of the bunker and meets the walls approximately at a right angle, and the walls are covered with sod or, in some cases, wooden railroad ties (called "sleepers" in Scotland). What this amounts to is that a player is at the mercy of where the ball comes to rest in a bunker. Any time the ball settles within an inch or two of the angles formed by the sand and the walls, the golfer has a big problem. If it lies toward the target side of the bunker, he will not be able to lift the ball quickly enough for it to clear the front wall. The player can attempt to play a shot that will clear the incline, and if that fails, hope the ball deflects off the wall and settles in the center of the bunker where he'll have enough room to successfully get it out. If the ball sets at the wall of the bunker opposite the target, there is no room to swing the club back, and the player is forced to play the shot on a line perpendicular to the target.

If a ball caroms off the fairway and into the rough or is off-target all the way and finds the rough on its own, the grass it settles into will vary in terms of length and thickness. In some places it will be wispy and offer little resistance to the player. In other spots it will be thick and perhaps as high as his knees. The courses used for Open Championships have few, if any, trees; off to the sides of the fairways, however, native plants lurk like highwaymen waiting to visit bad news upon the unsuspecting traveler. The most menacing of these is gorse, a bush that is a brilliant yellow when it blooms around May. Lovely to look at, gorse is Alcatraz to a golf ball, its limbs too thick and numerous to allow a club to pass through.

The Open challenge does have a conspicuous weakness: Since the courses are wide open and have mostly flat greens, and if the weather is calm for an entire day, a links course offers little challenge to a world-class professional at the top of his form. There are calm days during Open Championships, and on them the scoring can be very low. Seldom, though, are there four consecutive such days during the Open.

ARNOLD PALMER'S STATURE was such among his fellow professionals on the American tour that his play in the Open had a trickle-down motivational effect on their desire to cross the Atlantic. Perhaps their curiosity had been piqued by the televised images of Palmer at Birkdale and Troon. The appearance of Palmer at the Open on television screens across America was the result of the small budget that ABC Sports had compared to the other two networks (CBS and NBC) at the time. Unable to afford the broadcast rights to professional baseball or football, ABC Sports executive Roone Arledge was forced to look elsewhere for inexpensive programming. A keen golfer, Arledge landed the rights to broadcast the Open on *Wide World of Sports*. ABC paid the R&A £11,000 for the permission to broadcast sixty minutes' worth of the Open, and in years to come, American sports fans would become familiar with *Wide World*'s identity as the show that "spanned the globe" to bring them the "constant variety of sport, the thrill of victory and the agony of defeat." In the early 1960s, however, producers of the infant show had to go to great lengths to air footage of the Open.

The first challenge to Arledge's troops was a technical one. The standard picture shown to the viewers in Britain by the BBC consisted of 625 lines per image; American television used 525 lines per image. The conversion from the BBC format to one suitable for broadcast in America whittled away at the quality of the image. After conversion and editing in England, the tapes were flown to New York and later aired. Between the unfamiliar look of the golf courses and the fuzzy imagery, an American viewer might have thought Palmer was playing golf on the moon. In an eerie sort of way, however, the images presented the fact that golf history was being made in a far-away place.

In the gray stone home of the R&A in St. Andrews, action was being taken to capitalize on the renewed interest in the Open. Most significantly, Keith Mackenzie, a former marketing executive with Shell Oil, was named secretary of the organization after responding to an advertisement for the post in *The Times* of London. The work of golf administrators is of little interest to anyone other than themselves, but in Mackenzie's case the R&A had appointed a man who was both a realist and liked a good fight, and his impact was immediate. Years later he was recalled by Michael Bonallack, who would eventually succeed Mackenzie as R&A secretary. "He was a larger than life character, Keith," said Bonallack. "He had been in the army and with the Gurkhas during the war, and then he was marketing director at Shell in Burma. When he came back here he decided that the R&A needed to smarten up its image."

The first thing Mackenzie decided was that the small amount of prize money available to competitors in the Open could no longer be ignored. Tradition was all well and good, but reality must be faced head on. "Together with Mark McCormack," said Bonallack, "Keith dreamt up the idea of having hospitality areas, and the expanded product exhibition area that today is known as the tented village. He started to promote the Open as a spectacle as well as a golf championship. This attracted more money into the championship through television coverage and through sponsorship of the tented village, so it was possible to up the prize money."

While Nicklaus was frittering away the old championship in 1963, he was doing so in front of an Open crowd that for the first time had the option of grandstand seating: Four thousand seats at eight locations were stationed around the course. Also for the first time, the playing areas were completely roped off, or in some cases fenced off. In the tented village there was a fashion show, of all things, and in something called the Bunny Club, spectators could be entertained while seeking shelter from inclement weather. Those with access to the clubhouse or specific hospitality tents could watch the proceedings on closed circuit television.

In the manner one might expect of an old army hand, Mackenzie decided to leave nothing to chance in terms of luring American players to the championship. "Keith would go over to tournaments in America every year," said Bonallack, "and persuade the young Americans that this [playing in the Open] was the thing they should go and do. He got great help from people like Jack and Arnold who saw it as part of their life's ambition to come and win this tournament. Keith was largely responsible for making the Open what it is today." The amount of prize money for the Open would grow slowly, but Mackenzie had laid the foundation for future growth. Along with the awareness of what Palmer had done, Mackenzie's efforts at cajoling young American players to stake their claim in history were equally important to the future of the championship. In fact, they were necessary, because the golf fantasies of young boys in America did not include winning the Open. Hubert Green, the 1977 U.S. Open champion and one of the top Americans at Turnberry in 1977, was thirteen years old when Palmer went to St. Andrews in 1960. "When I was a kid," said Green at the age of fifty-four, "I never dreamed of winning the British Open. Back then it wasn't a very important event. It never even crossed my mind. When I was playing I would tell myself I had a putt to win the U.S. Open or the Masters, but never the British Open."

By early 1971, when Green was named Rookie of the Year on the PGA Tour, American players would be heading to the Open Championship in droves. Part of the reason for this was that the seeds sown by Palmer and Keith Mackenzie eventually bore fruit. The other powerful influence on the new generation of American players competing in the Open was that Nicklaus considered his record in the major championships to be the measuring stick of his career. "Jack talked about the majors like there were no other tournaments that mattered," said Green. "That meant if you were going to be considered a great player, you *had* to play in the majors. All of them."

As of 1964, the heady days of an Open field packed with Americans still lay in the future. In the meantime, enough Americans played to build on Palmer's successes at Birkdale and Troon. The Open returned to the Old Course in St. Andrews in 1964 and was won by a darkly handsome, smiling American from Oakland, California, named Tony Lema. Before "Champagne Tony" was able to share forty bottles of bubbly with the golf writers covering the event, he had to outlast Nicklaus, who closed with rounds of sixty-six and sixty-eight after a wobbly start of seventy-six and seventy-four. The day before the first round of the Open, Nicklaus played a practice round with his pal Phil Rodgers and a skinny, young Australian named Bruce Devlin. Striking out down the first hole's fairway shortly after noon, the three made an odd sight. Nicklaus and Rodgers, two stout men who could physically pass for brothers, had their hands stuffed in their trouser pockets and walked with a noticeable swagger. Devlin strode beside them, a frail-looking Ichabod Crane sort in a cardigan sweater, hands clasped behind his back and leaning nervously into the conversation between the two Americans. Atop Nicklaus's blond head he wore a white baseball cap with an emblem of a golden-colored bear on the front of it. The year before, an Australian newspaper writer had dubbed him the Golden Bear, and as anyone looking at his hat could see, the nickname had stuck. Nicklaus wore the same hat for Saturday's two rounds, but custom hat or no, the Golden Bear could not catch Champagne Tony. Nicklaus finished second, just as he had done at the Masters (behind Palmer) and would do a few weeks after the Open at the PGA Championship in his hometown of Columbus. By year's end, Nicklaus had piled up enough money ($113,285) to lead the American tour in earnings, won four tournaments, finished runner-up in six others, and third in three more. Teamed with Palmer he won the Canada Cup in Hawaii, and he picked up an additional victory at the Australian Open.

Nearly any one of his contemporaries in professional golf would have cut a Faustian deal in exchange for the year Jack Nicklaus had in 1964; Nicklaus, meanwhile, was not happy with it. While leading the money list would give nearly any golfer in history reason to dance in the streets, Nicklaus didn't give a damn that he had done so. He had not won a major championship, and in doing so felt like his career had taken a step backward. In the coming years, Nicklaus, golf fans, and the media would all regard any season in which he did not win a major championship as an off year. On the part of Nicklaus, such years served only to stoke his ambition.

IN SUCCESSFULLY DEFENDING HIS TITLE in an eighteen-hole playoff at the 1966 Masters, Jack Nicklaus became the first player to win back-to-back Masters and clearly assumed the mantle as the best big-game player in golf. Only the claret jug awarded to the winner of the Open Championship had eluded him. After dealing with a spate of personal tragedies and illnesses in his family in the early summer of 1966, Nicklaus went to Scotland for the Open Championship at Muirfield, home of the Honourable Company. (A freakish series of events befell Jack and Barbara Nicklaus over the course of two months: They lost two of their closest friends, Bob and Linda Barton, in a small-plane crash while the couple were headed to the Masters; a few weeks later, one of Barbara's uncles died suddenly; two of their children required surgery, and they were worried a third might as well; and Charlie Nicklaus was admitted to the hospital for abdominal surgery.) Nicklaus was hoping the challenge of finally winning the Open would shake him out of a mental funk, during which he briefly considered retiring from professional golf, and was excited to once again be playing at Muirfield, where he had played so well in the Walker Cup. When he arrived in Scotland a week before the championship, he settled into the stylish and cozy Greywalls Hotel just a few seconds' walk from the clubhouse of the Honourable Company.

Anxious to see Muirfield for the first time in seven years, Nicklaus popped out the backdoor of Greywalls and was greeted by a site that anyone but a golfer would have found lovely. The rough on the golf course had been allowed to grow to beyond knee-high, and as the muted gold-colored fescue grass rocked back and forth in the gentle breeze, it made Nicklaus think that "the only thing anyone could compete for here was a harvesting championship." The grass was so deep that during the tournament, a caddie laid his player's bag down in the rough to join the search for his man's ball and could not find the bag once the ball had been located. To make matters worse for the competitors, there was no buffer zone of short rough between the towering grass and the fairways. Since the lack of loft on the clubface of a driver makes it the most difficult club to hit straight, Nicklaus's ability to thump 300-plus-yard drives would do him no good here; a single shot shoved or pulled slightly off-line could lose him the tournament. The 1966 Open would be a game of position, which would bring all of Muirfield's 170 bunkers into play. Shunning his initial negative reaction to the course setup, Nicklaus forced himself into a state of mind that he alone could among his contemporaries at the time: The rough would eliminate half of the serious contenders right from the opening shot, and he had a week to play the course and set a plan of attack. By the end of his practice rounds he had decided that he would play the driver only a few times each round, opting instead on the long holes for a three-wood or one-iron, both of which had more loft than a driver and made for better accuracy. (At least for a professional golfer. Nicklaus always maintained the one-iron was his favorite club to hit, a preference that must boggle the mind of the weekend player.) He also correctly concluded that his power advantage had not been taken from him since he could hit the three-wood and one-iron as far as most players could hit their drivers. This meant that unless the other players in the field wanted to face a day of unbelievably long approach shots created by playing shorter tee shots, they would *have* to hit the driver more often than Nicklaus. This meant more opportunities for them to make mistakes.

The errors came early and often for most of the competitors. An Italian player competing in his first Open made a nine on the first hole in the first round, and by day's end *Golf Illustrated*'s Tom Scott reported that "on the [score] board were one nine, one eight, one or two sevens and dozens and dozens of sixes." Nicklaus, though, made it around the penal colony in seventy strokes, one under par. The 1966 Open was the first to be played over four days, the first round being played on Wednesday, and Nicklaus was in control of his game and the tournament until halfway through Friday's round, when he bogeyed four of the last five holes. While he was doing that, Palmer, having grown weary of playing it close to the vest, was unsheathing his driver and attacking Muirfield. He played the back nine in thirty-two for a round of sixty-nine to pull within two of Nicklaus. More disconcerting to Nicklaus was the furious rally of Rodgers, who after going out in forty strokes brought it to the house in *thirty* blows. That remarkable nine on the vicious course setup put Rodgers two shots ahead going into the final round.

At the eleventh hole of the final round, it occurred to Nicklaus that he was playing one of the finest rounds of his life. He had pured a one-iron off the tee and followed it with a pitching wedge shot that ended up just seven feet from the hole. For a putter of his skill, the birdie seemed almost assured. He had played the front nine in thirty-three strokes, which left him two shots clear of Rodgers and American Doug Sanders and three ahead of Palmer and Dave Thomas of Wales. This birdie would for all intents put him in the lead for good since Palmer and Rodgers had tussled with the rough and lost. No one could have found a bookmaker insane enough to even give odds on Nicklaus taking three putts from seven feet, but that's what he did. Now Nicklaus's mind, the clearest in the game, became muddled. He bogeyed two of the next three holes, and a secret doubt he'd harbored since botching his chance at Lytham in 1963 came roaring to the forefront of his psyche: He may never win the Open.

There was more on the Golden Mind than its own poor play. A British player had not won the Open in fifteen years, since Max Faulkner had done so in the only Open played in Ireland. Now, Thomas, playing ahead of Nicklaus, was in position to win one for the home crowd. When Thomas made a birdie two at the thirteenth he was tied with Nicklaus. At the par-three sixteenth, Thomas's tee shot hit the flagstick—nearly an ace!—but ricocheted ten feet away. Despite the urgings of the Scots fans ("Go on, Dave!"), Thomas was unable to coax the birdie putt into the hole. On top of all this, Sanders had not faded away either. When he made a par at the eighteenth hole, it put both him and Thomas in the clubhouse at 283. Nicklaus learned of this as he played the fifteenth hole and quickly realized he would have to close with four consecutive pars to tie Thomas and Sanders. Years later, Nicklaus said he was so discombobulated by the goings-on that he "doubted his ability" to make four straight pars.

Nicklaus made the first two pars and made his way to the seventeenth hole, a 528-yard par five. He had played a one-iron from the tee the three previous days, but now he decided to play the tee shot with a three-iron to make certain the ball did not run through the dogleg fairway and leave him handcuffed by the rough. He creamed the ball—after it finally stopped skidding along the hard fairway it had traveled 290 yards—and it stopped just six feet shy of the rough. Suddenly, the Golden Calculator was working again. Facing a shot of 238 yards to the green and under extreme pressure, Nicklaus ran through the equation for his club selection: one club less than normal for the small ball, one and a half fewer clubs' allowance for the downwind, one less club because the ball would bounce considerably on the hard ground, and a half-club less to accommodate the adrenaline pumping through the Golden Veins. In the end he selected a five-iron for a distance from which, under normal conditions, he would typically hit a one-iron. The ball was struck fully and well, and the last sight Nicklaus had of it was as it bounced eight yards short of the green. While the ball trickled along the ground there was silence from the crowd around the green, and then a tremendous boom of shouts went up. Nicklaus half-ran to the green and saw the ball hole-high, just fifteen feet to the left. With two putts he had a birdie four, and the Open Championship belonged to him.

When presented with the claret jug, Nicklaus was unable to speak. The secret doubt that he would never win the Open now vanquished, tears formed in his eyes. The Scots had treated Nicklaus well from his very first trip to the country in 1959, even though he himself felt he must have appeared brash to them in his younger days. The most savvy golf fans in the world, the Scots had never begrudged Nicklaus his success at the expense of Arnold Palmer, and on this day they had cheered him on even though it meant him beating a British player in Thomas. As he posed for photos clutching the claret jug and medal awarded to the Open champion, he grinned the contented grin. His pretty wife, head wrapped in a fashionable scarf, stood beside him. His hair was longer than it had been in the past, a slight wave visible in his mane.

Nearby, the scoreboard told another story. Among the top fifteen finishers there was an Irishman, a Welshman, a Spaniard, two South Africans, and three Australians. The other seven names were Americans: Nicklaus, Sanders, Rodgers, Dave Marr—the young gadfly who had won the PGA Championship the previous year and was immortalized by Dan Jenkins as "the pro from Fifty-second Street," Palmer, Dan Sikes, and Julius Boros, who by then was a two-time winner of the U.S. Open. The cash prize of £2,100 awarded to Nicklaus meant little to him, but it was £700 more than Palmer had won at Birkdale five years previously. Thomas and Sanders, tied for second, each received £1,350, which was £150 more than Kel Nagle got for winning in 1960.

The week after the Open, the Slazenger company ran an advertisement in British periodicals featuring Nicklaus with the claret jug and winner's medal. The copy read:

Jack Nicklaus played Slazenger clubs.
Jack Nicklaus played the Slazenger ball.
Jack Nicklaus wore Slazenger golf clothing.
Jack Nicklaus won the 1966 Open.
Q.E.D.

HISTORY IS NOT A TIDY SUBJECT. Things cannot be neatly compartmentalized since, like the families in the Bible, a moment begets another which begets another. To borrow a phrase from Winston Churchill, however, the end of the beginning of Jack Nicklaus's major championship career came the summer after he won at Muirfield when he won the 1967 U.S. Open at Baltusrol Golf Club in Springfield, New Jersey. After six years as a professional, he had won each of the professional majors at least once and had a total of seven of the big titles to his credit. At the same moment in time, Arnold Palmer was reaching the end of the end of his championship run, and the collapse at the 1966 U.S. Open turned out to be a foreshadowing of things to come. At the '67 U.S. Open he was paired with Nicklaus in the final group, and Nicklaus was in control throughout most of the day. Despite the vocal strength of Arnie's loyal-to-the-end Army, it was never much of a contest. In the end, Nicklaus won by four shots, and Palmer faded from his position as one of the elite players in professional golf. Palmer and his Army never gave up, and over the next ten years the golfer the Scots called the "great mon" would nine times finish in the top ten at a major championship, but there were no more major victories. This left Nicklaus alone at the top of the game. There *were* other outstanding players—notably Gary Player and, soon enough, Lee Trevino—but none, including Player and Trevino, ever had the game to be considered the best without Nicklaus's name being mentioned in the same breath.

There had never been a golf champion as popular as Arnold Palmer, and the fact that he had been shouldered aside at the very height of his power was a clear signal that the usurper must have been some kind of sporting demigod. Perhaps Nicklaus was the first of a new breed of golfer, and maybe others would quickly follow who were capable of knocking him from his pedestal as he had done to Palmer. The underlying urge to identify the newest great player was as old as the search for a successor to Allan Robertson, which led to the creation of the Open Championship in 1860. Thus, with Palmer having peaked and no one else on the scene capable of completely toppling Nicklaus, the watch began on the part of the press and golf fans for the conveniently alliterative Next Nicklaus. It would be a long wait.

As Nicklaus's Teutonic forefathers in Robertson's time might have put it (if they'd ever heard of golf), their descendant was an *übergolfer,* and his arrival in professional golf marked a big change. If they had seen him play, they would have immediately noticed how he differed from other professional golfers: His tee shots flew as if launched from a cannon, while the other players seemed to be using peashooters in comparison; his tee shots were played with steady accuracy, while the other players frequently sprayed the ball left and right; while others missed more critical putts under pressure than they made, Nicklaus had them shaking their heads at his ability to hole the important ones. The biggest difference, however, was that Nicklaus had an endless well of nerve and everyone else went limp at the prospect of facing him down. Weiskopf, a wonderful player who joined the professional tour in 1965 and one of the earliest players thought to be a Next Nicklaus, knew the feeling. Thirty-five years after his rookie year on tour, Weiskopf put the experience of playing against Nicklaus into terms he felt as a young touring pro. "When you stood on the first tee and you looked at Jack Nicklaus, and he looked at you, you knew that he knew that he was going to beat the shit out of you," said Weiskopf. "I tried not to look at him. He was pretty intimidating." (This sentiment has been repeated by countless tour players over the years, but Weiskopf was the first to articulate it.)

The astonishing thing about the Next Nicklaus phenomenon was that it began long before Nicklaus defeated Palmer at Baltusrol, and even prior to his Open victory at Muirfield or his back-to-back wins at Augusta National in 1965 and '66. The very first Next Nicklaus was probably Rodgers, who was being touted as such before Jack had even secured his position as First Nicklaus. Before the 1963 Open at Lytham, *Golf Illustrated* columnist Tom Scott wrote of Rodgers that "behind that poker face I detect a burning desire to be top dog, the man who can topple Palmer and Nicklaus from their perches." After that, arrivals of the Next Nicklaus were as common as post-mortem Elvis sightings. There was even a mini–Next Nicklaus in the tented village at the 1964 Open. A caption that ran next to a photo in a British magazine of a young boy crouched over a golf ball read: "A budding Nicklaus tries out his putting style in the marquee housing the Trade Exhibition."

The Next Nicklauses came in all shapes and sizes. In 1964 a British magazine reported that "they've started calling him the new Nicklaus, this bullshouldered, muscular twenty-two-year-old whose poise on the golf course belies his youth. His name is Raymond Floyd. . . ." If Floyd was wide in the shoulders, Weiskopf was the "tall" Next Nicklaus. At six-feet-three, Weiskopf towered over the real Nicklaus and had the added burden of being from the same state and of having attended the same university (Ohio State). In 1967, an amateur from Port Arthur, Texas, named Marty Fleckman led the U.S. Open at Baltusrol after three rounds. Here, for certain, was a Next Nicklaus candidate. Fleckman carded an eighty in the final round, but reemerged later in the year to win the first event he entered as a professional, the Cajun Classic in Louisiana. He never won another significant tournament. The emergence of the Next Nicklaus prototype occurred in 1969 in the person of Johnny Miller, a tall, skinny, blond-haired young man from California. The hair was important; if you were going to be *the* Next Nicklaus, you couldn't have Floyd or Fleckman's dark hair or Weiskopf's kinky coif. A blond mane was required even if, like Miller, the player didn't possess the same girth as Nicklaus. Miller had a pedigree, having won the 1964 U.S. Junior Championship and, as he put it, a penchant for "firing the ball right at the stinking flag."

The rub of being a Next Nicklaus was that while all players aspired to play the game at Nicklaus's level, they didn't welcome the comparisons. It was like being compared to Zeus. The result was that once a player was saddled with the Next Nicklaus tag, it was just one more thing to worry about. Conquering self-expectation is the most basic challenge in golf and it is occasionally too much for even professional golfers to handle. For a player to have the expectation that he might be the Next Nicklaus foisted upon him by the press was not just an annoyance, but a millstone around the neck.

The first Next Nicklaus of the 1970s was Ben Crenshaw, who arrived on the PGA Tour in the fall of 1973 after winning three consecutive NCAA Championships while at the University of Texas. (He was coholder of the '72 NCAA title with another Texan, Tom Kite.) Crenshaw won the first tournament he played in after turning professional, the San Antonio–Texas Open. He had everything required in a Next Nicklaus, including longish blond hair in the style of the day. Crenshaw had a syrupy swing and uncanny touch with the putter and also possessed the one thing Nicklaus hadn't had as a young man, an abundance of natural charm. People liked Ben Crenshaw. Nearly thirty years after his rookie season, Crenshaw recalled the Next Nicklaus phenomenon. "I had a lot of expectations written for me, because I *had* started well. I thought that I could accomplish things in golf, but I certainly didn't consider myself the next Nicklaus. I was trying to be the best *I* could be. The whole notion of a next Nicklaus was ridiculous. He was such a rare exception. I was just one of a lot of very good young players who were trying to climb the ladder. There couldn't really be a next Nicklaus because the real Nicklaus was still there, and still beating everybody, and would continue to for more than another decade."

AMID THE CLAMORING for a Next Nicklaus, or a "Bear Apparent" as some preferred, the man himself lay fallow during the campaigns of 1968 and 1969. Nicklaus won five PGA Tour events over the two years and finished second and third respectively on the money list, but there were no major championship victories. The best Nicklaus could muster was runner-up finishes at the U.S. Open and Open Championship in 1968. He missed the cut in the PGA Championship that year and rolled that anemic performance right into the worst year of major championship performances he would suffer during his prime: twenty-fourth place at the Masters, twenty-fifth at the U.S. Open, eleventh at the PGA Championship, and sixth in the Open Championship. In later years he demurred from all the reasons proffered by press at the time for his slump, namely that having grown up a rich kid he was unable to cope with adversity, that he didn't play enough tournaments, that his swing was fundamentally unsound, that he was in poor physical condition, or that his desire had waned. Instead, said Nicklaus, he had gotten "mentally lazy, or complacent, or both." When his game went awry, as happens to all golfers, he was unwilling to work hard at fixing it and believed that because of his natural talent, his game would fix itself.

Nicklaus was wrong on that count, and there were plenty of hungry players around who took advantage of the situation. Foremost among them was Lee Trevino, a former Marine who had finished unnoticed in fifth place behind Nicklaus at Baltusrol. Trevino was everything but a Next Nicklaus. As a Mexican-American, Trevino had dark hair and dark skin, and he had learned the game at Hardy's Driving Range in his hometown of Dallas. He was a year older than Nicklaus, but throughout most of the 1960s the only golfers who had ever heard of him were those he hustled in betting games in Dallas. In the 1968 U.S. Open at Oak Hill in Rochester, New York, Trevino shocked everyone but himself when he won. Bounding along the fairways in bright red socks to match his red shirt, Trevino wore a Band-Aid on his forearm to cover a tattoo he'd gotten during his days as a Marine. Golf fans loved Trevino and loved to laugh with him as he nervously wisecracked his way through a round of golf. During the countless hours of pounding practice balls at Hardy's, Trevino had produced an effective (if flat and unorthodox) swing and as a result had masterful control of the golf ball. He didn't hit the ball far, but he hit it straight and could maneuver it brilliantly. Moreover, Trevino was undaunted by Nicklaus—he knew Nicklaus was great, but he wasn't afraid to beat him. Trevino did so for the first time at Oak Hill by becoming the first player ever to have four rounds in the sixties in Open competition. (Trevino had three rounds of sixty-nine and one of sixty-eight.)

Over in Great Britain, a young English player named Tony Jacklin was emerging as the great hope of Britain's golf fans. He won the Open Championship in 1969 at Lytham, becoming the first Briton to win the Open since Faulkner in 1951. It was the third straight year that a non-American had won the Open. Roberto De Vicenzo had beaten Nicklaus by two shots in 1967 to become the first South American to win a major championship, and Gary Player had won his second Open title with a victory at Carnoustie in 1968. Nicklaus was once again second.

While Trevino and Jacklin were taking what they could get while Nicklaus was dormant, Tom Watson was a student at Stanford University, in Palo Alto, California. Stanford, the alma mater of Watson's father, is a school known foremost for its academics, although it does field very competitive teams in athletics. (Stanford golfers over the years include Tiger Woods and Lawson Little, the latter won both the U.S. Amateur and Amateur Championship in 1934 and 1935. He also won the 1940 U.S. Open after turning professional.) When Watson first arrived in Palo Alto he did not do so with visions of being a collegiate golfer. The Stanford golf coach, Bud Finger, had to ask Watson to try out for the team. More than two decades after his graduation from Stanford, the golf program decided to honor Watson by placing a plaque on the first tee of the campus golf course. Watson's friend Sandy Tatum was there that day and recalled a great deal of needling directed at Watson. "Tom was a wild player in college," said Tatum. "The joke was that rather than putting the plaque on the tee, it should be installed about one foot inside the out-of-bounds markers along the side of the first hole—the place Tom's drives always ended up." Watson's reputation for being erratic in terms of accuracy with his driver would follow him onto the PGA Tour, where it would be compounded by a new belief that he was unable to keep his game together under pressure.

# FOUR

★

AS THE 1960S DREW TO A CLOSE, JACK NICKLAUS'S pants were still too tight. His thunderous tee shots were now mythical, his record for the decade was rivaled only by Palmer's, and his ability to think and focus on the golf course was the envy of everyone who played the game. (In the 1964 Masters, Nicklaus hit a driver 340 yards at the 500-yard fifteenth hole. With a persimmon driver and a golf ball that felt like a rock compared to current-day golf balls, that distance is incomprehensible.) Few doubted that his off years of 1968 and '69 were anything but a passing phase. Lee Trevino, for one, was hopeful that people would quit trying to figure out what was wrong with Nicklaus for fear that such probing would cause him to stir. "Don't disturb the Bear while he's sleeping," said Trevino over and over again, "because you know what's going to happen when he wakes up."

Trevino's wariness was well-founded, but the fact remained that toward the end of 1969, there was still one thing preventing Nicklaus from rising to the status of full-blown legend: He did not *look* like a legend. Nor did he feel like one, a point that became obvious to him in England at the Ryder Cup that autumn. On the final day of that competition at Royal Birkdale, Nicklaus played two eighteen-hole matches against Tony Jacklin. Ryder Cup competitions of that era were typically lopsided affairs in favor of the Americans, but that year's was a cliffhanger, and Nicklaus was front and center in the drama. He lost his morning match to Jacklin by a score of four and three, leaving the Americans a single point behind the team from Britain with eight points up for grabs in the afternoon. (The Ryder Cup is currently a biennial match-play competition between teams of professionals from the U.S. and Europe. Prior to the 1979 match, however, only players from Britain competed versus the Americans; the change was made to make the matches more competitive. The matches alternate between venues in the U.S. and Europe, and the structure of the matches, while always match play, has changed constantly through the years.) In their afternoon match, Jacklin holed a putt in excess of forty feet for an eagle at the seventeenth hole to draw even with Nicklaus, but American captain Sam Snead had allowed Nicklaus to play in only one match on each of the first two days so Nicklaus would be strong for just such a finish. But now with the two teams tied and Nicklaus and Jacklin playing the final hole of the competition, Nicklaus was tired. The pressure was immense as the British team looked for its first victory in the competition since 1957.

Sensing that the moment was probably especially difficult on Jacklin, Nicklaus asked him how he was feeling as they walked down the final fairway. "Bloody petrified," said Jacklin. After holing a five-foot putt for his par, Nicklaus conceded Jacklin's par putt of a few feet and the Ryder Cup ended in a draw. "I don't think you would have missed that putt," said Nicklaus to Jacklin, "but under these circumstances I would never give you the opportunity to do so." While that moment lingers to this day as a clear indication that Nicklaus always maintained the highest possible sense of sportsmanship in the heat of battle, the fact remained that he may have faltered in those two matches because he was in lousy physical condition.

On the flight back to the States, Nicklaus mentioned to his wife that he thought his fatigue during the final match was a sign that he should lose weight. Barbara Nicklaus concurred, and upon arriving home her husband started a Weight Watchers program (minus the meetings); he stayed off the tour for three weeks, and when he played practice rounds he carried a handful of clubs and jogged between shots. Within three weeks, he had dropped twenty pounds—an inch around the waist and seven inches around his hips. When Nicklaus went back out on tour, he won the first two events he played in and finished second in the third. He never got tired on the course, and when he arrived back home after playing in four tournaments, he had lost five more pounds.

The 1970 season was now on the horizon, and with a fresh slate of major championships before him, Nicklaus could battle the upstarts like Trevino knowing that the Golden Trousers would not burst at the seams.

TOM WATSON WASN'T ESPECIALLY COMFORTABLE at Stanford University. He was born and raised in Missouri, which is a long way from Northern California both geographically and philosophically. In the late 1960s and early 1970s, the nation's college campuses, including Stanford's, were flashpoints for protests against the American military presence in Vietnam. Watson never took part in the war protests, and in later years said he "was somewhat of a fish out of water" at Stanford and that he "was unhappy at times." It wasn't that Watson was in favor of the young men of his generation getting shot up in Southeast Asia; the first time he voted in a presidential election, he cast his vote for George McGovern, who was adamantly opposed to American troops in Vietnam. ("You're an idiot," said Ray Watson to his son upon learning of the vote.) The greater and more probable reason for his discomfort was that Watson, intrinsically a deep thinker, was struggling with Life's Big Questions as do all young people.

One place he could get away from the noise was at Pebble Beach, America's most famous seaside golf course, just a short drive down the California coast from Stanford. While most of his future contemporaries on the PGA Tour were playing golf at big state universities from which they would not graduate, Watson pursued his education and his game in a more solitary manner. "On Saturdays," said Watson years later, "I would get up at five in the morning and drive to Pebble Beach. The starter was a man named Ray Parga, and he would let me play for free. I'd be the first one off. Later in the day, after everyone else had finished playing, I'd go out for another round." It is safe to say that Watson did not feel lonely during those rounds; he reveled in them. When he played the last three holes, he would imagine that he needed three successive pars to beat Nicklaus for the U.S. Open Championship.

If those around Watson at Stanford thought him different—and they did—there was a simple reason for it: He *was* different. His selection of psychology as his major area of study was not the typical nonsense curriculum of a future professional golfer. Nor, as it turns out, was it any hint of a possible career path. "I had no intention whatsoever of making a career out of psychology," Watson said thirty years later. "I just liked it." After he graduated and began playing professional golf, the press was always quick to point out that Watson had studied psychology and that such training must have provided him with some sort of edge over other golfers. It made for an intriguing image: The future professional golfer sitting in the classroom arming himself for championship clashes yet to come; but it was hogwash. When asked if he ever applied *anything* he learned in the classroom on the golf course during his competitive years, Watson answered, "Not really. No, not at all."

In discussing his studies at Stanford, however, Watson said that "I've always subscribed to the fact that you are what your parents are." Therein lies the only bit of psychological insight anyone would ever need to figure out Tom Watson, the golfer. His father, a member of the toughest generation of

American men of the twentieth century, played hard on the golf course and so would his son.

Tom Watson did not look tough, and he most emphatically did not look like a Next Nicklaus. After the 1977 Open Championship at Turnberry, Herbert Warren Wind would write in *The New Yorker* that Watson's face looked like it belonged to a boy "sucking on a stem of grass as he heads for the fishing hole with a pole over his shoulder." This caricature of Watson was strengthened by his reddish brown hair and a slight gap between his two front teeth; when he was a young man on tour there was no end to the delight television commentators derived from comparing his appearance to Mark Twain's most famous character, Huck Finn.

Those who knew Watson even as a young man knew his harmless-looking exterior belied the instincts of a competitive killer. At his Missouri high school, Pembroke Country Day, he quarterbacked the football team with such intensity that his coaches referred to him as "Huckleberry Dillinger." He showed a capacity to adapt to change as well. "When I started out," said Watson, "we ran a single wing offense, but later we changed our offense to the run-and-shoot." The run-and-shoot offense in football depends heavily on a decisive quarterback, and the coaches at Pembroke Country Day knew they had their man in Watson. "I was a pretty good running quarterback," said Watson. "I couldn't pass, but I could run."

It was during these years that the quarterback with the suspect arm started getting noticed on the golf course by the other young guns of his generation. In 1965, the Trans-Mississippi Amateur Championship was played at Kansas City Country Club, where Ray Watson regularly played with his friends and his teenage son. The Trans-Miss, as the match-play tournament is commonly known, is one of the most important amateur events in the United States. First played in 1901, the Trans-Miss is used by the USGA as one of its guides for selecting players to its Walker Cup team, and the list of Trans-Miss champions prior to 1965 included Jack Nicklaus in 1958 and 1959. The year before the Trans-Miss was at Watson's home club, he won the Kansas City Match Play Championship, so it was only natural that he would want to test himself against national competition when it was right in his backyard.

One of the players in the field at the 1965 Trans-Miss was future PGA Tour player Mark Hayes, who is the same age as Watson. "I guess you could say I was a hotshot player in Oklahoma, and Tom was something of a local legend on the rise in Kansas City," said Hayes thirty-five years after the event. "We ended up playing each other in the Trans-Miss and I beat him one-down. Even though I won, it was obvious that Tom was a special player."

Another player in the field was a seventeen-year-old out of Midland, Texas, named Terry Jastrow. In later years, Jastrow would become the director and producer of golf telecasts for ABC Sports, including the U.S. Open and Open Championship. At the time, however, Jastrow was another young golfer with a bag full of game. In 1966, Jastrow would be the medalist at the U.S. Junior Amateur with a qualifying score five shots better than anyone else in the field. (Jastrow lost in the second round of match play in that junior amateur to Lanny Wadkins, a seventeen-year-old from Richmond, Virginia. Wadkins would go on to win the 1977 PGA Championship and become the most storied American player in Ryder Cup history.) Thirty-five years after the 1965 Trans-Miss, Jastrow recalled Watson from that week at Kansas City Country Club. "I remember seeing this local kid that was a little younger than me," said Jastrow. "That was the first time I ever saw him. He had a very loose swing at the time, but anybody who played junior golf in those days knew Tom Watson was coming."


ON FEBRUARY 19, 1970, Charlie Nicklaus died from cancer at the disturbingly young age of fifty-six. Jack Nicklaus had just turned thirty when his father died, and it was the first time he had lost a close family member. Beyond the obvious trauma of losing his father, friend, and supporter, Jack Nicklaus was shaken for another reason by Charlie's death; it was his guilty feelings over refusing to try harder to fix his golf game when it soured on him in 1968 and 1969. Years later, Nicklaus recalled how when the realization hit home that his father would not recover from his illness, the son had an awakening. "Here was a father," said Nicklaus, "who had done so much for me. He had seen what he believed to be a rare potential and he struggled and sacrificed so selflessly to make that dream come true. And now, here was his son, grown complacent, faltering, taking the easy way out and accepting second best from himself. By the time Dad died, I had decided those days were over. I might never fulfill it, but now at least I had recovered the will to do everything in my power to live up to his dream." Even though *Golf World* awarded "man's estate" to Nicklaus after he had won the 1961 U.S. Amateur, Barbara Nicklaus thought her husband reached full maturity only after losing his father. In later years, Jack Nicklaus would agree with that assessment.

As the championship season began in 1970, Nicklaus was leaner and longer of hair, but the position he had established atop the game was threatened in two ways: by his own erratic play in the major championships the previous two years and by a group of talented insurgents bent on trying to shove him aside. He had noticed over the preceding five years that with the exception of a few isolated incidents galleries at tournaments in America had become more and more inclined to cheer him on. Now as he moved into the 1970s, his more appealing physical appearance and his status as something of a vulnerable giant made it possible for golf fans to appreciate not only Nicklaus the golfer, but Nicklaus the man as well. As he dug his heels in for a fight, he did so with the backing of golf fans realizing that here was a man who was not a malevolent conqueror, but one that *they had chosen* to misunderstand because it suited them. Seen anew, Nicklaus was a man of honor—as illustrated by his concession to Jacklin in the 1969 Ryder Cup—and as he set about to fend off challenges to a crown that was rightfully his, he would have the fans on his side.

Like a medieval ruler returning from a far-off battle to find his immediate kingdom threatened, Nicklaus had to fight ferociously to reestablish order. The place Nicklaus took the first step toward advancing his claim was at St. Andrews, ten years after Palmer had first gone there. The final three rounds of the 1970 Open Championship were played in stiff winds and chilly temperatures. At times the winds registered gale force—gusts as high as fifty-three knots were recorded—and Nicklaus wore as many as three sweaters during some rounds. This was the Open at its most punishing, a mentally and physically draining experience. On the final day of regulation play, it all came down to a putt of slightly more than two feet on the final green. The player facing the putt was American Doug Sanders, and if he made it he would nip Nicklaus by a single shot and his name would be engraved on the claret jug.

It was an exasperating few moments while Sanders lingered over the putt. He locked himself into position to draw the putter back, and just when it seemed he must do so or remain frozen in that crouched position forever, he bent down to pick up a loose blade of grass. After settling back into his address position, Sanders again waited what seemed an eternity, bracing himself against the raging wind. Then he made a feeble jab at the ball and it skidded by the hole. In agony, he momentarily reached for it while the ball was still moving, like a weekend golfer wanting to slap a similarly wretched try back toward the hole.

In the playoff the following day, Nicklaus was one shot ahead of Sanders as they played the same hole. In the past, Nicklaus had reached the green on this hole from the tee with a three-wood with the wind at his back. Now under the same conditions, Nicklaus eyed the green, 348 yards away.

Sanders was the first to play, and even with his short swing managed to slap his ball to a spot just thirty yards short of the green. Nicklaus decided to play the driver, but before doing so paused for a moment to remove one of the sweaters he was wearing. The removal of the sweater has gone down in golf history as a dramatic omen of what was about to happen. It has even been suggested that it was meant to intimidate Sanders, but Nicklaus was above such hokum. He simply wanted to make sure he was unencumbered while making a big swing.

Nicklaus settled in to play the shot as methodically as he did every stroke. Standing behind the teed-up ball, he picked his end target. In this case, that was the flag rippling in the wind on the eighteenth green. He then picked out a spot on the ground just in front of the ball and on the same line. When he settled into his setup position, he aimed the club at the short target. Then, while gently moving his body to keep from tensing up, he turned his head slightly to view the short target, and finally turned it even more to eye the flagstick. Those two glances were quickly repeated just prior to the signature move that signaled the start of Nicklaus's mighty swing—the cocking of his head to the right. By doing so he created enough room for his left shoulder to turn fully away from the ball without bumping into his chin. With that extra bit of shoulder room, the clubhead could travel on the longest and widest possible path away from the ball.

Then the downswing: The left foot, after being raised slightly to allow for the body turn, slammed to the ground to create a solid brace against which the torque of his body could unwind. And then mayhem—the upper body turned back toward the ball while the shaft of the club hung for a moment in suspended animation, waiting for the delayed tug of the arms. The shaft of the club was bowed and building up energy as the clubhead traveled toward the ball. Then the smashed click of persimmon wood colliding with the golf ball, and in a matter of seconds, the ball was on the ground just in front of the green and then leapt, nearly hitting the flagstick! But it didn't, and instead it ran through the green and almost out of bounds. Nicklaus here caught a break, as the ball settled into high grass leaning toward the hole. After a delicate chip shot, he holed the putt for a birdie three and was Open Champion once again. As the putt dropped, an exuberant Nicklaus flung his putter into the sky. In a darkly comic moment, spectators and television viewers gasped as the putter soared through the gray sky and Doug Sanders ducked for fear of being hit by the club as it descended. The club didn't strike Sanders.

Afterward, Nicklaus said to the gathering, "There is no place in the world I would rather win a championship than here. It has been quite a while since I won a major championship—three years, in fact. I don't think I've ever felt so excited in my life."

The next day in *The Times* of London, Peter Ryde wrote, "The putter of Jack Nicklaus somersaulting through the air above the eighteenth green at St. Andrews yesterday signaled victory. . . . Now he is the only player to have won the American and British Opens and the Masters twice . . . and he is back once more at the top. . . ."

In the ensuing five years, Nicklaus would play fewer and fewer regular tour events—1970 was the last year he played in more than nineteen. In the major championships, however, he energetically clashed with insurrectionists. For certain, he was bloodied and at times battered, but he would not relinquish his power. In 1971, he won the PGA Championship, finished tied for second with Johnny Miller at the Masters, two behind Charlie Coody, and lost an eighteen-hole playoff to Trevino at the U.S. Open at Merion. In 1972 he won the Masters and the U.S. Open at Pebble Beach and headed to Muirfield for the Open Championship in search of the third leg of golf's Holy Grail, the Grand Slam. Six shots behind at the start of the final round, Nicklaus surged toward the lead with a frantic crowd of Scots chasing after him. He shot sixty-six, but it wasn't enough to beat Trevino. In 1973, Nicklaus won the PGA Championship during a year when Next Nicklauses flexed their muscle: Miller won the U.S. Open with a record-shattering closing round of sixty-three, and Weiskopf won the Open Championship at Troon, but Nicklaus's win at the PGA Championship put him in front of Bob Jones as the all-time leader in major championship victories. Gary Player was the man in the major championships of 1974, winning at Augusta National and the Open Championship at Carnoustie. Nicklaus's best finish in a major that year was one stroke behind winner Trevino at the PGA Championship.

At the Masters in 1975, Nicklaus would once and for all quash what for any other player would have been a withering assault on his prominence. That year, golf fans witnessed a final-round shootout without equal in Masters lore. At the par-three sixteenth hole, Nicklaus hit a less than pure five-iron that left his ball on the front of the green about forty feet from the back right hole position. The other member of the Nicklaus twosome arrived at the green only to find his ball unplayable at the edge of the pond by the green and had to walk back to the tee to play another shot. While that was happening, Tom Weiskopf and Johnny Miller stepped up to the sixteenth tee. Fresh off a birdie at the fifteenth hole, Weiskopf led Nicklaus by a single stroke and Miller by two.

Weiskopf and Miller were primed to topple Nicklaus. Miller had won three tournaments in the Southwest early in the year, repeating a sizzling run he had in 1974 that earned him the nickname "Desert Fox." Weiskopf had finished runner-up in the Masters three times previously and badly wanted the green jacket. Twenty-five years after that Sunday in Augusta, Weiskopf described the scene. "When you get in there and you have a chance to beat someone like him [Nicklaus], you experience something that you will never feel at any other time in your life. Everything was moving in slow motion, and I wasn't aware of the people around me, just the colors around me. My emotions were running fast, but my capability to think was moving slow. There wasn't a lot of confusion in my mind. When you're play-ing badly, everything speeds up. But I was confident, and a tremendous sense of relaxation came over me."

Nicklaus's fellow competitor hit his second tee ball into the water, too. After finally getting a third ball on the green, he made his way once again to the green. Meanwhile, Nicklaus surveyed his long birdie putt as Weiskopf and Miller watched from the tee. As he took a last look at the line of the putt, Nicklaus thought to himself, "Make it." When the ball was still twelve feet from the hole, Nicklaus was so certain it would go in that he stabbed at the air with his putter. Once it did, Nicklaus and his caddie broke into what he later referred to as a "war dance." The rattled Weiskopf three putted on the same green to drop out of the lead, and despite a birdie at the seven-teenth, Miller couldn't catch Nicklaus. For the fifth time, Nicklaus was Mas-ters champion. Later in the year he won the PGA Championship for the fourth time. The rebellion was crushed, and at the end of 1975, Jack Nick-laus once again stood alone atop the world of golf.


THE THEATRICS AT THE SIXTEENTH HOLE in the final round of the 1975 Masters were brought about in part because of the calamitous quadruple bogey made by Jack Nicklaus's fellow competitor that day. If that player had not been forced to return to the tee to play a second ball (and, as it turned out, a third one), Weiskopf and Miller might have avoided the jar-ring blow to their psyches caused by watching Nicklaus's putt and its im-mediate aftermath. The golfer playing with Nicklaus was Tom Watson. He had played himself out of contention by the time they left the sixteenth hole that day, and at the time that pretty much summed up what golf fans knew about him. They knew he could get close, and they knew he could fall apart when he did. Most of the people watching Watson that day at Augusta Na-tional had little clue that it was his first Masters Tournament or that it was only his fifth major championship as a professional. What they did know was that Watson had blown the lead at the 1974 U.S. Open at Winged Foot, and that as a result he bore golf's scarlet letter: a "C" for "choker."

That Tom Watson was branded a choke artist when he was just twenty-four is perhaps the most presumptive judgment ever passed on a professional golfer. No one seemed to care that Nicklaus had finished fifteenth in his first Masters as a professional, compared to Watson's eighth-place finish in 1975. The truth was that Watson was playing superbly for a man who just a few years previously wasn't even certain if he had the game to survive on the professional tour. Twenty-five years after that day at Augusta National, he recalled that "when I first went out on the tour all I was trying to do was make a few birdies every round. Heck, I didn't even know if I *could* make birdies on the tough pro golf courses."

Watson had every reason to be uncertain about how he would fare as a professional. He never won the U.S. Amateur like Nicklaus or Lanny Wadkins had. He had never played in the Walker Cup, and he hadn't won the U.S. Junior Amateur like Johnny Miller had. He hadn't even been the medalist in an important tournament as Jastrow had been. In 1971, Ben Crenshaw won the first of three straight NCAA individual titles when Watson was in his fourth year at Stanford. The only wins Watson had in college were the Stanford Invitational and the Fresno State Classic, hardly big-time events. Watson did compete in the U.S. Amateur four straight years, and he played well. In all four years that Watson entered the tournament, the U.S. Amateur was a stroke-play competition. In 1967 he finished tied for sixteenth (with Miller); in 1968 he finished tied for twenty-fifth (Bruce Fleisher won; Hubert Green was third); in 1969 Watson finished joint fifth; and in 1970 he finished tied for twenty-sixth (Wadkins won; Crenshaw's college teammate Tom Kite finished second). As good as Watson's record in the U.S. Amateur was—and it is a fine record considering that tournament easily has the best field of any amateur event in the world—it certainly did not serve as a harbinger of coming glory.

Midway through his final year at Stanford, Watson phoned his girlfriend and future wife, Linda Rubin, and told her he had decided that after graduating from Stanford he was going to try playing professional golf. Rubin was far from thrilled with her boyfriend's decision. When he proposed marriage shortly after graduation, she initially declined. Years later she recalled her reason, saying, "I did not want to be a professional golfer's wife. I didn't want my husband to be a stranger to my children." The two finally reached a compromise; Linda would marry Tom on the condition that he would play the tour for five years, and if he wasn't doing well by then, he would put away the clubs and pursue another career.

So it was with the blessing of his future wife that Tom Watson made his way to Florida in the autumn of 1971 to compete in the tournament known as the PGA Tour Qualifying School. In the days when Palmer and Nicklaus turned professional, a player simply declared himself as such and that was that. In the intervening years, the Qualifying School evolved to sort out the pretenders from the future contenders. In 1971 the tournament was played at PGA National, in Palm Beach Gardens, the very same course where Nicklaus had won the PGA Championship that February. The mustachioed Watson was one of many long hairs who showed up that year to take a shot at big-league golf. Others in the field included Wadkins, Fleisher, John Mahaffey (the 1970 NCAA champion), and Leonard Thompson. All these young men played well enough to get their tour cards, the magic pass that allowed them to compete professionally.

Watson did not wait to join the fray. He immediately got on a plane and flew to San Francisco to compete in one of the final events on the tour that year, the Kaiser International at Silverado Country Club in Napa, California. Since he had no track record as a professional, Watson had to play in the Monday qualifying round to get into the tournament, and there he was amid the "rabbits," a term used by more established pros at the time to describe players who had to qualify each week to play in tournaments. (Prior to 1983, only the top sixty money winners from the previous year and golfers who had made the cut the week before could just show up at any tournament and play. The remainder had to play in a Monday qualifying round. When the PGA Tour introduced its plan for an "all-exempt" system in 1983, Monday qualifying became a thing of the past.) Watson got through the qualifying round and into the tournament proper, and once in, he discovered he could indeed make birdies on those tough pro courses. He scored sixty-eight in each of his first two rounds as a PGA Tour professional but faded over the final two. Watson played in five events before the end of the calendar year, and made the cut in all five. For his trouble he earned $2,185.

If he was only going to have five years to make it on tour, Watson was going to make the most of that time. In his first two full seasons on tour he played in thirty events each year. The results were less than promising. In 1972, while Nicklaus was chasing the Grand Slam, Watson's best finish was second place behind Deane Beman at the Quad Cities Open in Bettendorf, Iowa. It was Watson's only top ten finish of the year. He played in only one major championship, the U.S. Open at Pebble Beach, and he finished tied for twenty-ninth place. With $31,081 in prize money on the year, Watson ranked seventy-first among U.S. tour players. Meanwhile, Wadkins and Mahaffey were doing much better. Wadkins won a tournament, finished second twice, and third once. By year's end, and after playing in thirty-three tournaments, Wadkins had won $116,617, enough to earn him the fifteenth spot on the money list. (Nicklaus was first, with $320,542.) Mahaffey finished second twice and third twice and made $57,779.

Watson played better during his second full year on tour, recording eight finishes in the top ten and winning $79,974. He was not keeping up with the pacesetters from his Qualifying School class, however. Wadkins won twice during 1973 and had three runner-up finishes and three third-place finishes. He ended the year ranked fifth on the money list with $200,456. (Nicklaus was first again, with $308,362). Mahaffey had his motor running at full speed, too. He won a tournament, came in third in another, and twelve times finished among the top ten ending up in twelfth place on the money list with $112,537. Watson again played in only one major championship in 1973, finishing tied for twelfth at the PGA Championship at Canterbury Golf Club in Cleveland. Since Nicklaus was busy breaking Bob Jones's major championship record that week, Watson's finish went unnoticed by golf fans and the media.

As the 1973 season ended, any talk of new stars on tour centered around Johnny Miller, who had desecrated the feared Oakmont course with his final-round sixty-three at the U.S. Open. Even with that, however, Miller finished ninth on the money list, four spots behind Wadkins. Two spots behind Miller was Hubert Green, who won two tournaments that year and earned $114,397. Green was rookie of the year in 1971 when he won the Houston Champions International and finished twenty-ninth on the money list. As such, he knew a hot young golfer when he saw one, and even though he and Watson occasionally shared hotel rooms to keep expenses to a minimum, Green did not see Watson as a comer. "Tom couldn't play at the beginning of his career," said Green many years later. "He was a very marginal player his first couple of years on tour. He was a great collapser."

The meaning of that bizarre word—*collapser*—would become clear at the 1974 U.S. Open.

THERE ARE TWO COURSES at the Winged Foot Golf Club in Mamaroneck, New York. Both were laid out by Albert Tillinghast, the mad genius of American golf course design during the first part of the twentieth century. In 1974, the U.S. Open was held on Winged Foot's west course, and the course preparation by the USGA must be ranked right up there with the Royal and Ancient's mangling of Muirfield for the 1966 Open Championship. The mood for the championship at Winged Foot was set during the first round when, on the very first hole, Jack Nicklaus gingerly stroked a putt from twenty-five feet above the hole and watched his ball roll *thirty feet past the cup and off the front of the green.* The USGA had determined that the ignominy visited upon its championship by Johnny Miller's sixty-three at Oakmont the previous year would not be repeated. In addition to the greens being as fast as any in U.S. Open history, the rough was maniacally grown to a height of twelve inches in some places.

Prior to the U.S. Open at Winged Foot, Watson was having a very solid year. He had not won a tournament, but he made the cut in seventeen events, and seven of those times he finished in the top ten. That he held the lead after three rounds at Winged Foot was not a big surprise to him, but it did represent a slightly more accelerated pace than he had imagined for himself. "I was still really trying to figure out if I could make it on the tour at that time," said Watson twenty-five years later. "So I took it one step at a time with my goals. At first I was just trying to make the cut in tournaments so I wouldn't have to play in Monday qualifying the next week. Then once I started making cuts, I thought about how much money I needed to make to be in the top sixty, so I didn't have to qualify for tournaments at all. And once I made the top sixty [1973], I thought, well, let's think about winning here. *Maybe* I can win. I still had to learn how to win, and I would lose a lot before I learned to win. For sure I had dreamt that I would one day contend in the major championships. Every time I was out hitting balls, that was the goal in staying out there until it was dark every day. I wanted to get into a position where I could play against the best and beat the best, but I didn't fully expect it to happen as soon as it did. Being in that position in the 1974 U.S. Open felt very sudden to me. I guess I knew I had enough good rounds in me that if I could put them together I could win. The question was whether I could put them together."

As he prepared to play the final round at Winged Foot, he had put three rounds together and led by one stroke after posting scores of seventy-three, seventy-one, and sixty-nine. In the final round, he was paired with his closest pursuer, Hale Irwin. Four years older than Watson, Irwin wore eyeglasses that made him look like a nerd of the first order, but his geeky appearance was as deceptive as Watson's Huck Finn looks. Irwin had been the 1967 NCAA golf champion while attending the University of Colorado *and* was a two-time all-conference defensive back for the school's football team.

The final twosome that day at Winged Foot was an amusing sight: the nerd and the huckleberry marching along. Their caddies wore light blue overalls, but even they looked better than Watson and Irwin. The two golfers looked as if they had gotten dressed with the lights out. Irwin wore dark trousers and a hideously patterned blue-and-white shirt, with a fat white belt, and Watson's wardrobe was even worse: He wore a white shirt and light blue pants. He, too, wore a white belt, but forgot the age-old style dictum that a man's belt and shoes should be of the same color—Watson's shoes were black. This mismatched ensemble was capped off with a yellow golf glove, and the net effect was that Watson looked like someone who had sneaked onto the course by parking near the woods and starting his round on the second hole.

Watson looked as young as the caddies, a fact that was not lost on the ABC Sports announcers. Two of them, Keith Jackson and Jim McKay, repeatedly referred to the leader as "Tommy" Watson, as if he was the kid next door come over to see if little Jimmy could come out to play. On the greens, Watson choked down several inches on the shaft of his putter to the point that it brought to mind a toddler at a miniature golf course.

The course setup at Winged Foot had caused sloppy play from the get-go on Thursday, and the final round was no exception. After eight holes, Watson and Irwin were tied for the lead at six over par for the tournament. Irwin birdied the ninth hole and bogeyed the tenth to stay at plus six, while Watson drifted to plus seven after three-putting on the tenth. From that point on, Watson slid farther and farther from the lead. The most notable thing about Watson's play over the closing nine holes was that even when it was apparent he would not win, he never assumed the body language of a beaten man. He continued to grind on each shot, just like his father had taught him. He never lost complete control of his game until the seventeenth hole. There, his drive found the rough, and attempting to play a small shot back onto the fairway, he sent his ball scurrying across it and into some trees. He then successfully played his third shot out to the fairway and struck his fourth shot from about one hundred yards out. Even while this minidisaster was occurring, there were positive signs if one looked closely enough. Watson made the putt for a bogey five and in doing so displayed a nervy willingness to jam the ball into the hole on the slick greens. In the end, Watson carded a seventy-nine and finished tied for fifth place. He was quick to shake hands with Irwin, the champion (who finished seven over par), after they finished play at the eighteenth hole. As Watson exited the final green, he flipped his ball to a couple of young boys who had been watching him play.

Only a neophyte would suggest that Tom Watson choked during the final round at Winged Foot. The setup of the golf course was asinine and everyone in the field struggled. Years later, the then chairman of the USGA

Championships Committee, Sandy Tatum, said that he was "seriously disappointed in his [Watson's] final round at Winged Foot." The truth was that Tatum should have been disappointed in *everyone's* final round at Winged Foot. During the course of the week, Tatum was quoted as saying that the USGA was not trying to embarass the best golfers in the world but rather "to identify them." Tatum is a highly intelligent man, but he could not have genuinely believed that Irwin's topped four-wood from the rough on the seventeenth hole was an identifying sign of the world's best player; nor was Johnny Miller's final score of twenty-two over par; nor were the conversations in the locker room, where players compared their experiences to find that it was the norm to have played eighteen holes without a single birdie. Jack Nicklaus had to shoot a sixty-nine in the final round to finish at fourteen over par. When asked afterward what he thought of the closing holes at Winged Foot, Nicklaus said, "The last eighteen are very difficult."

Watson did not play in the Open Championship the following month when Gary Player won at Lytham. When Watson finished tied for eleventh at the PGA Championship that August it was only the third major championship of his professional career. Viewed with a modicum of common sense, his finishes of twelfth, fifth, and eleventh in those three championships were indicative of a player on the rise, not a choke artist.


WHEN TOM WATSON made the decision to become a professional golfer, he had, in his own words, "dedicated my life to trying to be the best player that I could be." Such decisions do not come easy, and most people live their entire lives without committing themselves to be the best at anything. Terry Jastrow was a person who realized the enormity of making the kind of decision Watson made. "When I was playing golf at the University of Houston on a golf scholarship," said Jastrow, "I certainly had thoughts about turning professional. But then it occurred to me that great golfers must have a singleness of purpose that I did not have. There were too many other things in life that I enjoyed—skiing, tennis, travel, the arts. When the opportunity to work at ABC Sports came along and they were doing all that spanning the globe stuff, I realized that would be a lot more fun than trying to make sidehill five-footers."

Watson had the single-mindedness to which Jastrow referred, but he also had some other assets; he could play exceedingly long tee shots with his driver. In the 1969 NCAA Championships, he averaged 294 yards with the driver, the longest of anyone in the field. Tom Weiskopf said years later that "Watson could hit it out there with Nicklaus and myself no problem."

Watching Watson swing the club, an observer would never imagine that he generated such power. In Nicklaus's swing, one could *see* the power building, and the same could be said of Weiskopf's swing, although in his case it had more to do with the enormous arc the clubhead traveled on due to his height. Watson was only five-feet-nine and weighed 160 pounds; the source of his power was in the tempo and length of his swing. Watson did everything quickly—he made quick decisions on the course, he did not dilly-dally in addressing the ball, and moving from shot to shot he walked faster than any player of his time. He also swung the club quickly. While such an attribute can be death to the weekend golfer, in Watson's case it was a perfect match for the speed of his internal motor. Besides, the fact that he swung the club quickly did not mean that he swung it in a herky-jerky manner. On the contrary, when he was playing well the tempo of his swing was exemplary. He started the club swiftly away from the ball, but he *maintained* that pace throughout his swing. He allowed the power to build without forcing it, but since he started the club moving quicker than other players, the end result was that it was moving measurably faster at impact. Watson was able to keep the tempo of his swing under control because his swing was elegantly simple. When Nicklaus prepared to play a shot, his body language was that of a man about to *pound* on something. When Watson addressed the ball, his body language was almost silent except for the slightest tightening of his mouth. Once the club was in motion, Watson moved his body with great economy: His hands swung high into the air, and the shaft of the club went beyond parallel with the ground at the top of his backswing, but the overall impression was of a tight yet smooth swing.

As long as Watson was off the tee, he possessed an even more deadly weapon in his putting. Like everything else, Watson went through his putting routine faster than other players: He took brisk practice strokes, and when he briefly settled into position to strike the putt, it represented a moment of perfection. His eyes were directly over the golf ball and his left wrist was locked in place, staying there until the stroke was finished. The stroke was simple—the arms simply rocked back and through—but firm. He putted aggressively, unafraid of the consequences of sending the ball scooting well past the hole if he missed. Unlike most great putters, Watson held the club with a death grip. Twenty-four years after seeing Watson play at the 1977 Open at Turnberry, Ben Crenshaw's caddie Bobbie Millen recalled that "Watson mesmerized me on the greens. He gripped the club so tightly that his knuckles went white. Like most fine putters, Ben held the club so lightly it looked like it might fly out of his hands. But not Watson. Even on the fastest downhill putts he squeezed the club so hard it was frightening. My

God, he hit the ball so hard that if he missed there was no telling how far by the hole the ball would go. Ben mentioned to me several times that he was simply amazed at how firmly Tom gripped the putter."

The key to such nakedly aggressive putting was confidence. Twenty-eight years after his rookie season on the PGA Tour, Watson recalled a round when he was paired with veteran tour player Jim Colbert. "Jim was from the same area I'd grown up in," said Watson. "I played with him in the first round of some tournament. I'd knock a putt three feet by the hole and say, 'I'll finish,' and just casually knock it in every time.

"Jim said to me in a real friendly way, 'Man, you better take a little more time with those short putts.'

"I said, 'Why?'

"That," said Watson, "ended the conversation. Any time I knocked it by I *knew* I was going to make it coming back."

There was, of course, a chink in Watson's game. Mark Hayes, who finally joined the PGA Tour in 1973 after a stint in the army, knew exactly where the weakness lay in Watson's swing. "Tom always swung the club on the same path," said Hayes years later, "but he sort of hung on his left side throughout his swing. It seemed like he trusted that move until the final round of tournaments. We knew that once he got out of the 'reverse C' position that led to, he was going to be tough to beat. It was only a matter of time before he controlled his swing. We all talked about him and we all said the same thing: Once he wins that first tournament, look out."

That first tournament victory came just a few weeks after the U.S. Open at Winged Foot. It was in the Western Open at Butler National Golf Club, outside of Chicago. The Western Open is one of the oldest tournaments in America, first played in 1899, and to this day it is one of the premier events on the tour. Watson defeated Weiskopf and J.C. Snead by two strokes. The time to "look out," as Hayes put it, was still a few years away, and in the meantime, Watson would follow his 1975 Masters debacle with another botched chance at the 1975 U.S. Open, where he led after two rounds. Blown chances or not, it was beginning to look more and more like Tom Watson would break through in a major championship. When he finally did, it came in a tournament that even he considered the least likely place that he would win.

# FIVE

⋆

ARNOLD PALMER CROSSED THE ATLANTIC IN 1960 IN search of glory at St. Andrews. In 1962, Jack Nicklaus went to Troon to fulfill his own dream and the dreams of others. When Tom Watson made his first trip to the Open Championship, he was a man in search of a tee time. Upon arriving at Carnoustie in 1975, Watson decided he would play his first practice round on the Sunday prior to the Wednesday start of the championship. His play on the American tour had earned Watson an exemption into the championship proper, so he had three days to become familiar with the course, or so he thought. When he arrived at the starter's hut by the first tee on Sunday, he was informed he could not play the course. It was reserved that day for players who had made it through local qualifying. The man who informed Watson of the situation was none other than Keith Mackenzie.

It's a bit ironic that Mackenzie had spent countless hours over the years trying to persuade young American golfers to play in the Open, and here he had one standing directly in front of him and was forced to tell him he could not accommodate him for the moment. On Watson's part, there was more than just irony involved; he was a bona fide contender for the Open Championship title. Earlier in the year he won the Byron Nelson Classic in Dallas, and his play at Augusta National and the U.S. Open at Medinah, where he held the thirty-six-hole lead, were clear markers that he could play well enough to win one of the game's big championships. Despite his increasingly solid play, however, Watson's chances were mitigated by the fact that he had never played a *single hole* of links golf before arriving at Carnoustie. His countless rounds on Pebble Beach's seaside layout may have been scenic, but they amounted to little more than extremely beautiful target golf. (During an interview for this book, Watson was emphatic when he said, "Pebble Beach is not a links course." It did, however, play firm and fast when Watson played it during his college days, before excessive irrigation of golf courses became the norm.)

In addition to the lack of experience he had on humpy, bumpy linksland courses, Watson was not even certain he would like playing links golf. In fact, many years later Watson said that it wasn't until 1979 that he grew fond of that punishing and capricious style of golf. Prior to then, he said, "I was not enamored with links golf. I thought the luck of the bounce played too much a part in the outcome of things."

Watson could take little solace in recalling that Ben Hogan had not played links golf prior to his victory at Carnoustie in 1953; the Wee Ice Mon practiced for two weeks at Carnoustie before he hit a shot that counted. On top of that, Ben Hogan circa 1953 was the most consistent ballstriker the game had ever known, and his typical shot was drilled with a low flight that was perfect for links golf. Watson was a high-ball hitter, like most good target golfers, and nowhere near as consistent with his direction as Hogan had been.

Like St. Andrews, Carnoustie is on Scotland's east coast. Driving north from St. Andrews, one crosses the Firth of Tay on the Tay Road Bridge, and then swings hard to the east for the road to Carnoustie. Like many towns in Scotland, Carnoustie is a small and gray place, but once into town a traveler can almost smell the golf. These days, a vacationing golfer is more than likely to stay at the plush Carnoustie Hotel, a palace of a place that sits directly behind the first tee and eighteenth green. Sipping a pint of one's choice on the veranda facing the course, a casual glance to the right reveals a golf store called Hogan's Alley, a reference to Hogan's four birdies at the 578-yard sixth hole during the '53 Open. A pause in conversation will reveal the sounds of the ocean surf drifting in from the left and out beyond the golf course the chatter of small arms fire from a nearby military range. When Tom Watson showed up in 1975 the Carnoustie Hotel did not exist, but the overall feel of the place was much the same. (The lack of a large hotel in the town of Carnoustie was one of the reasons the Open did not return to the vaunted links for twenty-four years after the 1975 Open.) Specific also to the town is the ever-present sense that the weather might turn nasty at any moment. If a maelstromlike front of weather such as the one that parked over St. Andrews during the 1970 Open Championship happened upon Carnoustie in 1975, Tom Watson would be in for an experience the likes of which he could, at that point, only imagine.

Although Tom Watson didn't know it yet, he had a lucky charm with him at Carnoustie in the person of Alfie Fyles. Up until that point, when Fyles wasn't caddying for Gary Player in the big championships, he was a regular looper at Royal Birkdale in England. He had caddied for Player when the South African won the Open at Carnoustie in 1968, and his brother, Albert, had worked for Tom Weiskopf when he won the 1973 Open at Old Troon. With the exception of a few years spent in the Royal Navy, Alfie Fyles had caddied for most of his life. He was of the old school and would have none of the nonsense of pacing off yardages and tossing grass into the air to see which way the wind was blowing. That stuff was for amateurs, something Alfie Fyles most certainly was not. Bobbie Millen did not caddie in the '75 Open (Ben Crenshaw was injured at the time), but he saw Fyles and Watson work together many times. "The yardage book didn't play a big part in things for Alfie," said Millen twenty-five years later. "He was an old style caddie. Guys like Alfie would eyeball a shot. In other words, they'd just go with a gut feel for a situation. Even in practice rounds, when you watched Alfie and Tom together, it was Tom who was taking all the notes. Those fellows [old school caddies] were characters. There wasn't a night that would go by when Alfie and his pals wouldn't visit the local hostelry and partake of beverage."

Like a lot of serious caddies, Fyles was a fair golfer himself. He was a short man with a weathered face, and his wild, thinning hair was perpetually covered with a cap. Fyles peppered his speech with the rhyming Cockney code used in the part of England where he resided. Fyles and his fellow old-schoolers would meet at the Jack Tar (a bar) for a few Kitchen Sinks (drinks). Fyles might have a Mick Jagger (a lager) while his mates might have a Vera Lynn (a drink of gin). Twenty-six years after their first meeting at Carnoustie, Watson fondly recalled Fyles. "Alf was a hard-drinking guy with a great smile. He loved to smoke cigarettes and go to the bars and tell stories and get in fights. One time he showed up at Muirfield and he had a little shiner right underneath his left eye.

"I said, 'What did you do last night, Alf, get in a little altercation?'

" 'Yes, sir.'

" 'Who won the fight,' I said.

"Alf said, 'Who do you think, sir?'

"He was a beauty," said Watson. "He always called me 'Mister.' Never Tom or Mister Watson. Just 'Mister.' "

What Mister lacked in knowledge about Carnoustie would be somewhat compensated for by the presence of Alf Fyles. A little break in the weather wouldn't hurt Mister's cause either.


ON THE MONDAY AND TUESDAY before the championship, Tom Watson got his practice rounds in at Carnoustie. Before play began on Wednesday, Player told Watson that Carnoustie was the most demanding and punitive links course in the world. The last four holes in particular represented as brutal a finish as any in the game. Even though Watson hadn't played any other links courses, he could scarcely disagree with Player's opinion. The course was 7,065 total yards in length, about 200 yards *shorter* than it had played for the 1968 Open, though that in itself wasn't much of a problem for a player who could hit the ball as long as Watson. Consistently controlling the ball over such a vast distance in the wind could prove another story, however.

It is not uncommon for American professionals to have heard and read about the wild weather conditions at the Open only to arrive in Scotland for the first time and find things rather benign. It's a fact that even the greatest of links courses are toothless without a stiff wind. There is a reason for this: Since the wind is typically gusting all day long on the links, allowances must be made in the layout of the course so it can remain playable in inhospitable conditions. This is especially true of the approach shots to the greens; if the greens were elevated and fronted by bunkers, as is often the case in America, even the world's finest golfers would shoot amazingly high scores in the gales. The greens on most links courses are level with the general roll of the terrain, and the bunkers are set off to the sides of the greens to allow entry for a low, running approach if the wind dictates such a shot. The wind does not *always* blow hard in Scotland, nor does it always rain. It just seems that way.

Over the first seventy-two hours of the 1975 Open, Tom Watson got lucky. It did rain steadily, but only at night. During the day, the wind did not kick up to any significant degree, and with the greens softened by the nighttime rains, the Goliath of Carnoustie was reduced to a mushy dart board. While the sight must have been anathema to the townspeople of Carnoustie, the players took a bite out of the proud old links. South African Bobby Cole scored sixty-six in both the second and third rounds. Twenty-five-year-old Australian Jack Newton set the course record with a sixty-five in the third round. Alfie Fyles and his Mister found the going to their liking as well; Watson scored rounds of seventy-one, sixty-seven, and sixty-nine. That was a nine-under-par score for fifty-four holes, and it placed Watson close enough to the lead to make something happen on Saturday. He played in the penultimate group the final day with Johnny Miller, who was at ten under par, while the final group was Cole, at twelve under par and Newton at eleven under. With the course playing so easy, Bobby Cole knew that there was a slew of players still in contention. "Anyone within four shots of the lead has a chance tomorrow," said Cole after the third round. It's very likely that before making that statement, Cole knew that Jack Nicklaus was among those precisely four shots behind.

There was every reason to believe that Nicklaus might be the champion come Saturday evening. He was clearly the supreme player of the moment after his win over Miller and Weiskopf at the Masters. Practicing before the tournament, Nicklaus had twice scored rounds of sixty-five on Carnoustie. And there was another factor. Nearly twenty-five years after the tournament, Johnny Miller recalled a feeling common among his contemporaries, saying: "When you looked at the scoreboard and saw Nicklaus's name near the lead you could be certain of one thing: It wasn't going backwards."

Angelo Argea was on the bag for Nicklaus at Carnoustie and years later said, "Jack was on his game at Carnoustie. Hell, he was on his game that whole year." Even though Argea had been Nicklaus's tour caddie since the mid-1960s and helped his man to what Argea estimates at "close to fifty" wins in tour events, the 1975 Open Championship was among the first major championships he worked with Nicklaus. "We weren't allowed to caddie in the majors at home back then," said Argea years later, "and Jack had a regular caddie in Britain. A fellow named Jimmy Dickinson had caddied for Jack since he started going to the Open and had worked for him when he won at Muirfield and St. Andrews. The only reason I went to Carnoustie was because Jimmy was sick. I had never been to Scotland or England before." (At the time, the Masters required players to use club caddies, and use of professional tour caddies was not permitted in the U.S. Open.)

On Saturday, the day of the final round, the wind came. It was not the kind of wind that would rip the tented village into the sky and carry it to Oz, but rather a constant breeze of approximately fifteen miles per hour; certainly enough to make the last four holes show a bit of fang. Years later Watson recalled how just prior to teeing off he had a chance meeting with Byron Nelson. One of the finest players in history, Nelson had long since retired from competitive golf but was in Carnoustie as part of the ABC Sports announcing team. "Tom," said Nelson in his calming Texas drawl, "the way the wind is blowing today, par is going to be a good score. You're playing the best golf of anyone here. Don't give up or get discouraged. Just remember everyone has to play those last four holes."

Watson was the only one of the leaders to play the front nine under par, but as he hit the middle of his round, things went haywire. His dead-eye putting temporarily deserted him and he took three putts on the tenth, eleventh, *and* twelfth holes. The slide continued when he bogeyed the very long (235 yards) par-three sixteenth hole for the fourth day in a row. Tom Watson was one over par for his round as he made his way to the seventeenth tee, and he had reached a critical moment in his career. Should he fail here, he might (to borrow a phrase from the then recently resigned Vice President Spiro Agnew) prove the nattering nabobs of the media correct in their assessment of him as a choker.

The 459-yard seventeenth hole was playing directly into the wind, and Watson had to be wary of the Barry Burn, the creek that zigs across the fairway at one point, and then zags back again closer to the green. Watson made his par of four after drilling a three-wood onto the green on his second shot, and then turned for home. The eighteenth at Carnoustie has no equal in terms of difficulty as a closing hole on the courses used for the Open Championship. Royal Birkdale's eighteenth is nearly as arduous, but it is shielded from the wind to a certain extent by huge sand dunes. Carnoustie's final hole was playing 478 yards, and here the Barry Burn zigged, zagged, and then zigged again across the fairway, putting the same stream in play at three different points on the same hole. (Those who watched the closing holes of the 1999 Open Championship on television may recall that this is the hole where Frenchman Jean Van de Velde perpetrated one of the most brainless finishes in Open history. His ball ended up in the Barry Burn and he made a triple bogey. He lost in a four-hole playoff involving American Justin Leonard and Scotsman Paul Lawrie, who won.)

When Watson and Miller approached the eighteenth tee all hell was breaking loose behind them. Newton held the lead at twelve under par through fifteen holes, and Cole was at eleven under par. With their concentration clamped down tight on their own games, Watson and Miller had no idea that Newton and Cole would stagger home like a couple of guys at closing time. *Everyone* was making bogeys, and up on the eighteenth fairway Jack Nicklaus knew it. He had held steady all day long and was still at eight under par. As he paused for a moment over his ball, Nicklaus said to Argea, "A birdie will take it, Angie, because those guys are going to fly apart back there." Nicklaus's iron from the fairway just missed the green. He nearly holed a little chip shot, but did not and stayed at eight under par.

Back on the tee, Miller was nine under par for the tournament and Watson was eight under. Pressing for what he thought was a needed birdie, Miller drove into a fairway bunker and left his second shot there as well. Miller got the third shot up around the green, and needed to hole a chip to stay at nine under. He did not do so. Meanwhile, Watson throttled his drive and was left with only a nine-iron to the green. He played the short iron neatly to the green and—finally—his putter came through. He made a twenty-foot putt for birdie and was in with an even par round and a nine-under total.

Down the eighteenth came Newton and Cole, both with a chance. A birdie would win it outright for Newton, and a three would tie Cole with Watson. Both players hit their second shots within twenty-five feet of the hole. Newton putted first. Later he would describe the putt. "I was never confident of the line and I could see where if I putted past the hole the ball would duck down an incline. So I hit a dreadful putt and left it three feet short. That last putt was a knicker twitcher." With his par, Newton had forced an eighteen-hole playoff with Watson. Cole's putt did not come close to going in. Many years later Watson would say of that moment, "Compared to the guys who were chasing us, Newton and I were two no-names in that playoff."

Newton couldn't have agreed more. When asked by writers covering the event what he planned on doing that Saturday evening, Newton responded, "The first thing I'll have to cancel out of a pro-am I'm supposed to play in Dublin tomorrow. Then, I guess, get drunk again."

AS THE PLAYERS ARRIVED at the first tee that week in Carnoustie, they were greeted by Ivor Robson. Just prior to them teeing off, Robson would announce who the players were to the fans gathered around the first tee. Robson had never worked as a first-tee announcer before the 1975 Open, and twenty-five years later he would say that "only the laundry maid knew how nervous I was" at the prospect of his first week on the job. But he loved his new position from the start, saying, "it is the greatest honor in golf to be the first tee starter for the Open Championship." It beat the hell out of his old job, which had been playing on the Scottish pro tour from 1964 to 1974 while still holding down his club job at the Moffat Golf Club in central Scotland, just to the north of Lockerbie. As a player, Robson said, "I lived in utter fear of being on the first tee and having my name announced. I got to shaking so much from nerves that I finally had to stop playing in tournaments. I suppose it is ironic that I ended up doing the very thing that drove me mad."

Robson had lived in the area of Scotland known as The Borders for his entire life. (The Borders begins just south of Edinburgh and includes Peebles and Berwick to the north and Selkirk and Roxburgh to the south.) He had the lively wit of a Scotsman and also the trademark characteristic of not wasting words. There was no one to teach Ivor Robson his new job, so he just made it up as he went along. One of the first things he decided was that there was no point in singling out a player as American or Taiwanese or English or Spanish. That might create some sense of prejudice, and there was no room for that at the Open. In other tournaments, when a player was ready to play away, an announcer would rattle off previous tournament victories by the player, where the player lived and sometimes even commercial endorsements the player had. ("Now on the first tee, playing out of Palm Beach, Florida, winner of the 1962, '67, and '72 U.S. Opens; 1963, '65, '66, '72, and '75 Masters; 1966 and '70 British Opens; the 1963, '71, '73, and '75 PGA Championships, representing the MacGregor Company, Jack Nicklaus. . . .") Robson eschewed such blather. When Nicklaus was ready to begin a round at Carnoustie, Robson would speak gently into his microphone: "On the tee, Jack Nicklaus." And that was it. Ivor Robson would not conduct himself like a carnival barker.

The rookie first-tee starter for the Open Championship had also decided that it would be inappropriate for him to show even the slightest hint of bias at any time. He would not even follow the playoff once the players had teed off for fear that it might indicate he somehow preferred Watson and Newton over all the others who had played that week. Even at that, Robson could not help but notice the look on Watson's face as he stood on the first tee preparing for the noontime start to his game with Newton. Twenty-five years later Robson remembered thinking to himself, "Here's a chap who is going to make it. You could see Tom Watson had everything. He had the determination, the physique, the mentality. And you could *see* that. I thought to myself that I wouldn't be surprised if he won many Opens."

The playoff was an odd affair. At the second hole, a wee boy in the crowd happened upon Newton's ball and picked it up as a keepsake. That got a few laughs, but no one was laughing at the next hole when a camera whirred while Watson was in midswing, distracting him and causing him to hit a sharp hook off the tee. In later years Watson would have let such an incident pass, but perhaps feeling some pressure he barked in the direction of the offending camera operator. The two golfers played steadily along, neither player pulling far ahead of the other. At the par-five fourteenth, Watson played a long second shot that cleared two cavernous bunkers known as the Spectacles, which front the green. Newton played his third shot dead stiff to the hole and was looking at a certain birdie. Watson played a chip of about thirty feet with his pitching wedge, and the ball went in the hole for an eagle. He was now one shot ahead of Newton. Watson gave the shot right back at the sixteenth hole, which he bogeyed for the fifth day in a row, and the two players reached the eighteenth hole all square. It should have been a dramatic moment, but back at the fourteenth hole a heavy rain had started to fall. Only a few stouthearted spectators remained on the course, the rest having sought shelter in the tented village. Under horrid conditions, both players were left with two-iron shots into the final green. Newton was slightly away and played first. He came off the shot just a hair, and it slid to the right, landing in a greenside bunker. Years later Watson recalled feeling a "surge of adrenaline as his [Newton's] ball caught the bunker." Watson played safely to the middle of the green and took two putts. Newton's putt for par from ten feet looked good when he struck it but swung wide at the hole. With his seventy-one, Watson won the Open by one stroke.

In the press tent, Dan Jenkins hammered out his copy for *Sports Illustrated*. "Another authentic American hero was born . . . out of the gloom and crusty old atmosphere of golf on the linkslands of Britain. In a playoff for the British Open . . . young Tom Watson finally became a champion, a new person and one hellacious player."

A story that didn't make news at the time involved Watson and Fyles. When Watson handed Fyles a check for his week's work, Fyles thought the amount written on the Goose's Neck (check) was insufficient. The two men had a verbal scrape, during which Fyles tossed the check on the floor and averred that Mister must need the money more than he. Linda Watson told her husband to have Fyles leave the room, and the caddie shot back that the Trouble and Strife (wife) should keep out of it, that this was between the golfer and the caddie. Fyles grew Tom and Dick (sick) over the discussion, and snapped up the Gregory Peck (another way of saying check) and left the room. The payday struck Fyles as Pony and Trap (crap), a sentiment he most certainly shared with his friends at the Jack Tar. When the Open was played at Royal Birkdale the following year, Alf Fyles would certainly not be caddying for the young Sherman Tank (Yank) from Missouri.

THE GOLF WORLD did not stand still while the two "no-names" fought for the claret jug. On the very day that Watson was winning his first major championship, a twenty-four-year-old PGA Tour rookie from San Jose, California, won an American tour event called the Ed McMahon Quad Cities Open in Moline, Illinois. His name was Roger Maltbie, and he shot a sixty-four in the final round to come from seven shots off the lead and win his first tour title, passing Mark Hayes along the way. Seeing no reason to stop, Maltbie won again the following week at the Pleasant Valley Classic in Massachusetts. Twenty-five years after that jackrabbit start to his career, Maltbie recalled what it was like to be a rookie professional golfer. "It was more of a struggle to get started on tour than it is today. Today, with the all-exempt tour, you see a lot of fellows play not-so-good for ninety-five percent of the year, then have a few good weeks and be exempt for the following year. You couldn't do that back in 1975. We were playing for our livelihoods, and there wasn't much money involved. [Maltbie won $15,000 for his win at Quad Cities. Watson won the American equivalent of $16,600 at Carnoustie.] The other big difference from today is that when I started on tour, you really learned your craft on tour. You may have had some game, but you learned the rudiments of how to play professional golf on the job. Between college programs and junior tours, kids today hit the tour with loads of tournament experience. I couldn't even afford to play in the U.S. Amateur.

"Back when I started, we were bridging an era from what professional golf *was* to what professional golf *is* today. If I wanted to learn something, I'd talk to the veteran players while I bought them a drink or two at the bar. And if you were going to be in the bar, you'd better have a sports jacket on. That's just the way it was back then, and I think it was a good thing."

Maltbie was right, two eras were being bridged. Nicklaus had domi-nated the end of the old era and was now dominating the start of a new one. The other great players of the old era weren't finished as winners, but men such as Trevino, Player, and Jacklin couldn't fully cope with Nicklaus and the young lions. "If you saw Nicklaus's name on the leaderboard," said Maltbie, "you knew he wasn't going to make any silly mistakes. You knew you were going to have to *play* to beat him. And after Tom won at Carnoustie the same week I won at Quad Cities, we were looking at a whole new ball-game. Before we used to *think* Tom Watson could be great, but we knew he could be as wild as a March hare off the tee. He could thump the ball—and I mean *thump* it—but he had no idea where it was going. Once he won at Carnoustie, we saw a different Tom Watson. He found a way to get bullet-proof through those losses at Winged Foot and Medinah. Somehow he found the way, and from that point on, he wasn't afraid of anyone. He would never be the ballstriker that Nicklaus was in terms of consistency, but there was no comparison in their short games. Watson had the best I've ever seen. And that was all because he believed in himself."

Watson himself acknowledged years later that his win at Carnoustie gave him the confidence he needed to succeed. It's easy to agree with that sentiment in retrospect, but based on his play in 1976 it would have been a stretch to think that Watson had truly broken through at Carnoustie—the pages of golf history are littered with the names of players who have won a single major championship only to fade from prominence. At the end of the 1976 tournament season, few people aside from Watson himself would have looked askance at the suggestion that he might drift into the rank-and-file of golf professionals who play out their careers working tirelessly on their games, collect enough checks to make a living, have their skin ravaged by the sun, and never again win a significant golf tournament.

NEXT NICKLAUSES both old and new dominated play throughout 1976. Raymond Floyd, who all those years ago had been touted as a Next Nicklaus, won the second major championship of his career, at Augusta National. A super-cocky twenty-two-year-old out of the University of Alabama named Jerry Pate won the U.S. Open with a dramatic closing birdie. Pate had won the '74 U.S. Amateur, and his win at the U.S. Open, as well as his arrogance and talent, seemed to indicate a major star on the rise. This belief was strengthened when he won the Canadian Open later in the summer. In the Open Championship at Royal Birkdale, Johnny Miller ran away from the field with a total of 279. It was Miller's second major championship victory, and he finished six strokes ahead of Jack Nicklaus and a nineteen-year-old from Pedrena, Spain, named Severiano Ballesteros. Ballesteros had also played in the Open at Carnoustie the year before, missing the cut with rounds of seventy-nine and eighty. Even at nineteen, Ballesteros was a brilliant player with more natural talent and imagination than anyone had ever seen. Ballesteros was wildly emotional and hot-blooded, and he had a smile that lit up his entire face. When journeyman American pro Dave Stockton won the PGA Championship, it meant that Nicklaus had been shut out in the major championships for the year; though he did win two tournaments, led the American tour money list, and was named player of the year. As was well-known by that time, however, Nicklaus did not consider that a quality season. There was, however, a significant event in Nicklaus's career in 1976: During that year when America was celebrating the two hundredth anniversary of its break from England, the inaugural Memorial Tournament was played on the PGA Tour. The Memorial was Nicklaus's tournament, played on a golf course he designed in Dublin, Ohio. The course was called Muirfield Village, in homage to the designer's first win in the Open Championship, and the tournament played on it was associated with its founder in much the same way the Masters was associated with Bobby Jones. The first Memorial Tournament was won in a playoff by Roger Maltbie over Hale Irwin.

While all this was going on, Tom Watson was missing in action. He played in twenty-three American tour events and survived the thirty-six-hole cut in twenty-two of them. Watson finished in the top ten in eleven tournaments and was runner-up in two. His twelfth place finish on the money list ($138,203) was more than respectable, but for a player Dan Jenkins had described as a new American hero, Watson's play in the major championships in 1976 was dismal: He finished tied for thirty-third at the Masters, seventh at the U.S. Open, missed the cut defending his Open Championship (minus Alfie Fyles), and tied for fifteenth at the PGA Championship.

"I was a little bit discouraged at the time," said Watson, "but I kept on fighting, kept on practicing—the wrong things it turned out—and always thinking there are better times ahead. I never gave up, because I knew that if you give up once there's always the chance you'll do it again. I refused to give up."

In October 1976, Watson traveled to Roanoke, Texas, to spend a few days with Byron Nelson. Nelson thought Watson was "too fidgety" in his address position prior to swinging the club. Nearly all good players waggle the club gently before starting the swing as a means of blocking the onset of tension, but "Tom's waggle was too nervous," said Nelson, and that hindered Watson's ability to maintain his swing tempo. Always a fast swinger, he was waggling the club with such force that he was programming an initial move in his backswing that was too quick even for him to handle. Nelson also told Watson to "relax his right side and keep his legs driving through the shots." The old pro knew what he was talking about. In his playing days Nelson swung the club so beautifully that when the USGA acquired its first mechanical golfer for club testing, they named it "Iron Byron."

In November, Watson won a tournament in Japan, but it mattered little. His place in the game's history—either footnote or titan—would be determined during the 1977 tournament season and that year's four major championships.

SPANISH DICTATOR FRANCISCO FRANCO died at the end of 1975, and seven months after his death the nation held its first free elections since the end of the Spanish Civil War in 1939. It marked the first time in history that all of non-Communist Europe was under democratic rule, but democracy didn't much help Seve Ballesteros. In February 1977 he was called up for compulsory national military service. As a member of the air force, Ballesteros would make eight pesetas a day. The good news was that the young *caballero* had received an invitation to play in the Masters. Since basic training for the Spanish air force lasted six weeks, Ballesteros would make it to Augusta in April. "Normally I spend six hours a day playing golf," said the new recruit, "now I must learn to be a soldier. The next six weeks will be rougher and tougher than any golf course I've ever played." The colonel commanding Ballesteros's training unit was aware of his trainee's rare talent but was unimpressed. "We know he is a great golfer," said the colonel, "but we cannot make exceptions. He'll be drilled and trained like every other recruit. And like everyone else he will have to learn to obey orders."

As the new year broke, sports fans around the world could not have suspected the state of rapture that awaited them. In the World Series, Reggie Jackson would put the TNT back into the Bronx Bombers with three successive first-pitch home runs in the final game of the Yankees' win over the Los Angeles Dodgers. It was the Yankees' first championship in fifteen years. On the track, Seattle Slew would win the triple crown, and on the lawns at the All-England Championships at Wimbledon, Sweden's Bjorn Borg would win his second of five straight titles. Borg beat the rambunctious American Jimmy Connors, but that was not the biggest news out of Wimbledon. In the women's final, Virginia Wade of England was the winner, and her countrymen were delirious with joy.

In America, college basketball was becoming one of the most exciting games on the planet. In the NCAA championship game, a street-savvy coach from the streets of New York named Al McGuire led the Marquette Warriors past North Carolina. On America's gridirons, the University of Notre Dame won the college national championship, and the wild, long-haired Oakland Raiders won the Super Bowl behind their popular coach John Madden. The losers for the fourth time in the history of the Super Bowl were the Minnesota Vikings. It would be another long winter for football fans on the American tundra. There was no such gloom in the industrial town of Manchester, England. There, in the *real* football championship, the boys from Manchester United traveled from their fabled stadium of Old Trafford to the big show: the Football Association (FA) Cup final against Liverpool. The FA Cup is the world's oldest and most famous football competition, and Man United had not won it since 1963. They did this time by a score of two to one, the winning goal coming on a shot by Lou Macari that was redirected into the net by Jimmy Greenhoff. That goal marked the beginning of Manchester United's eventual position as the world's most popular sports franchise at the end of the twentieth century.

In golf, the sleepy game that often struck sports fans as anything but a sport, new heights of goofiness were being reached. The popularity of the movie *Saturday Night Fever*, starring John Travolta as the white-suit-wearing, disco-dancing New Yorker Tony Manero, had far-reaching effects on the wardrobes of American men. (Coincidentally, Tony Manero was also the name of the 1936 U.S. Open champion.) The men's fashions of the time—already horrific—plunged to new and more ridiculous depths because of the movie; the collective fashion sense of America's country club members and professional tour golfers became so skewed that even nongolfers knew touring pros dressed in obscenely bright colors and, frequently, unbearably plaid trousers. Everyone made fun of the way professional golfers dressed to the point that they became caricatures. The tournaments themselves didn't help matters. On the American tour, the comically clad players teed off in the preposterously named Joe Garagiola Tucson Open, the Andy Williams San Diego Open, the Bob Hope Desert Classic, the Glen Campbell Los Angeles Open, the Jackie Gleason Inverrary Classic, the Danny Thomas Memphis Classic, and the Ed McMahon Quad Cities Open. If that weren't bad enough, former president Gerald Ford seemed to show up to play in all of them. Ford was not a good golfer and frequently beaned spectators with wayward shots, a fact that led to Bob Hope's description of him as "the man who made golf a contact sport."

The ancient game of golf as interpreted on the American golf tour was stuck somewhere between being noble and being groovy as the tournament season began in 1977. The tour had always had elements of a circus atmosphere about it, but now it was creeping closer toward becoming just plain silly. Fortunately for the game, an ultradramatic year of major championship play was about to blind everyone to the wackiness that had descended upon professional golf.


GOLF'S FOUR MAJOR CHAMPIONSHIPS are the keystones of every tournament season. In 1976, Raymond Floyd won the Masters Tournament by eight strokes. While that was undoubtedly pleasing to Floyd, it was disappointing to fans of the game. That sentiment had nothing to do with Floyd, but simply put, watching any golfer win by eight strokes is a numbing experience for golf fans. Wins by large margins are particularly unappetizing at the Masters, a tournament golf fans depend on to rekindle their excitement for the game after seven months with the absence of major championship golf.

Awaiting the 1977 Masters, golf fans had reason to be optimistic regarding the chances for a good dustup at Augusta National. Jerry Pate, the reigning U.S. Open champion, won the first tournament of the year in

Phoenix and thereby marked himself as a player to watch for the first part of the season. Two of the next three tournaments were won by Tom Watson. The time he had put in with Nelson was paying off, and Watson won big at the Bing Crosby Pro-Am and the Andy Williams San Diego Open. The win at the Crosby was Watson's first tour win since he won at Carnoustie, and his total of 273 was four shots lower than the previous tournament record. (Three courses were used for the tournament in 1977: Pebble Beach, Cypress Point, and Monterey Peninsula Country Club. The last was a replacement for Spyglass Hill, but isn't nearly as demanding. The record Watson broke was set by Billy Casper in 1958 over the same three courses played in 1977.) The next week in San Diego, Watson set another tournament record—this time by three strokes—finishing at nineteen under par. Four weeks after that, Jack Nicklaus registered his first win of the year at the Jackie Gleason Inverrary Classic in Florida. After two more events in Florida, the Tournament Players Championship (TPC) was the next on the tour schedule. That tournament, now known as The Players Championship, was in only its fourth year of existence in 1977. Even then, however, it had the biggest purse and one of the best fields of any tournament in golf.

The wind was slashing across Sawgrass Country Club during the first two days of the TPC, and Watson's score of sixty-eight the first day was a dandy. He followed that with two rounds of seventy-four and shared the lead with Mike McCullough, who had posted a sixty-six in the first round. Others were sniffing around the lead: Mark Hayes was one shot back, Hale Irwin and Raymond Floyd were two shots back, and Nicklaus was three behind. When Watson played the front nine in level par on Sunday, he opened up a three-stroke lead. With two wins in the book for the season already, Watson seemed a good bet to walk away with the tournament. Instead, he bunkered shots at the tenth, twelfth, thirteenth, and fourteenth holes, making a bogey each time. Hayes, who was playing with Watson, made three pars and a single bogey over the same stretch and unexpectedly found himself in the lead. By the time they reached the eighteenth tee, Watson was one shot behind Hayes. Since Hayes had bogeyed the seventeenth hole, Watson was first to play from the tee. He promptly drove his ball into a water hazard, essentially gift-wrapping the tournament for Hayes. Afterward, Watson said he felt he wasn't playing well enough to win, so the loss wasn't unexpected. For Hayes the win *was* unexpected and very sweet. He won twice during 1976 and now was taking home the biggest paycheck in golf. "I felt like I was finally catching up to guys my age like Watson," said

Hayes. "They got out on tour quick while I was in the army. That throws you for a loop when you're in basic training and those guys are out there gaining experience."

By the following weekend, Watson *did* feel he was playing good golf, and it seemed a logical conclusion. With a sixty-six in the third round, Watson took a four-shot lead into Sunday at the Sea Pines Heritage Classic on the tricky Harbour Town course on Hilton Head Island, South Carolina. But by the time he finished playing the front nine on Sunday, Watson had frittered away his lead. When he reached the fourteenth tee, he was tied with Australian Graham Marsh. Television viewers who had watched Watson splash away his last chance at the TPC must have thought they were watching an instant replay at Harbour Town. Watson hit his tee shot at the fourteenth into the water, and Marsh waltzed home with the title. This time Watson felt the sting more acutely. "I was playing well," Watson said later. "I was pretty dejected by what happened at Harbour Town."

With only two weeks until the Masters, Watson led the tour in earnings and top ten finishes and had won twice. What most people wanted to talk to him about, however, was his two most recent collapses. He was ready for them. "I expect the questions about choking," said Watson. "If you lead a tournament and don't win, people say you choke. Either I haven't won the right tournaments so far, or I've lost the wrong ones."

Two days before the first shot was played at the Masters, most of the men in the seventy-seven-player field were practicing at Augusta National. Watson went off to a nearby golf course to work on his game with Byron Nelson. They went over the same things they had during the previous fall in Texas. Nelson urged Watson to slow everything down—the pace at which he walked, his setup to full shots, and the lining up of putts. When Watson showed up at Augusta National the next day he said, "I've got a swing now that I think can hold up under pressure."

With the wind swirling around Augusta National on Thursday, Hubert Green took the tournament lead with a sixty-seven during which he missed only two greens in regulation. (A green is "hit" in regulation when the player has his ball on the putting surface in two or more shots less than par for the hole.) Green was sometimes overlooked as one of the game's leading players at the time, but that Thursday afternoon in Augusta the fact was that he had won more tournaments during his career than either Tom Weiskopf or Hale Irwin, who *were* considered top players. Green's crazy setup to the ball and his equally loony split-handed putting grip were two reasons why he was often overlooked: Green set up to the ball with his hands very low and with the clubhead dancing around behind the ball as if it were doing the tango, while his head repeatedly jerked back and forth between looking at the ground and his target off in the distance. On the greens he used an old-style blade putter called a "Great Lakes," and unlike most players he placed his hands several inches apart on the shaft of the club. "I started with the split grip when I was putting poorly in college," said Green. "It evolved the same way anything else does for a golfer. I was doing something poorly, so I decided to change it."

The other thing holding Green back from the recognition he deserved was that there were no major championships among his ten professional titles, but he was fixing to change that. "I've geared myself to win a major this year," said Green, and there was no question he had the potential to do so. He was primarily a feel player (as opposed to a swing technician), and when he got in a groove he could rip off scads of birdies. His first round score could have been even lower but for a missed eagle putt at the fifteenth and a missed birdie try at the seventeenth, both of which were from distances that presented him with a realistic chance of making them. Green's round placed him two strokes in front of Bill Kratzert and Don January, and three ahead of Pate, Watson, Irwin, Tom Kite, and the surprising Rik Massengale, a young American player who had already won twice on tour in 1977. The group four shots behind Green included Floyd, Hayes, Gary Player, and Crenshaw. With an even-par round of seventy-two, Nicklaus was five shots off the pace.

Green got himself into deep trouble at the nasty little par-three twelfth hole on Friday. The middle of the three holes Herbert Warren Wind called Amen Corner is a place where the wind swirls, starts, and stops like none in golf. Watson said years later that "I was never fooled by the wind much, except at Augusta National. No one can figure out the wind there." Green spent a lot of time making his club choice and finally settled on a seven-iron. The ball carried the green and buried in a bunker. When he hacked at the ball in the sand, Green sent it flying into the water that fronts the green; he eventually made a double-bogey five. At day's end, the lead was held jointly by Watson and Rod Funseth. Watson told the press he had hit a lot of thin iron shots because he was struggling with his tempo and that his round of "sixty-nine was about the best I could have done." Watson was actually asked the question, "Why do you choke?" and could only say he wasn't sure what would happen over the next two days. No one had to ask Funseth about choking. He wasted no time in declaring that "I can't win." He was not asked to explain himself. Nicklaus had stayed close enough to the lead to strike, but would have to get his putter working if he was going to make any noise. He took thirty-seven putts on Thursday and thirty-six on Friday.

Pate was tied with Nicklaus at two under, but a shoulder problem that would dog him throughout his career was just then becoming excruciatingly painful. He almost withdrew on the eighth hole, but toughed it out the rest of the way. After the round he said, "If the shoulder doesn't get any better, I won't play again until the U.S. Open."

The weekend began with Rik Massengale shooting sixty-seven and posting a total of six under par through fifty-four holes. It was not good enough to get Massengale the lead, however. Watson took seventy strokes on the day, and that tied him for the lead at seven under par with Crenshaw, who shot sixty-nine. There was no one at five under par, but at four under there was the one name that got every golfer's attention: Nicklaus. He had hit the ball solidly, putted poorly, and there he was, just three shots behind on a golf course he knew better than any player in the field. Nicklaus completed his third round while the eventual leaders were still on the course, and when a writer suggested that a three-shot deficit wasn't much of an obstacle for a player of Nicklaus's eminence, the Golden One said, "If Crenshaw makes a few birdies on the closing holes, it won't be that close." He made no mention of Watson.

At the time, the Masters used a different system for pairing players than other tournaments did. The Masters system paired players on an even-odd basis rather than starting at the top of the leaderboard and working down; as a result, the final pairing on Sunday was Watson and the third-place Massengale. Crenshaw, the joint leader, was paired with Nicklaus. This positioning of the groups would prove critical to the day's histrionics.

Nicklaus crashed out of the gate with two birdies and made the turn in thirty-three. Crenshaw wilted under the heat of Nicklaus's assault and the pressure of being paired with a legend in action. By the time he played the eleventh hole, Crenshaw said, "I had begun thinking about next year's Masters." Watson was zoned in on the Masters at hand, however, and made four consecutive front-nine birdies for an outward half of thirty-two. Later Nicklaus would say it "was pretty sobering to shoot thirty-three on the front and lose ground." Watson led by four strokes at the turn.

Nicklaus had gotten something going though, and when he birdied the tenth hole and Watson bogeyed the same hole just behind him, Nicklaus was within two. Watson was on the eleventh green as Nicklaus stood over a birdie putt on the twelfth. The two greens are close to each other, and Watson watched as Nicklaus's ball dove into the hole for a two. Nicklaus was now within a single shot. The proximity of Nicklaus and Watson to one another on the course led to some faux drama at the par-five thirteenth hole.

Because that hole runs along the border of the Augusta National property, spectators cannot walk down the left side of the hole or get anywhere close to the green. Nicklaus carried the tributary of Rae's Creek, which fronts the green, with a three-iron, and when he holed a two-foot putt for birdie to draw even with Watson for the moment, he turned and waved to acknowledge the cheers of the distant crowd. Standing in the fairway, Watson thought the gesture was directed at him, as if Nicklaus were saying, "Let's see if you can top that, kid." Watson was steamed. He played his second shot to the back of the green and chipped down to close-in birdie range; he made the putt and once again took the lead by one. By now, all the other players had faltered and it was just between Watson and Nicklaus. On the very next hole, Watson three-putted and the two were tied.

At the par-five fifteenth, Nicklaus made a two-putt birdie and a few moments later Watson did the same. Both players made par at sixteen, and at the seventeenth Nicklaus hit his eight-iron second shot twenty feet from the hole. He later said he "was sure he could make [the putt] because it didn't look like it was going to do anything [movementwise]." But the putt slid just to the right of the hole, and Nicklaus moved to the eighteenth tee while Watson was playing his approach to the seventeenth green. Watson's nine-iron shot stopped twenty feet from the hole, and after surveying the line, he determined it would break eight inches. As Watson prepared to play his stroke, Nicklaus was in the eighteenth fairway planning his approach to the final green. He decided he would play a full six-iron beyond the hole position and take his chances that two putts would get him into a playoff with Watson. Just as he settled on that thought he heard the roar of the crowd back at the seventeenth green. Twenty years later, Crenshaw said he could still hear the thunder of noise rolling up the eighteenth fairway toward him and Nicklaus. Watson had made the birdie putt.

Now Nicklaus knew he had to fire directly at the flag on eighteen. In attempting to take a little something off the six-iron shot, he caught too much turf and the ball drifted into a greenside bunker. "Tom's birdie at seventeen changed my strategy and my mind couldn't handle it," said Nicklaus shortly afterward. Nicklaus came into Watson's view only after the latter had reached his tee ball in the fairway, and at first when he saw Nicklaus looking over a putt, he thought it must be for birdie. Watson asked a person in the gallery what was going on and learned that Nicklaus was putting for a par. When Nicklaus missed the putt, Watson said to himself, "Let's go." He made a safe par and with it won the Masters title. No one would dare suggest that Nicklaus had choked, but Watson had turned the table on the five-time Masters champion. Watson applied the pressure, and Nicklaus *had* cracked. "Why do you choke?" was never asked of Tom Watson again.

In the immediate aftermath of the tournament, a weird scene took place. Even though he had won, Watson was still smoldering over what he thought had been Nicklaus's taunting of him back at the thirteenth hole. He accosted Nicklaus about the incident outside the scoring tent behind the eighteenth green. Nicklaus was at first shocked, then patiently assured Watson that he had only been waving to the spectators. It was a sign of Watson's relative youth that he had accused the greatest sportsman in golf history of gamesmanship. Embarrassed, Watson apologized.

The perceived slight may have had a greater impact on the outcome than even the psychology-loving Watson realized. A few weeks after the Masters a psychologist named Thomas Tutko gave an interview to the *Atlanta Constitution* newspaper. In the interview, Tutko, who had authored a book called *Sports Psyching,* suggested that "the incident at the thirteenth hole produced a subtle psychological shift, mobilizing psychological forces Watson didn't have before. In the long run, that might have won the tournament for him. Those are the kinds of things that win and lose games." Incredibly, Tutko went on to say that he "didn't think Watson could have handled the situation had he interpreted Nicklaus's gesture as a friendly one." Tutko's hypothesis was no doubt offered up with the intent of selling more copies of his book. The fact was that Tom Watson had shown with his front-nine thirty-two that he was not going to back down from Nicklaus.


WITH ALL THE MARCHING and saluting he had to do in the weeks leading up to the Masters, it was no surprise that Seve Ballesteros finished in the middle of the pack in his first major championship in America. In the tiny Masters field, he was one of only eleven non-American professionals, if one counted David Graham, an Australian who by that time lived and played full time in the States. Nonetheless, when Ballesteros returned to Europe where the professional tour was just getting under way for the year, he did so at the forefront of a golf renaissance in Britain and on the European mainland.

The godfather of the movement was England's Tony Jacklin, who had won the 1969 Open Championship and the 1970 U.S. Open. In doing so, Jacklin gave Britain and, by association, Europe, its first genuine golf hero since Henry Cotton. Despite Jacklin's inability to maintain his position at the top of the game and the resultant ganging up on him by the British press, he had accomplished something of vital significance in the revival of European golf: He had shown that European players could compete, and win, against the mighty Americans, Australians, and South Africans who always seemed one step ahead of the players from Europe.

Twenty-year-old Ballesteros was the boy genius of the new movement. As a young boy in the Basque region of Spain, he rose to greatness from the caddie yard. That path, which had long since vanished in America and never existed to any great extent in Britain, was one blazed in part by one of Ballesteros's uncles, Ramon Sota. Sota was known as the "Bull of Santander," and he won eight tournaments in Europe between 1963 and 1971. In 1963, Sota and Sebastian Miguel, the younger brother of the equally talented Angel Miguel, finished second to Palmer and Nicklaus in the World Cup in Paris. Angel Miguel won three tournaments in Britain between 1964 and 1966, making him the first Spaniard to achieve such success in Britain. By 1977, there was a bumper crop of former caddies from Spain threatening to break out in the golf world, and the young Spaniards were girded for their fight by thirty-four-year-old Angel Gallardo, a player who served as a link to the Bull of Santander and the Miguel brothers. Gallardo's influence was especially necessary in the spring of 1977, as that was when the British PGA and the Continental Tournament Players' Association merged to form a single entity known as the European Tournament Players' Division (now known as the European PGA Tour).

With a single tournament schedule for the best professional golfers in Europe the fields for tournaments became more integrated. Spanish golfers had always been regarded as second-class players by the British, even to the extent that British players and officials openly accused them of the most low-brow attempts at cheating on the course. One British Ryder Cup player referred to the Spaniards as a "bunch of cheats" who routinely improved their lies in the rough with the "leather mashie" (shoe-clad foot) and who wandered the course "carrying golf balls, all with the same number, to push down the trouser leg through a hole in the pocket when the five minutes allowed to search for a lost ball were nearly up, and no ball had been found."

Such accusations were ludicrous, but Gallardo was aware of them and knew the youngsters coming up must conduct themselves in a manner that would keep their actions above reproach. The young Spaniards called Gallardo *el Abuelo*, the Grandfather, but he did not coddle the impetuous youths like a grandfather. When Salvatore Balbuena skipped a pro-am appearance the week before the 1977 Open Championship, Gallardo read him the riot act. When Ballesteros walked out of a hotel because he didn't think the lodgings were suitable, Gallardo ripped into him. "I told Seve how it was when I first flew to London from Barcelona to play in 1965," said Gallardo. "I had only a return ticket and £75 to keep me going for three months. More than ten times I slept on a bench in a railway station. I thought it was fantastic when I could afford to pay £2.50 a week for an attic room. I'tell Seve, 'The more care you take with people, the more you will win in the end.' "

There were eleven tournaments on the European Tour before the Open Championship in July, and Spanish players won seven of them. Manuel Ramos won the Portuguese Open; Antonio Garrido won the Madrid Open and the Benson and Hedges International; Gallardo himself won the Italian Open in a four-hole playoff with Scotsman Brian Barnes, and his young charges followed the playoff on foot to cheer him on; and Manuel Pinero won the British PGA Championship at Royal St. George's. But it was Ballesteros who caused the greatest stir. His swarthy looks, radiant smile, and the charisma that gushed from him in torrents caused one of the oddest sensations in the history of golf when teenage girls—hardly core golf fans—began showing up at golf tournaments to get a look at him.

More than his looks and machismo, however, the thing that fascinated people most about Ballesteros was that he played the game as if the ability to do so were channeled to him from some distant point in the universe. His swing was so fluid, his imagination so elastic, that he played as if he knew something secret about the soul of the game that no one else could fathom. He won the French Open, and then he won the final regular tournament before the Open Championship. It was called the Uniroyal International, and it was played just north of London at the Moor Park Golf Club.

At Moor Park, Ballesteros was suffering from his first bouts with chronic back pain that years later would have an increasingly detrimental impact on his play. He ignored the advice of his doctor in Madrid who had told him to rest on a wooden plank for two months and instead took pain-killing injections for his injured vertebrae. Still on leave from the air force "until September or until my colonel calls me back," Ballesteros displayed his game at its best. In the third round he drove the ball wildly from the tee, putting the ball in the fairway only eight times. Yet he still shot sixty-seven, which put him in the lead, one shot ahead of a nineteen-year-old Englishman named Nick Faldo, who was in his second year as a professional. In the final round, Faldo birdied the eighteenth hole to force a tie with Ballesteros. In the sudden-death playoff, Ballesteros birdied the first hole to win.

The most shocking news of the week to British golf fans was not Faldo's defeat, for he was still a relatively inexperienced player. Instead, the big blow came from Peter Oosterhuis, the most talented British player of the time. Oosterhuis announced to a shocked press corps that he would skip the Open Championship to return to playing the American tour. "I cannot afford to miss three tournaments on the U.S. Tour," said Oosterhuis, "and that's what playing in the Open would mean. I must get into the top sixty money winners [in America] before the end of the season, and I am too far down the list to be taking time off from that circuit."

With the Open dead ahead, that meant that English (and British) hopes of winning the championship rested with Faldo, the quirky Scotsman Brian Barnes, who sometimes wore tartan Bermuda shorts during competition, and the veteran English professional Tommy Horton, who was playing the best golf of his career at age thirty-six. Horton finished tied for fifth in the 1976 Open behind Miller, Ballesteros, Nicklaus, and Floyd, and felt good about his chances as the 1977 Open approached. Yet Horton felt the weight of being one of only a handful of home players at the Open, especially in light of the Spanish dominance of the early tour season. Years later, Horton said that "we [British players] very much considered the Open to be our tournament. We didn't travel much in those days except to South Africa in the winter, so the Open was very much a British thing. Here were all these players coming from all over the world to try to take our title away from us, and we desperately wanted to hang on to it. There was no question we were playing for our country."

In addition to the Spaniards and the Americans, there was one more player from "all over the world" that the British players had to worry about. Two weeks before Ballesteros beat Faldo at Moor Park, a twenty-two-year-old Australian player had won the Martini International tournament in Blairgowrie, Scotland. The Aussie scored a sixty-six on the final day, and he was described by British writer Michael McDonnell as having "blond hair, a Tarzan-like physique and a powerful golf swing." The young man's name was Greg Norman, and in only his second professional event in Britain, McDonnell wrote that Norman "was not prepared to feel his way cautiously around a British golf course that was totally alien to him. He attacked whenever possible with his driver through the narrow tree-lined fairways, and he ripped into the last round with five birdies in six holes to leave his more experienced rivals in complete disarray."

THE WEEK AFTER THE 1977 MASTERS, Jack Nicklaus won the Tournament of Champions at La Costa Country Club in Carlsbad, California. In those days, the Tournament of Champions was considered a big event on tour even though it had only a thirty-two-player field. Nicklaus skipped the tournament in 1976 because it conflicted with his children's spring vacation from school, so he showed up in 1977 even though he didn't feel like it. "If this were any other tournament I wouldn't be here," said Nicklaus early in the week. "But as the week goes on, if I can stay in competition, I'm sure I'll get more excited." When he birdied the third playoff hole on Sunday to defeat Bruce Lietzke, it was the sixty-second American tour victory for Nicklaus, a number that represented two victories more than Palmer and just one less than Ben Hogan. Angelo Argea, who caddied for Nicklaus at La Costa, said that at the time there was "still no doubt that Jack was the best player in the world."

Watson was in the field at La Costa but finished well down in the pack, eleven shots behind Nicklaus and Lietzke. He spent the week being awakened at all hours of the morning and night by telephone calls to his room at La Costa. On the other end of the line were reporters wanting to talk to the game's newest star. Another player on the bottom half of the leaderboard that week was Crenshaw. After the thriller at the Masters, Nicklaus had suggested that pairing Crenshaw with him on that Sunday at Augusta National had been unfair to the young Texan. Asked how he felt about the pairing, Crenshaw said, "I don't know if it made any difference. All I know is that I'm bitterly disappointed in my performance."

As the schedule moved toward the U.S. Open in June, however, Crenshaw got his game back together. It turned out what he needed was some home cooking, and he found it during the tour's three-tournament Texas swing that began two weeks after the Tournament of Champions. The second tournament of that swing was the Byron Nelson Classic in Dallas, and Crenshaw finished second in that tournament to Raymond Floyd. The following tournament was in Fort Worth, at Colonial Country Club, one of the best courses in regular use on the PGA Tour. Crenshaw started out the final round one shot behind thirty-one-year-old Californian John Schroeder, but quickly fell back with four bogeys on the front nine. At that point, it seemed that if any charge was to be made it would be by Watson, who started the day four strokes off the lead and was closing with a sixty-seven. Crenshaw, however, got hot with the putter the press had affectionately dubbed Little Ben and flew home in thirty-one strokes, enough to overcome Schroeder's six-shot advantage by a single stroke. Schroeder said afterward, "I didn't choke coming home. I played good solid golf. Two over par is not bad on this back nine. Ben just went out and put it to me." It was the second time in two years Schroeder had been overtaken with a six-shot lead on the final nine of a tournament; Hubert Green had done it to him in the 1975 Southern Open. Watson finished third behind Crenshaw and Schroeder in Fort Worth.

As summer approached, the level of play on the PGA Tour grew stronger.

The week after Crenshaw won, the tour swung north to Ohio for the Memorial Tournament. Since Nicklaus was the host of the event and had countless details to worry about, it seemed unlikely that he would ever win the Memorial. But by week's end, that notion had been put to rest. It was the third victory of the year for Nicklaus, and he accomplished it by beating Green by two strokes and Watson by four.

The biggest names on tour continued to dominate: The week after the Memorial, Hale Irwin won in Atlanta, and one week later Tom Weiskopf won the Kemper Open in Charlotte, North Carolina. Just when it seemed the pace could not get more frantic, it did. The week after the Kemper Open, eighteen-year tour veteran Al Geiberger shot a *fifty-nine* in the second round of the Danny Thomas Memphis Classic; it was the first time anyone had broken sixty in a PGA Tour event. Remarkably, Geiberger did not run away with the tournament. He won, but starting the back nine on Sunday he was two shots behind Gary Player. Geiberger made a couple of birdies heading in, and they, combined with a mini-collapse from Player, gave Geiberger a three-shot victory. His other three rounds that week were seventy-two, seventy-two, and a final round seventy.

The U.S. Open was next on the schedule. Played at Southern Hills Country Club, it lacked any of the pure golf drama of the Masters, and neither Watson (tied for fifth) nor Nicklaus (tied for tenth) seriously threatened to win. The eventual winner was Hubert Green, who finally got the major championship he had sought to give him credibility in the minds of golf fans. The most serious threat to Green's chances of winning came not from another player but rather from an anonymous death threat that had been telephoned in to the Oklahoma City office of the Federal Bureau of Investigation. Green had a one-stroke lead when he was informed of the threat after holing out on the fourteenth hole. Presented with the option of withdrawing from the tournament, asking for a suspension in play, or just continuing on, Green chose the last. He finished par, birdie, par, bogey and won by a single stroke over 1975 U.S. Open Champion Lou Graham.

Watson had closed with a nifty sixty-seven at Southern Hills, and that good round carried him into the Western Open the following week where he won his fourth tournament of the year by a single stroke over Johnny Miller. It was the best showing of the year to that point for Miller, and it couldn't have come at a better time. The Open Championship was only two weeks away, and the best American players vacated the American tour after the Western Open to head to Europe.

The week previous to the U.S. Open, Watson admitted in an interview with the *Tulsa World* newspaper that he had a growing fascination with the major championships. "It's clear to me," said Watson, "that they mark the road to fame and fortune." The public's interest in golf's big four events was increasing, too, as shown by the fact that the 1977 U.S. Open was the first golf tournament to have all eighteen holes of the leaders' weekend rounds telecast live to America's living rooms. Terry Jastrow was directing the telecast from the ABC Sports control trucks at Southern Hills, and nearly twenty-five years later he recalled how "golf was beginning to emerge in those days as a mainstream sport in America. Back in the 1960s when I was playing it was considered very esoteric, almost like badminton or croquet. But by 1977 the audience was starting to grow, and that season was just week after week of outstanding tournaments.

"It was clear to me that an event was destined to happen in golf that year that would define the generation. All of the big names were playing super, but Nicklaus and Watson were headed at each other like two trains coming from opposite ends on the same track." The collision would take place on Scotland's southwest coast in the Open Championship. The name of the golf course was Turnberry.

# SIX

★

THE OPEN CHAMPIONSHIP THAT BEGAN ON JULY 6, 1977, was the one hundred sixth playing of the tournament. Nearly all of the previous Open Championships had been played on a rotating basis over a small group of golf courses that came to be known as the rota (short for rotation). The concept of an Open rota didn't exist in the earliest days of the championship since the first twelve Opens were played at Prestwick. In 1871 there was no Open because Tom Morris, Jr., won the Challenge Belt with his third consecutive championship victory in 1870. During the off year of 1871, Prestwick was joined by the R&A and the Honourable Company in conducting the Open, and when the Open resumed in 1872 with its new prize, the claret jug, the rota was born. For the next twenty-two years the championship was played alternately at Prestwick, the Old Course at St. Andrews, and Musselburgh, the home of the Honourable Company. When the Honourable Company moved to Muirfield, the golf course at Musselburgh dropped from the rota. Muirfield was first used in 1892.

Over the years the rota expanded to include new courses, and sometimes a course was dropped because it could not facilitate the growing championship. Royal St. George's in England was added in 1894. Hoylake, also known as Royal Liverpool, was added in 1897 and held its tenth and (as of this writing) final Open seventy years later. Deal was added in 1909, but used only once more (1920). Troon was added in 1923. Royal Lytham, in England, was added in 1926, and Carnoustie was added in 1931. Prince's, a course in England, was used once, in 1932. In 1951 the Open was played at Portrush in Ireland, the only time the championship left Scotland or England. Royal Birkdale, in England, joined the rota in 1954. Prestwick, the grand club that started it all, was dropped after 1925. It hosted the championship twenty-four times. The current-day rota includes St. Andrews, Muirfield, Troon, Carnoustie, and Turnberry in Scotland. In England the rota courses are Birkdale, St. George's, and Lytham. In Febru-

109

ary 2001, the R&A cleared the way for Hoylake to rejoin the rota, possibly in 2006.

When the Open went to Turnberry in 1977, it had been twenty-three years since a new course had been introduced to the rota. Despite the tradition that oozed from the other courses used for the Open, not a single one could compare to the delightful assault on the human senses presented by Turnberry. The fact that it had a comparatively anemic championship golf history was more than made up for by the all the other history surrounding it.

If an American player who had never before been to Turnberry—and as of 1977, that would have been most of them—purchased a map to locate the place, he still could have easily missed it. There is no town or village of Turnberry. There is the Turnberry Hotel and the Turnberry lighthouse, both of which take their names from Turnberry Bay. The hotel and its golf courses sit along the southwest coast of Scotland in the county of Ayrshire, approximately fifty miles south of the industrial city of Glasgow, and a straight line running west from Glasgow would hit the coastal town Skelmorlie. While a motorist would not go from Glasgow to Turnberry via Skelmorlie, the latter town is a useful point of reference in understanding that the southwest coast of Scotland is pure golf country. By the time a driver winding down the road from Skelmorlie to Turnberry reaches Girvan—a town just to the south of Turnberry—he has passed thirty-seven golf courses. Among those courses are Troon and Prestwick, as well as Western Gailes, Glasgow Gailes, and Barassie, which are used on occasion as qualifying sites for the Open.

At some point during that drive along the Firth of Clyde, the driver would begin to glimpse a giant form rising from the sea. As long ago as the ninth century, travelers made note of this enormous rock formation sitting alone in the water, ten miles off the coast. In the *Book of Leinster,* written in the twelfth century, there are accounts of battles involving people known as the *Gall Ghaidhil*; these are the foreign Gaels who invaded Ireland with the Vikings around the year 852. They came from what is today known as Scotland, and the area known as Galloway (southeast of Turnberry) derives its name from these people. The allied Vikings and Gaels sailed to the coast of modern-day Northern Ireland, where they engaged the ships of Aed, King of Ailech. Ailech was near the modern-day county of Londonderry, and it was the seat of the northern kings of Ireland. The Gaels were described by the Irish as "Scots and foster-children of the Norsemen . . . they were men who had renounced their baptism. They had the customs of the Norsemen, and though the real Northmen were bad to the churches, these [Gaels] were far worse."

For the Vikings and the Gaels to arrive off the shore of Ailech, they would have sailed across the Firth of Clyde and into the Irish Sea, then through the rugged North Channel. Ten miles off the coast of Scotland, where the Firth of Clyde meets the Irish Sea, the warriors passed the giant rock. *"Aldasain .i. carrac etir Gallgedelu Cendtiri I n-a camar immuigh"* is how the *Book of Leinster* describes the rock. *Aldasain is a rock between Galloway and Kintyre, facing them out (in the sea).*

Those ancient mariners could not possibly have grasped how Aldasain came to exist. They could not have known that roughly 500 million years before their voyage, giant land masses had collided and, over an excruciatingly long period of time, formed the Caledonian mountain chain. That chain was comparable in scope and size to the Himalayas, and it sutured together a giant supercontinent. When that suture eventually ruptured, the land mass split and formed modern-day North America and Europe. (The Caledonian chain would vanish as slowly as it had been created.) The strain on the earth's crust caused by these cataclysmic events allowed molten rock to rise from beneath. At first the molten rock was devoid of structure, but as it cooled over millions of years it evolved into a rock formation known as batholith. As the batholith lost its heat, it began to crystallize. What was left was solid granite: Aldasain. Eventually, the sea crept in—there were no large bodies of water in the vicinity when Aldasain formed—and covered the base of the granite rock. Year after year, ice sheets, sunlight, wind, rain, lichens, and the sea shaped what one sees today when looking across the firth from the Turnberry links. The rock is two miles in circumference and towers 1,129 feet above the surface of the water.

As the Gaelic tongue evolved over the years, so too did the name of Aldasain. Out of Aldasain came the simplified Ailsa, and out of the Gaelic *carric* and then *carraig* and the Welsh *carreg*, all three meaning "rock," we have the word craig. Today, the giant block of granite John Keats referred to as "thou craggy ocean pyramid" is known as Ailsa Craig.

Ailsa Craig sits almost due west from Turnberry. Although it can be seen from other golf courses along the coast, it is only at Turnberry that the rock takes on a spooky, quiet omniscience. Robert Burns, the famous Scots poet and author of "Auld Lang Syne," was born in 1759 in the nearby town of Ayr. Burns understood that Ailsa Craig, though silent, was an observer of all that happened within sight of her. The poet wrote of Duncan Gray, who was in love with a lass named Meg. To Duncan's persistent wooing, Meg remained as "deaf as Ailsa Craig."

As much as Ailsa Craig dominates the scene, it is only part of the visual and emotional mix that overwhelms the human soul at Turnberry.


THERE IS A GENUINE but comfortable sense of isolation about Turnberry. The nearest towns are Maidens to the north and Girvan to the south, and heading inland one eventually comes to the small town of Maybole. Before local fishing industries around the world collapsed under the weight of giant conglomerates with processing ships, Maidens and Girvan were fishing towns. Maidens, the tiniest of villages, got its name from a nearby rock formation that sailors thought resembled a comely young woman. Girvan is bigger than Maidens, a small town with a main street of shops and pubs, and a medium-sized marina. On the back wall of the Harbour Bar in Girvan there is a fading photograph from World War I. It's a photo of the six Ingram brothers, each looking smart in his service uniform. Beside the photo is a framed letter addressed to their father from the Privy Purse Office, Buckingham Palace. The letter is dated November 18, 1915:

> Sir,
>
> I am commanded by The King to convey to you an expression of His Majesty's appreciation of the patriotic spirit which has prompted your six sons to give their services to the Army and Navy.
>
> The King was much gratified to hear of the manner in which they have so readily responded the call of their Sovereign and their country, and I am to express to you and to them His Majesty's congratulations on having contributed in so full a measure to the great cause for which all the people of the British Empire are so bravely fighting.
>
> I have the honour to be,<br>Sir,<br>Your obedient servant,<br>Keeper of the Privy Purse

The deep footprints of the two great wars of the twentieth century do not simply linger at Turnberry. The impressions made by the wars are so prevalent that they imbue Turnberry and the surrounding area with a sacred aura. To the west of Turnberry, north of Ailsa Craig, is the island of Arran, easily visible on a clear day. To the west of Arran is the peninsula of Kintyre, and the water separating the two is known as Kilbrannan Sound, and it was there on February 23, 1943, that the submarine HMS *Vandal* submerged with her complete crew in a training exercise. The ship was only three days old. The *Vandal* and her men never surfaced. Almost precisely two years later, the Royal Navy ships *Loch Scavaig, Nyasaland, Papua,* and *Loch Shin* were patrolling the North Channel, just to the south of Kilbrannan Sound. One of the ships detected a Nazi U-boat—*U-1014.* Depth charges were launched, and soon a two-square-mile slick of oil appeared on the surface of the water. In the midst of the slick bobbed a lone German sailor's cap. The were no surviving *kriegsmariners.*

However, it was the advent of mechanized air warfare that left the most visible scars on Turnberry. In a letter dated January 4, 1917, Major Richard Bel-Irving wrote to his father:

Dear Father:

At times supplies and delays are reported as ordered by the War Office. Was given this position as commandant of the new aerial gunnery school to be formed . . . the general evidently took a fancy to me. And here I am. The establishment will eventually be over 700 men including three squadrons of about 12 machines each. This is a most delightful spot and couldn't be more suited for a school. The whole hotel—one of those fashionable ones for the Glasgow golfers—the golf links and two large fields have been taken over by the government . . . [I] have already taken over the various extensive garages and work has commenced on erecting hangars for the machines. . . . There is nothing here except a station hotel and a few small cottages. The nearest village is five miles away. Kitty and two other wives will be the only ladies in the neighborhood. Love to mother.

Son,
Dick

The golf links described in the major's letter were the two golf courses at the Turnberry Hotel. In those days the air arm of the British military was known as the Royal Flying Corps, and its pilots and gunners zipped about the skies over Turnberry and the Firth of Clyde in a series of aircraft known as the Bristol M.1c. The zipping, though, was mixed with a fair amount of crashing. The lightweight aircraft of the day did not need the kind of massive landing strips required by the next generation of war planes, and no serious permanent damage was done to the golf courses or the hotel.

When war came again in 1939, the conflict was bigger and so were the tools used to wage it. Turnberry was again taken over by the British government for training airmen to become part of a three-letter unit that became the most famous in the history of air warfare: the RAF (Royal Air Force). The fighters, bombers, and scout planes of World War II were rugged and durable machines, which meant that they were more heavily armored. As such, they could not just bound along the fairways of Turnberry's golf courses and lift into the air like the twin-winged butterflies of World War I. The new planes had powerful engines, and if they thudded across the turf to take off, the surface would have been reduced to mush in a matter of days. Heavy equipment was brought in and eighteen-inch-thick concrete runways were poured. To this day, portions of runway are still fully intact on the property and are put to use as equipment and parking areas when Open Championships are played at Turnberry. It does not take much imagination to stand on the runway at Turnberry and hear the drone of heavy Vickers bombers as they lumber into the sky with the surreal northern light and Ailsa Craig as a backdrop.

The airmen trainees came from all over the Allied map: England, Scotland, Australia, New Zealand, Canada, the United States, and South Africa. Fatalities were not uncommon during training; the base log shows the records of numerous crashes. One occurred on September 1, 1942:

> Hampton and Beaufort aircraft collided in mid-air when coming in to land from north on northeast, southwest runway. Both aircraft crashed and burst into flames. The crew of the Hampton . . . were killed instantly. From the Beaufort, First Sgt. Goodsend escaped with severe burns . . . the almost unrecognizable body of Young was recovered when the fire subsided. . . .

Two weeks later, another report in the log shows that:

> . . . Pilot Sgt. Walters experienced engine trouble near Ailsa Craig. Machine had to be ditched. Crew of six took to dinghy, and were picked up by the motor vessel . . . owned by Mr. J. Alexander, fishmonger.

In November, Beaufort number L9865 and its two crewmen crashed into the sea soon after taking off on a night-flying training mission. The log records that a search was made. The two occupants composing crew could not be found. Shortly thereafter, the log notes:

Remains of occupants Beaufort L9865 washed ashore west of aero-drome.

Out on the championship golf course at Turnberry, to the right of the twelfth green, there is a hill that is higher than any other on the course. On top is a monument made from granite. Once atop the hill, a person is af-forded the best possible view of the links, but it's hard to focus on the scenery. Instead, the eyes are drawn first to the flowers or wreaths held to the monument with a thin wire and then to the words inscribed.

*To the memory of the officers and non-commissioned officers and men of the Royal Flying Corps, Royal Air Force, and the Australian and United States Air Services, who gave their lives to their country while serving in the school of aerial gunnery and fighting at Turnberry. MCMXVII–MCMXVIII [1917–1918]. Their names liveth for evermore.*

Just under that inscription is another:

*Also those commemorated below who died in the 1939–45 war.*

There are many names below the inscription. There are more than forty from the RAF, almost twenty from the Royal Canadian Air Force, twelve names from the Royal Australian Air Force, seven names from the Royal New Zealand Air Force, and four names from the United States Army Air Force. Among these names, one is more disturbing than the others: *R.N. Makepeace, Lt., RAF.*

TURNBERRY WAS NEVER MEANT to be the last stop for young men before the slaughter. It was supposed to be a spot for a restful vaca-tion. By the time players started arriving for the 1977 Open Championship, Turnberry had long since recovered from its years as an air base and re-turned to its glamorous existence as a resort. Aside from the very con-siderable interruptions caused by the two wars, recreational golfers on holiday had been keen about the Turnberry Station Hotel for most of the twentieth century. They owed this feeling to Archibald Kennedy, the third Marquess of Ailsa, and a man with an eye for a good thing. Kennedy lived in Culzean Castle, just up the coast from where Turnberry stands today. (Visitors to Culzean Castle who admire its wonderful gardens can also thank the third Marquess. They were his idea.) Befitting a titled man, Kennedy had a wide range of interests, and golf was one of them. He had been the captain of Prestwick in 1899, and in 1900, the good Marquess had a heck of an idea: Why not combine his considerable land holdings and his interest in golf and create a cracking golf course? The idea got even better; Kennedy held a directorship with the Glasgow and South Western Railway company, and he knew that in 1896 an application had been made for permission for a single railway track running from Girvan to the town of Ayr.

Kennedy saw that all of the pieces were in place to do something spectacular. If the railway company were to build a golf course and a luxury hotel along the new rail line, golfers from all of England and Scotland would have something they'd never had before—a golf resort. The building of the railway line was authorized in 1899, and construction on the almost twenty-mile length of track began in 1902. In the meantime, the Marquess knew just the spot for the golf course and hotel. He owned 175 acres along the shore at Turnberry Bay that would be worthy of inclusion in any traveler's plans. The Marquess contacted Willie Fernie, the golf professional at Troon and the man who won the Open Championship in 1883, and asked Fernie to lay out a golf course on the land. Fernie routed thirteen holes in 1901 and later he added thirteen more. Things got cooking at Turnberry on May 17, 1906, when the Golfer's Railway and the Turnberry Hotel both opened for business. The railwaymen called the line the Shore Road, and to cut down on construction costs, it had been built to accommodate small trains puttering along at a maximum speed of twenty-five miles per hour. The Marquess could board the train at a ministation at his castle and get off at the hotel along with curious golfers making the trip to Turnberry from Glasgow.

The real expectation, however, was that golfers would come from all over the island nation. They were encouraged to do so by an artful series of advertising posters with the words:

> Turnberry Hotel
> On the Ayrshire Coast
> The Sunshine Corner of Scotland

Newspaper advertisements sold readers on the new light railway between Ayr and Girvan and the Turnberry Hotel's "over 200 apartments, always found comfortable and complete, its arrangements perfect. Heating, ventilation and sanitation, electric light, lift, lounge, hairdressing salon, billiard room, conservatory, garage and stables . . ." And so the golfers came. They came from London, almost exactly 400 rail miles away, by getting on a sleeping car in the evening and exiting the next day under the roof of the Turnberry Station. And they came from Birmingham, 296 miles away, and Liverpool (227 miles) and Newcastle (168 miles) and Edinburgh (92 miles). (There are many courses in Scotland the origins of which coincide with the expansion of rail travel at the end of the nineteenth century. Among them is the thrilling and breathtaking Cruden Bay, on Scotland's northeast coast, which was part of an expansion plan on the part of the Great North of Scotland Railway.)

Newspaper readers were also told that the golf course was "laid out by Fernie of Troon, and is second to none in the United Kingdom." In 1912, the British Ladies Championship was played at Turnberry, and it was won by a Miss Ravenscroft.

It was not until after World War I that the golf courses began to take on a form more recognizable to the modern golfer. In 1926, Major Cecil Kay Hutchinson, formerly of the Coldstream Guards, was brought in to give the golf courses a face-lift, and he focused first on the newer of Fernie's layouts. Hutchinson extended the course to eighteen holes and, while he was at it, eliminated most of the blind shots on the course. ("Blind" meaning the player could not see his eventual target.) The new course occupied the land hugging the coast, and it was around this time that the course got its name: Ailsa. The older of the two courses was also modernized and became known as Arran.

It was 1938 before Hutchinson fully completed the job. His work, combined with the natural setting, placed Turnberry among the elite destinations in the golf world. In time, however, his work would be for naught. That same year British Prime Minister Neville Chamberlain met with Adolf Hitler in Munich and returned to Downing Street to greet the citizens of the empire with tidings of "peace in our time." Never in history had a man been so wrong.

During the war, British writer Henry Longhurst was moved to write that "in those long periods inseparable from wartime service when there is nothing to do but sit and think, I used to often find myself sitting and thinking of the time when we once again might be playing golf at Turnberry. Then came the news that the two great courses, the Arran and the Ailsa, had been turned into an airfield. While it was easy to imagine turning a golf course into an airfield, it was difficult for the layman to see how you could ever turn an airfield back into a golf course. Turnberry, it seemed, must be reckoned a casualty."

NEARLY TWENTY-FIVE YEARS after the 1977 Open Championship at Turnberry, Tom Watson said of Turnberry's Ailsa Course that "it is right there before you. It's not hidden like St. Andrews. There's a lot more guesswork involved in playing most links courses than there is at Turnberry."

The noted golf course architecture expert Bradley Klein agreed with Watson. "The Ailsa Course at Turnberry is distinctly modern," said Klein. "There isn't a lot of random bunkering like other famous links courses. The bunkering pattern at Ailsa is very strategic. It's not as much of a ground game as Troon, for example. It's a little closer to Muirfield, which was rebuilt in the 1920s. The dramatic dunes along the edges of the course make a tournament played there very theatrical. They used a natural setting and cut the holes below the dunes."

That the Ailsa Course even existed in 1977 borders on the remarkable, and the story of how it was brought to life after the war is one of innovation and determination. The determination was supplied by a man with a funny name: Frank Hole. During the immediate post–World War II years, Hole was the managing director of British Transport Hotels, which by that time was the owner of Turnberry on behalf of its parent company, British Rail. The very idea that Turnberry might be revitalized was optimistic to say the least. Hole knew that the Golfer's Railway had never made a profit even before automobiles became the primary mode of travel and that the line that took travelers to Turnberry had been closed to passengers in 1942 and never reopened. He also knew that British Rail would not foot the bill for rebuilding Turnberry's golf courses and that rehabilitating a golf resort was well down on the list of priorities of the government in postwar Britain. (Hole also had to worry about refurbishing the hotel, which had been used as a hospital during the war.) But Frank Hole must be considered among the shrewdest negotiators who ever lived, because in 1949 he convinced the British government to subsidize the reconstruction of the two golf courses at Turnberry.

The inspiration was injected into the Ailsa recovery project by Mackenzie Ross, a golf course architect who was nearing sixty years old when he was brought in to look at Ailsa in February 1949. Mackenzie Ross had the look of a fellow who could have been the Oldest Member in a P.G. Wodehouse story. He had silvery, thinning hair that he brushed straight back and a perky gray mustache the ends of which could be twisted during moments of contemplation. After fighting in World War I, the Edinburgh-born Ross was hired on as the boss of a golf course construction crew in 1920. The man who hired him was Tom Simpson, one of the best known British golf course designers of the early twentieth century. With the task before him at Turnberry, it proved useful that Ross had at one time been the foreman of a construction crew.

One of the hallmarks of Britain's magnificent links golf courses is that they look natural in every way. The effect of this is that even a novice golfer can look out over a great links course and think to himself that, yes, there could be no other use for this land. It *had* to be a golf course. One of the primary reasons for this is that when the links courses were created, the design approach was a minimalist one in terms of messing about with topography. The same could not be said of golf courses in the U.S., where since the 1920s heavy equipment was used regularly to gouge golf courses out of the earth.

When Ross inspected Ailsa in 1949, he must have been pleased when he realized that the dunesland along the sea had been for the most part left untouched. This would give Ailsa enough of a genuinely natural look that maybe—and only maybe—he could make it seem as if there had never been an airfield at Turnberry. It would have been easy to create perfectly smooth fairways, but that would have looked artificial. Ross would have to rip up the runways and then make the playing surface look, as Henry Longhurst was fond of saying, "all 'umped and 'ollowed." No golf course architect in Britain up to that point had ever attempted such a feat.

Ross had several things working in his favor. One was a technique of building plasticine models of golf holes, which had been used by Alister MacKenzie and the flamboyant Canadian course architect Stanley Thompson. Ross knew of it from Thompson's work, and at Turnberry he built models of the new fairways so that the men who would shape the ground could actually see the type of "movement" he wanted in it. Ross also had available to him men who were skilled with the heavy machinery that was still around from wartime days. "You have to keep in mind," said Bradley Klein, "that in order to create a golf course with bulldozers and steam shovels, you have to have the people to operate those machines. In all likelihood, they'd never built this kind of thing before. The hardest thing about creating a golf course is to convert two-dimensional plans into a three-dimensional place. That can only be done by a decent set of plans and a [ground] shaper that knows what he's doing. What is amazing about Turnberry is not only that Ross could see what he wanted, but that the shapers could do it. I'm certain some of the men working the machinery were the same guys who used it during the war."

While the work was going on, Ross invited Longhurst to stop by for a look. The writer later recalled "watching huge scoops, grabs and bulldozers heaving at the surface of the earth and giving to the ground what architects call movement . . . the tractor drivers were invariably intelligent men, Ross said . . . and they worked under the guidance of Sutton's [Seeds Ltd.] chief foreman, Mr. Chapman, who returned from recent retirement specifically for this work. As a result, and I should not have believed it if I had not seen it with my own eyes, it is quite impossible to tell which holes on the new Ailsa course were once part of the airfield."

The smashed bits of runway were trucked down the road to Maidens where they were used to make a new sea wall. The depth of the runways and their foundations ran as deep as four feet, which meant that when all was stripped away, there was no suitable topsoil left to allow new grass to take root. Ross estimated that he needed 30,000 cubic feet of topsoil to replace what had been stripped away. He was in luck; the soil could be had from land adjoining the course, but it would have to be dug out by hand to avoid mixing the topsoil with the subsoil. So Ross's men began shoveling. After filling in the stripped areas on Ailsa with the fresh topsoil and completing the shaping process, every tee, fairway, and green was covered with fresh sod, which was hauled out to the spot it was needed by farm tractors pulling flatbed trailers. Smoke puffed from the twin smokestacks on the front of the tractors as crews of six or so men unloaded the sod and set to putting it in place with spades and pitchforks and rakes. George Brown, the current greens superintendent at Turnberry, marveled at the feat nearly fifty years after it happened. "What Ross did was way ahead of its time," said Brown. "These days the cost of using all that sod would be prohibitive."

The Turnberry Hotel reopened on Easter Sunday in 1950. Astonishingly, nine holes of the new Ailsa Course were ready to be played upon by June, just a few months later.

BEN CRENSHAW HAD NEVER SEEN Turnberry before the week of the 1977 Open Championship. His recollection of his first look at it is clear, however. "I had only read about Turnberry," said Crenshaw twenty-five years after his eyes first swept over the landscape. "It was beautiful. There was a drought that summer, and the course had a lovely burnished look to it." Crenshaw more than likely took that first glance at Ailsa from just outside the back door of the hotel.

The roads leading to Turnberry from all directions eventually place one upon the tiny road known as A719, which provides access to the hotel's main driveway. If approaching from the north, the hotel is on one's left and the links and the sea and Ailsa Craig on the right. The driveway climbs a steep hill, swinging all the while toward the right side of the hotel. It then wraps around to the car park near the entrance to the building, obscuring any view other than that of the entrance to the hotel and, on the inland side, a herd of quietly grazing cows. The Turnberry Hotel, then, is backward—the front is the back and the back is the front. This setup is utterly logical, because it would be criminal to even slightly obscure the view from the top step at the rear of the hotel.

The Turnberry Hotel is long, running parallel with the coast, but not wide. As such it presents the most marvelous short walk in golf from its front entry to just beyond the rear door. To cross the threshold of Turnberry Hotel is to enter a world of perfect opulence. The hotel is staffed by exceedingly helpful and good-natured people who put to rest the nonsense about Scots being dour. After checking in, one must forgo heading to the room and wheel about toward the rear door just twenty or so paces away. On the way, one passes a spacious bar—the Ailsa room—with an enormous picture window. Once through the door, the visitor confronts a vista that renders him incapable of intelligent speech. It takes more than a few moments to drink in what is now at hand.

At forty-five degrees to the left, there is Ailsa Craig. If there are no clouds and the sun is reflecting off her, she appears as a barren, shimmering giant. If the sun is muted by light cloud cover, the rock looks less imposing and its abundant flora is visible. The flora is of course not visible in great detail at such a distance, but it is there. There are old Scottish faithfuls such as bracken and sea campion and heather and rarer species such as the delicately purple tree mallow, which has its most northerly home in all the world on Ailsa Craig. Seen in such light, it is easy to imagine that Ailsa Craig was once inhabited by a tiny group of thirty people—crofters, granite workers, and lighthouse workers, all of whom ate wild rabbits that were so abundant they nearly wiped out the flora on the rock.

At forty-five degrees to the right, out at what appears to be the tip of the links, is the Turnberry lighthouse, painted white with a flat mustard-colored trim. Immediately in front of and below the onlooker there is a small pitch-and-putt golf course. Further down, the opening and closing holes of the treeless Ailsa Course are plainly in view, but seem rather benign. Just a few bunkers are visible, and the only gorse to be seen is (from this viewpoint) to the left of the eighteenth fairway. There is more gorse apparent off to the right, on the Kintyre Course. (The Arran Course was redesigned, renamed the Kintyre Course, and reopened in 2001.) Beyond the links, a giant dune covered in native fescue grass rises up so high that it obscures the view of the shoreline. Past the dunes lies the sea. Off to the right in the sea on an even modestly clear day, there is Arran. The profile of its hilltops is called the Sleeping Warrior, and its highest peak is Goat Fell. To the left of Arran, on the clearest day, it is possible to make out the Mull of Kintyre, the promontory at the end of that peninsula that wraps around Arran like the arm of a proud older brother (and which Paul McCartney wrote a song about). Northern Ireland lies just beyond, which is why locals sometimes refer to Ailsa Craig as Paddy's Milestone. All of this is lit by the soft light of the northern sky that draws out the richest hue of every color. Turnberry is at something near fifty-five degrees north latitude, and the sun never seems to rise very high in the summer sky, but from early morning to almost midnight it hangs at an angle that produces these pleasing colors. (For the sake of comparison, consider that Chicago is at forty-two degrees north and that London and Paris are about forty-nine degrees north, roughly along the same line that separates Canada from the U.S. along the western part of the border.)

No matter how arduous the journey has been to get to Turnberry, the urge is too great now to go back through that revolving door. The golf course must be seen up close. The fact that the golf clubs are left behind for the moment is a good thing; it allows time to savor. Now it is down the 104 cement steps, past the pitch-and-putt, that take one to the roadside. A few good strides is all it takes to cross A719. The first tee is almost straight ahead.

Like many of the great links courses of Britain and Ireland, the holes on the Ailsa Course have names, sometimes denoting a landmark. The first hole at Ailsa is called Ailsa Craig, and the eighth is called Goat Fell. Other holes have names that reveal a bit of the nature of the game at that spot on the course. The first hole, a simple par four, plays to the south. The second hole, another par four, is Mak Siccar (Make Sure), and it swings back to the north. Walking down the fairway of Mak Siccar, one cannot help but look up at the hotel on the hill. It's as white as new snow, and the terra-cotta tiles on the roof make for a striking contrast. Thirteen white chimneys with burnt orange tops stand atop the building, and twenty-eight windows peer through the tiles of the roof. On the ground floor one can see the windows of four large rooms. Looking up from the course, the one on the far left is the formal dining room. To its right, and just to the right of the main rear door, the Ailsa bar. Farther right still, a reading room and then the writing room.

The third hole, Blaw Wearie (Out of Breath), swings back to the south before the fourth, a crafty par three called Woe-Be-Tide, swings hard along the coast to the north. Woe-Be-Tide is the start of a glorious march along the dunes to the lighthouse out on the point. The sixth hole is one of the longest par threes in championship golf at more than 220 yards, and it bears the singsong name Tappie Toorie. The Toorie in its name refers to "a thing on top," in this case the green which sits high atop a hill. The seventh hole is Roon the Ben (Around the Mountain), a 528-yard par five that players in the Open Championship can reach with two brave shots. On the eighth hole, the peak Goat Fell is visible in the distance and lends the hole its name. Walking along the fairway at the eighth an occasional clump of blue-bells and buttercups is seen. As the green is approached at Goat Fell, the expected surge of adrenaline is realized. The sound of ocean surf pounding against rocks can be heard now because the dunes have given way to a sheer drop-off to the sea. A ball ten paces to the left of the eighth green falls off the edge of the world. There is no wall or bunker to save it.

At the back fringe of the eighth green, only the very top of the lighthouse is visible. Exiting the green, the player walks on the same level as the green, but to the right the ground rises up and blocks the view of the lighthouse. About twenty paces off the green, peering to his left through high grass and rocks, the player sees Ailsa Craig staring directly at him. As he makes his way to the championship tee at the ninth hole, the wind blows harder and harder. The lighthouse comes into full view on the right, its white and flat mustard trim supporting its black cap. The player is on a footpath now and is aware that other than the path he is surrounded by the sea. After cresting a small knob in the ground, the teeing area comes into full view. Once there, the player turns to face what Tom Watson called the "toughest driving hole in golf, without question." In front of the player, there are only rocks and the sea. The carry of 200 yards or so is daunting for a weekend golfer, but the reasons Watson and others found the hole difficult is because the tee shot is partially blind (the player aims at a stone or the war monument off in the distance) and its fairway is hogbacked, a feature that causes it to reject almost every ball and send it scurrying into the rough.

The teeing ground itself is tiny and isolated, providing the feeling that one is in a boxing ring in the middle of the ocean. Immediately beyond the lighthouse (now on the left) but still out of sight are the ruins of a castle. If a man in a tight contest stood on the ninth tee of the Ailsa Course with the wind buffeting his body and his senses and felt for the first time that his game was a conflict versus nature and the spirit he possessed was that of a warrior, it would be with good reason.

In 1320, it was written in the declaration of Arbroath that Robert the

Bruce was a king "who, that he might free his people and heritage from the hands of the enemy, rose like another Joshua or Maccabeus, and cheerfully endured toil and weariness, hunger and peril." The declaration went on in words that became the cornerstone of Scottish independence. "For so long as one hundred men remain alive, we shall never under any conditions submit to the domination of the English. It is not for glory or for riches that we fight, but only for liberty, which no good man will consent to lose but with his life."

The road to those words was not an easy one for Robert the Bruce. He fought valiantly for years against Edward I of England, known in his day as *Malleus Scottorum*, the Hammer of the Scots. Edward I endured the rebellions of William Wallace and in 1305 had Wallace hung, drawn and quartered, and beheaded. To discourage other would-be revolutionaries, the Hammer of the Scots had Wallace's head displayed on a pike on London Bridge and had portions of the rest of his mutilated body sent to the corners of his kingdom. Robert the Bruce was not so easily put off. He went into exile, and in 1307 he hid out in a cave on Arran later named King's Cave. In that cave, Bruce watched a spider patiently spin its webs. While he slept, Bruce had a dream that the spider spun seven webs and took this to mean that he would have to persevere seven years before he could fight the deciding battle for Scotland's freedom. When he awoke, Bruce and his men made their way across the Firth of Clyde to the coast of the mainland. Once there, they routed the English garrison at the castle alongside Ailsa's ninth hole. Seven years later, on June 23, 1314, Bruce led his band of patriots against the army of the English king at Bannockburn. (By this time the Hammer of the Scots had died, leaving the throne to his fop of a son, Edward II. Fans of the movie *Braveheart* will recognize Bannockburn from that movie's final scene.) The Scotsmen were slightly more than 5,000 in number, and there were four Englishmen for every Scotsman on the battlefield. In the name of God and St. Andrew and against stupendous odds, Bruce and his men won Scotland its freedom for the first time in its history.

The ninth hole at Turnberry's Ailsa Course is called Bruce's Castle.

A FEATURE OF MANY of the courses on the Open Championship rota is that the front nine holes run in a straight line out from the clubhouse, and after nine holes, the course swings around and heads back in a straight line back toward the clubhouse. Tom Weiskopf, who became a noted golf course architect after his playing days, explained that "some of the links courses are built on narrow bits of land, so there's no room to continually change the direction of the holes. At Troon and Birkdale, for instance, you play the front nine with the wind from the same direction on every hole. On the back nine at those two courses, the wind comes from the opposite direction on every hole. Turnberry has a real good change of direction on the golf course, and that makes it different from most of the courses on the rota. Muirfield has the best continual change, but the Ailsa Course at Turnberry does a nice job of turning the player around."

The stretch of holes four through eight at Ailsa runs to the north. The eighth hole doglegs slightly to the left, so its green is at a northwest angle. Just behind the eighth green, the coastline hooks around to the right, so Bruce's Castle plays along a northeasterly line. The tenth hole, Dinna Fouter (Do Not Falter), runs in the same direction as the ninth. Dinna Fouter is a stellar par four of 452 yards. From the tee, the player feels elevated, but it's more accurate to say that just in front of the tee the ground falls sharply away from the player down to the fairway. A badly hooked or pulled drive can end up on the beach to the left, and the approach to the green must carry a huge bunker that is a classic, with sand encircling a big hump of turf in the middle. The short eleventh, Maidens, plays to the east, and after finishing this hole, it's just a short walk to the twelfth tee, where a moment's pause reveals a look back at the ground recently covered. Looking down the fairway, which runs to the southwest, the player still sees the now familiar Ailsa Craig and the lighthouse. He has a better look at the war monument now, better for certain than if he used the monument as his point of reference for the tee shot at the ninth. In just a few moments, he will pass directly to the left of the monument, and it is from the granite memorial that the twelfth gets its name: Monument.

Before leaving the tee at Monument, however, a glimpse at the Firth of Clyde is worthwhile, for now the course heads inland. Up the coast the Troon shipyard is visible, and on the surface of the firth there is a never-ending show provided by white birds with sharp beaks. They are gannets, and they live on Ailsa Craig. The gannets circle above the sea until they spot their meal of the moment, and then they dive with full speed toward the surface. For a split second they smash into the water and then rise up again, hunger sated for a minute or two. Gannets are such able hunters of herring that in days gone by the fishermen would track schools of fish by watching the gannets overhead. A gannet circling while looking intently at a certain spot was said to be "looking well," which was a tip-off to the men on their ships. When a gannet had a full stomach, it would sit on the water and rest awhile. But only for a while, because if the fishermen saw him "sitting heavy in the water," they knew the gannet was well fed. The boat would be turned toward the gannet in an effort to frighten it. To lighten its load to get airborne, the gannet would upchuck the contents of its stomach. These remains would float on the surface, and the fishermen could get a good look at them, thereby determining exactly what type of fish were in the vicinity.

There are still signs of the fishermen on the firth, and red flags dance in the water marking the place where crab traps have been lowered. The once plentiful cod have been mostly fished out, and the small fisherman concentrates mostly on prawns these days. On calm days, it's not uncommon to see swans floating along near the shore and farther off in the distance perhaps a fishing vessel struggling along or the outline of one Her Majesty's ships of war. Realizing the course is leaving the immediate coastline, a long inhale is taken to fill the lungs with the crisp, clean air. There is no overwhelming trace of salt in the nostrils or on the tongue. It is what expectant mothers refer to as a cleansing breath.

To reach the thirteenth tee of Ailsa, the player skirts to the right around the monument hill and up another incline. He is now playing southeasterly, and by the next hole (the fourteenth), Risk an' Hope, he will be heading straight west. The fifteenth hole, Ca' Canny (Take Care), is a par three of just more than 200 yards. The green at Ca' Canny is very narrow, and a ball drifting to the right will run down a steep embankment. In playing the fifteenth hole, the player has turned to the southeast for the remainder of the round until the final approach at the eighteenth hole. The sixteenth is Wee Burn, so named for Wilson's Burn, which cuts across the front of the green. Other than the ocean, the burn is the only water hazard on Ailsa that might come into play for the expert player. At 497 yards, the seventeenth green is reachable with two Lang Whangs (Good Whacks) for capable players. The eighteenth hole is a par four, Ailsa Hame (Home). For the vacationing golfer, this hole plays straightaway, very close to due east, but for the players in the 1977 Open Championship, a new tee was constructed off to the left side. The new tee forced an angled southeasterly tee shot toward a fairway that runs east, and it made for an awkward angle of attack. A drive hit too hard or pushed to the right would flirt with the only concentration of gorse on the golf course, which sat to the right of the fairway. It is the same gorse that can be easily seen from the back step of the hotel.

THE CADDIES AT TURNBERRY have a saying they love to share with visitors. "If you can see Ailsa Craig, it's going to rain. If you cannot see Ailsa Craig, 'tis already raining." This joke bolsters the image of golf in Scotland, and specifically at Turnberry, as a gloomy, wet, and cold trudge over the linksland. To be certain, it does rain often at Turnberry. Sometimes it is just squalls passing through, other times a front will park along the coast for days at a time. This is called a southwester, and it's usually the same front that a week before people in Boston and New York were calling a nor'easter. All the same, the weather on Scotland's southwest coast is just as frequently perfect.

The railway posters of the 1920s that referred to Ayrshire as the "Sunshine Coast of Scotland" were not making an idle boast. To this day a visitor to Turnberry is guaranteed that no matter what time of year he arrives, the temperature will be suitable for golf. This is not to say that it is guaranteed to be dry or balmy, but the golfer will almost certainly not freeze at Turnberry. Considering how far north Turnberry is on the globe, this is a remarkable guarantee made possible by the proximity of the mysterious Gulf Stream, which works its magic starting all the way down near the Gulf of Mexico. There, what are known as the North and South Equatorial currents get to know each other in the passage between the Windward Islands and the Caribbean Sea, and this eighty-degree (Fahrenheit) water flows to the north. Off the coast of Florida, the Gulf Stream is about eighty miles wide, and by the time it reaches New York, it has grown to nearly 300 miles in width. This is wide enough that John Glenn could actually see it—"a river of blue in the gray sea"—when he orbited the earth in February 1962.

The Gulf Stream continues north until it is just south of the Grand Banks in the North Atlantic, off the southeast coast of Newfoundland. There it makes a right turn and drifts northeast across the pond. Technically, the Gulf Stream at this point is referred to as the North Atlantic Drift, and it eventually splinters into separate streams that reach Europe, Iceland, the Azores, and the Canary Islands. The finger that heads toward Europe cuts directly between the east coast of Ireland and the west coast of the island shared by England and Scotland. Even though the temperature of the water has decreased by the time it has crossed the Atlantic, its effect is immense. Without it, western Europe would be a bitterly cold place. As it is, the effect of the North Atlantic Drift keeps western Europe as much as twenty degrees warmer in the winter than comparable latitudes elsewhere. On the west coast of the island it stays warm enough year-round to allow for a sight that to a visitor seems as bizarre as a walrus on Park Avenue: palm trees in Scotland.

The flow of the Gulf Stream is not perfect, and when it goes haywire meteorological chaos is the result. Ailsa Craig, sitting as it does where several bodies of water merge, is often the flashpoint for such chaos. In the summer of 1977, however, there was no such chaos, and the old joke about Ailsa

Craig wasn't making much sense: You could see it, and it wasn't going to rain.

George Brown was working at Sandwich in England at the time, and he recalled that the "whole of England and Scotland was parched that summer. It was a scorcher. Most of the water authorities put a ban on irrigation from the main water supplies, and the golf courses went brown." It was part of a larger weather cycle that had seen most of the Open Championships in the 1970s played in very dry conditions.

When Crenshaw looked out over the Ailsa Course for the first time and described it as "burnished," what he was seeing was dormant grass. There was a misconception on the part of some American players and television viewers that the grass was dead. "When you have native grasses as we do here," said Brown, "and they come under stress due to a lack of rain and heat, the roots will dig deeper and deeper into the ground to find water. When the grass goes brown, it is not dead. In fact, it is very healthy. The worst thing a greenskeeper could have done was to lash on the water and fertilizer and have the course go soft and mushy, and it makes the grass less tolerant. That's when *poa annua* and other shallow rooting grass takes over. Links golf should not be soft and mushy."

The long, dry summer leading up to the Open meant that Ailsa was going to play hard and fast, twin conditions that did not appeal to most American players. Nearly everyone on the American tour at the time had grown up playing the game on an endless green carpet of "soft and mushy" grass. This had increasingly been the case since expansive irrigation systems were introduced to American golf courses in the mid-1920s. "Green grass is a conceit of Americans," said golf course design authority Bradley Klein. The saturated golf courses of America even spawned a new term in golf: *target golf.* This meant that when a ball landed somewhere, it stayed in that general vicinity instead of running with the rabbits. Target golf changed golf from a game where the ground's effect on the ball was crucial, to a game that was played solely through the air. The net effect of golf as an air game was that American tour players became accustomed to having complete control over the distance a ball traveled. The only sprinklers at Ailsa were small ones near the greens, but even they didn't do a very good job. "The wind," said Brown, "blew all the water to the same side."

It *did* rain prior to the Open Championship, and on both June 30 and July 3 heavy rain fell over the Ailsa links. The *Glasgow Herald* reported that it gave Ailsa a "thorough and necessary drenching." The sandy and water-deprived soil sucked up the rain like a wino slurping a $2 bottle of grape, but there were no lasting visible effects. The tall rough bordering Ailsa's fairways was light and wispy. American television viewers used to seeing the thick, heavy rough at the U.S. Open would look at Turnberry and assume the course was playing easy; after all, who wouldn't want the ball to run forever and not have to worry about it getting tangled in impenetrable rough? The reality was that Turnberry would play very difficult. "It is very tough to judge how the ball will react out of dry rough," said Weiskopf. "It's easy to get the ball moving, but it's difficult to gauge how far it's going to fly, and you never know when it's going to stop. To shoot low scores, a pro would take a soft course over a hard and fast one any day."

Looking back on that week twenty-five years later, George Brown said, "Better that it didn't rain. Once it starts to rain around here, it can forget to stop."

# SEVEN

★

FOR A GOLF COURSE ABOUT TO HOST THE OPEN CHAM-
pionship, the Ailsa Course did not have much of a professional tournament
history. In fact, the most significant events at Ailsa prior to 1977 were amateur competitions: the 1961 Amateur Championship, won by future R&A
secretary Michael Bonnallack, and the 1963 Walker Cup, won by the United
States. The same year Turnberry hosted the Walker Cup, a young American
amateur golfer with aspirations of being a golf course architect visited Scotland for the first time. His name was Pete Dye, and he was in Scotland os-
tensibly to play in the Amateur Championship at St. Andrews. Since he had
made the trip, however, Dye took advantage of the opportunity to travel
around Scotland to see some of its more famous links, including Ailsa. Years
later when he was the best-known golf course architect in America, Dye
wrote, "Turnberry may be the most imposing of Scotland's great links . . .
seeing [it] was quite an eye-opener. I've always said Turnberry and . . .
Royal Portrush may be the two greatest courses in the world when you combine beauty and strategic play."

Throughout the 1960s, however, Turnberry hosted only two serious
professional events: the 1960 and 1963 PGA Match Play Tournaments (not
to be confused with the PGA Championship in America). In 1964, the Ailsa
Course hosted the Braemar Seven-Club Tournament for British professionals. As the name of the tournament suggested, players were permitted to
carry only seven clubs during the competition, in contrast to the fourteen allowed under the rules of golf. Many players carried their own clubs in can-
vas Sunday bags. The winner, Lionel Platts of England, shot a four-round
total of 288.

During the 1970s, Turnberry hosted four professional events prior to
1977. It was during the 1973 John Player Classic that hurricane force winds
flattened and blew away all the courtesy tents on the golf course; American
Charlie Coody won with a closing round of seventy-seven and a 289 total—

one stroke more than Platts had scored with seven clubs. The devastating wind of that year became an instant legend in golf, and players thought it possible that during the Open those gales might be repeated. They failed to consider that the '73 John Player Classic was held in October, a time of year when such blasts of weather were more likely.

The final professional event at Turnberry before the Open was the 1975 Double Diamond World of Golf Classic, a two-day pro-am that is best remembered for a scoring snafu involving Argentine Vincente Fernandez. Years later, Fernandez recalled that "I shot seventy the first day, and the second day I was playing with [Scotsman] Sam Torrance, who was keeping my score. Instead of writing thirty-four for my front-nine score, he wrote thirty-four on the ninth hole. My official score ended up being 104."

Fernandez was in the field at the 1977 Open along with his idol and mentor Roberto De Vicenzo, who by now was fifty-four years old, and for Fernandez the pursuit of the Open title was a matter of national pride. "In 1973 I wasn't having a very good year," said Fernandez. "I was in Switzerland with Roberto, and he approached me one day and said, 'If you need any money or anything at all, you just let me know. But I have to tell you something. I've been carrying the flag of Argentina for many years. I'm retiring. I'm not going to play so much around the world. So it's up to you to carry the flag from now on.' It was a very, very strong thing. And I felt like I was the only Argentinean who could do what he asked. I was not playing just for myself."

By 1977, the Open Championship had evolved into something far different than what it was when De Vicenzo first played in it. The purse for the 1977 championship was, for the first time, £100,000. The imposing steel arena around the eighteenth green could seat 6,500 bodies, and when the players approached it they would be entering the closest thing golf had to a gladiatorial setting. There were another 5,000 seats in grandstands scattered around the course. Looking down from the hotel, the tented village sat to the right of the stands surrounding the eighteenth green, and it was a commercial sprawl the likes of which have never been seen at a golf tournament in the United States. The village housed 197 exhibitors, and spectators wandering through could peruse things ranging from golf equipment (AMF International Ltd, Ben Hogan, Stand No. 43/44) to wool sweaters (Gleniffer Woolens, Stand No. 144) to the possibility of an exotic vacation (Mallorca Tourist Board, Stand No. 172). There were more than fifty corporate hospitality marquees in the tented village as well. For a bite to eat or a pint, the weary spectator could settle into the new clubhouse, which had been built at a cost of £180,000, and watch the action on closed-circuit television. The same could be done up the hill in the hotel. With the increase in prize money, the week was costing the R&A in the neighborhood of £400,000; which they were hoping to make up on ticket sales. Entry to the Open would cost £4 per day, and there was room (including some of the old runways) to park 13,000 cars. Fans who couldn't make it to Turnberry could watch the Open on BBC 1 and BBC 2, which would combine for almost nine hours of coverage a day. BBC Radio 2 and BBC Radio 4 would provide hourly reports from 10 AM until 7:30 PM. If that wasn't enough to satisfy the thirst for information, the Post Office would provide something new to the Open: Dial-a-Score telephone service that would inform listeners all over the United Kingdom of the ten leading players during a forty-five-second recording that was updated twice an hour. Before anyone turned on a television or phoned Dial-a-Score, however, 360 players from around the world would fight for the ninety-six spots still available in the Open field.

WHEN THE OPEN BEGAN in earnest on Wednesday, July 6, there would be 156 players in the field. After counting the sixty exemptions doled out by the R&A to top players and past Open champions, this meant that nearly two-thirds of the field was still wide open to the players participating in the two qualifying rounds on July 1 and July 2. Those two rounds were spread out over three golf courses: Glasgow Gailes, Western Gailes, and Barassie. If the Open proper was where dreams were realized, it was in the qualifying rounds that they were chased.

It was the two rounds at Barassie, near Troon, that served as the best microcosm of the Open qualifying experience. It was there that John Schroeder, the American tour player who only weeks before had lost out to Ben Crenshaw's charge in Texas, struck his first golf shot in the British Isles. "I had been playing on tour since 1969," said Schroeder years later, "and from the moment I arrived in Scotland in the summer of 1977, I regretted that I hadn't been there before. The biggest obstacle in going had always been the expense, but that year I worked out a deal to play in a tournament the following week, and that helped with the cost.

"Qualifying was on Friday and Saturday, so I had flown into Prestwick on Wednesday and had a day to get to know Barassie. I stayed at the Marine Hotel in Troon, and on Thursday I just walked around Barassie getting my yardages down for the two qualifying rounds. On the second day of qualifying it was overcast and exactly like what I had always imagined it would be. I worked as hard as I could to keep my game together through the jet lag, and I qualified in the middle of the pack. As soon as I realized I'd made it into the Open, it occurred to me that I had no place to stay. So I telephoned Keith Mackenzie, and he told me not to worry. He would make sure there was a room waiting for me at the Turnberry Hotel."

Also in the field at Barassie was Philip Jonas, a fifteen-year-old high school student from South Africa. Jonas had won the Junior World Championship when he was twelve years old, an accomplishment that years later he said meant "that I only had to beat a couple of people. I was nine under par on a course called Mission Bay in San Diego. Par there was fifty-eight."

Jonas's father was the manager of the Kyalami Country Club near Johannesburg, and a friend of the elder Jonas named Bob Landern wanted young Philip to play in a pro-am at his club in England. The father and son talked it over and decided that while he was there, Philip Jonas may as well try to qualify for the Open. Jonas recalled that "I was so young that I didn't have any sense of the history of golf in Scotland, or the Open. We didn't have television in South Africa until 1975, and even then there was no golf televised. When they had a big club tournament at Kyalami, they'd bring in the films of the Open on three or four reels, and we would sit there and watch the films. Those films were all I knew about the Open."

For a fifteen-year-old, Philip Jonas had traveled extensively, albeit mostly to the United States for several world junior tournaments. The trip to England for the pro-am at Landern's club was his first to Britain. "I traveled by myself," said Jonas. "The pro-am was the week before the qualifying at Barassie. I thought London was old and gray. Then Landern put me on a plane and I flew to Glasgow. He had arranged for me to stay with two ladies in Troon, a mother and her daughter, who was about forty years old. They looked after me and fed me, and the daughter would drive me to the golf course [Barassie] in the morning. I remember being amazed that a tiny town like Troon had seven or eight golf courses, and that the people seemed more working class than I was accustomed to at home.

"I think I played four practice rounds at Barassie, and I loved the links. It was a little cold and rainy for me, but I had fun playing because there was no one around. The first time I played I got to the third tee or so and I looked around and couldn't figure out which way the hole went."

Jonas scored a one-over-par seventy-two in the first round at Barassie, which put him in a fine spot to play his way into the Open. However, when a newspaper reporter asked him how he felt about his round, Jonas replied, "That round was absolutely stupid. I made so many bad club selections."

For his second round at Barassie, Jonas recalled "I played with this guy who'd gotten thrown out of the British PGA, but since this was the Open, anyone could play. This guy owned a bar, and he had cuts all over his face from bar fights, and he was a real rugged old Scotsman. I hit my drive on one hole and I guess he thought I was looking at it too long. While I was standing there watching the ball, he came up behind me and shoved me out of the way and said, 'That's enough looking, kid. It's in the fairway.' I was a little scared of him.

"I ended up playing the last six holes in four over par, and when I was playing them I knew that three over would have gotten me into a playoff for a spot and two over would have gotten me in [to the Open]. The weather was terrible that day, and those last holes were all playing into the wind. Par would have been a great score over that stretch. I ended up missing the playoff for the last spots by one shot."

One of the players who made it into the playoff at Barassie was forty-year-old John Philip, who seventeen years before had caddied in Arnold Palmer's group at St. Andrews. Philip became a golf professional in 1964, and nearly every year since then he had unsuccessfully tried to qualify for the Open. "In 1977 I was the pro at a club called New St. Andrews in Japan," recalled Philip years later. "Jack Nicklaus had built the course and asked me to be the professional there. I came home to Scotland for a vacation and to try to qualify for the Open. It was the ambition of every golf professional in Britain to play in the Open at least one time in their career. There was no question in my mind that I was getting pretty close to the end of my chances. I had some time to practice and I felt like I must give it my all, that this was my swan song. There had been times in the past when I struck the ball better, but in the summer of 1977 I thought I was as good an overall player as I'd ever been.

"I put more pressure on myself knowing that I wouldn't have many more chances. You have to remember that growing up in St. Andrews, we all played golf. Our moms would make us a wee pack lunch and we'd set off to play at seven in the morning and keep playing until eight at night. After that we'd have a swim and go home. We played for free on the Jubilee and Eden Courses until we were sixteen, and when we turned sixteen we were allowed to play on the Old Course. We watched our heroes like Peter Thomson and Bobby Locke and then Palmer. The Open was everything to us.

"What I remember most was that I missed a couple of really stupid putts in the second round. At the tenth hole I nearly knocked my second shot into the hole and I missed the bloody putt. When you're trying so hard, that's what happens." Philip ended up one of twelve players in a playoff for the last four spots available at Barassie. He did not do well. After the four spots were filled, the eight remaining players played on for spots as alternates.

Philip ended up sixth alternate; the first was veteran Scottish professional and former Ryder Cup player Harry Bannerman.

"If I had been the number one or two alternate, I think I might have anticipated getting into the championship," said Philip, "because it's unusual when a few guys don't pull out. But as the sixth alternate, I didn't think I had a realistic chance. All of the alternates got to play in the practice rounds at Turnberry just in case, so I played the practice rounds and hung around until Wednesday morning in case a miracle happened. We were given [identification] badges and all the privileges of someone playing in the tournament. That was as close as I ever got to playing in the Open."

When American player J.C. Snead withdrew from the Open on Monday, Harry Bannerman made it into the field. He was the only alternate to do so. Looking back ruefully twenty-five years later, Philip recalled how it felt for him, a Scotsman born in St. Andrews, to want so badly to play in the Open. "It was a matter of life and death, wasn't it?" said Philip.

The first player to grab one of the four spots in the championship in the twelve-man playoff was thirty-four-year-old Gaylord Burrows. The odyssey that took Burrows, who was living in Louisiana at the time, to Turnberry was nearly incomprehensible. His parents were British but he was born in India, where he lived until he started high school. The family then moved to Africa, and Burrows finished his high school education there. "Then I went to England to go to college," said Burrows years later. "I was there about five years and decided I didn't like it anymore, so I moved back to Africa. I was twenty-three years old, and that's when I started playing golf. I had played all sorts of sports at a pretty high level—soccer, cricket, field hockey, tennis—and I was looking for something new to try in Africa. The first time I swung a golf club I missed the ball, so I thought, 'Now, here's a challenge.' Within a year I was down to a three handicap and won the Uganda Open and the East African Championship at both match play and medal play. About then I thought I'd get serious about golf, and I thought the only way to get better was to get a scholarship and go to the United States. Eastern Illinois was the first school that offered me a scholarship, so I took it. When I got to Illinois, I found out that the University of Houston had offered me a scholarship in the meantime, but I didn't feel like transferring. So I stayed in Illinois, not knowing that I would only be able to play golf six months a year and that the rest of the time I'd be snowed in. I was twenty-six years old when I got there, and I made All-American every year and won the small college championship once. I played professionally in Asia in 1974 and finished in the top fifty money winners. Then I went to Europe that summer and played in six or so tournaments, and then I went home—which by then was Louisiana, and I had applied for U.S. citizenship—and started getting ready for the next year on the Asian Tour. You could say I played just about all over the world—South Africa in 1975, and a little in South America. In 1977, I won a tournament in Japan and was invited to stay and play the whole schedule there. I played a few more events, but getting by there without speaking Japanese was pretty difficult, so I headed home to Louisiana and my buddy and swing coach Johnny Mize talked me into trying to qualify for the Open. He went with me to Barassie and Turnberry.

"The first day at Barassie, the weather was nice and warm the way I like it, and I shot sixty-nine. I was playing with John Schroeder, and he was telling me all about his new swing and how he was going to win a million dollars with it. The next day it was cold and the rain was coming at us at an angle, and I shot seventy-five. I went to the first hole of that playoff and I said to myself, 'Let's end this right here.' And I birdied the first playoff hole and was in the Open."

The leading qualifier at Glasgow Gailes was Peter Dawson, a young left-handed player from England. The second qualifier behind Dawson was Nick Faldo, who scored sixty-six in his first round at Glasgow Gailes. Leading the way among qualifiers at Western Gailes at 142 was Lionel Platts, who thirteen years before had won the Seven-Club Tournament at Turnberry.

THE PLAYERS WHO WERE EXEMPT from the qualifying rounds made their way to Turnberry via varied routes. Severiano Ballesteros was in Germany the week before the Open, playing in an eight-man competition known as the Braun International Trophy, and on Sunday, July 3, Ballesteros scored a round of sixty-eight to win by two strokes over American George Burns. The young air force recruit with the aching back won $20,000, and it was the biggest payday of his career to that point. Others in the field included Gary Player and David Graham. In his victory over Faldo at the Uniroyal, Ballesteros's tee shots had avoided the fairways like they were no-man's land, but in the Braun International, he claimed he had missed "only four fairways" off the tee during the entire event. When Ballesteros arrived at Turnberry, he announced that he had ceased taking injections for his injured back. "I quit taking them last Wednesday," said Ballesteros. "The shots, they make me sleepy." When asked when he would be finished serving his time in the Spanish Air Force, Ballesteros said, "I get out of the service next April." He was then asked if he would go to play in America, where the year-long prize money had reached $9 million. "No," said Ballesteros.

"When April comes, I rest. When Americans come to Europe, they are welcome. But when Europeans go to America, it is very hard for them. I am not sure I ever want to play on the [American] tour. I think I can win here this week. If I win, maybe America give me a card for their tour."

The day before Ballesteros grabbed that big check in Munich, Tom Watson was in Barcelona shooting a final-round sixty-three to blitz the field by eleven strokes in the Barcelona Cup. The field was small there, too—just ten players—but it did include Raymond Floyd, Antonio Garrido, and Manuel Pinero. "I had won the Western Open pretty easily," said Watson, "and then when I won in Barcelona against some pretty good players, I felt like I was on a roll. I went into Turnberry on a real high."

While Ballesteros and Watson were picking up what for them were still much needed paychecks, Jack Nicklaus was flying to Scotland. Even though Nicklaus had only played Turnberry once many years before during a week when the Open was at Troon, he would arrive knowing that Angelo Argea had been doing advance work on the course. Earlier in the summer, Jimmy Dickinson had contacted Nicklaus to let him know he was too ill to caddie in the Open, and so Argea, who had now been with Nicklaus for fifteen years, made the trip to Turnberry a few days ahead of his man. He was then the most famous caddie in the world, a status obtained due to a lot of television time next to Nicklaus and the fact that he had a wild gray Afro and mustache. "I wasn't happy about Jimmy being sick," said Argea years later, "but I was happy to be there. The only other time I'd been to the Open we lost out to Watson, and it looked like we might be heading for another match with him. I knew Jack was on top of his game going into Turnberry." Nicklaus arrived on Friday, July 1, and played his first practice round the following day. (Some accounts of the week at Turnberry claim that Nicklaus had Argea at Turnberry as a security blanket of sorts, or that Nicklaus hoped Argea's presence would add to his intimidation factor. Argea called that "ridiculous" and said that "anyone who wrote that never talked to me or Jack about it.")

It certainly didn't hurt Nicklaus that Argea was as thorough in his preparations as the great man himself. Mark Hayes recalled that when he went out to play his first practice round at Turnberry "one of my first impressions was that I got to the third hole and I couldn't find any landmarks to use for reference points for yardage. It was such a natural course, there were no yardage markers or even sprinkler heads we could use as a starting point to pace off yardage. The natural part was nice, but you still want to have accurate yardages. I was looking around for little bushes, trying to find little spots on the ground to line up with the hotel up on the hill. Anything."

Argea found the same challenge, but he was determined to mark the course for Nicklaus. He picked up several scorecards to scribble on and walked around Ailsa on the days before Nicklaus's arrival. The white cards were simple looking enough: six and a half inches across and six inches high with a crease in the center. Across the top in black ink were the words:

106th OPEN GOLF CHAMPIONSHIP
THE AILSA COURSE—TURNBERRY HOTEL

Just below those words, on the left side of the card was a line with the word "Competitor" next to it. Below that were four columns labeled "Hole," "Length in Yards," "Par," and "Score." On the left side of the crease was the information for the front nine, and on the right the information for the back nine. Under the columns on the left were two lines marked "Signature of Marker" and "Signature of Competitor." On the right, an extended box ran below the two center columns for yardage and par. In that space was this information:

|       |      |    |
|-------|------|----|
| In    | 3420 | 35 |
| Out   | 3455 | 35 |
| Total | 6875 | 70 |

As Argea walked the course, he used crisp uppercase letters and numbers to mark each hole in pencil. At the third hole, he wrote the following directly across the width of the left side of the card: 1st CHIMNEY 2nd TEL' 188-33. This meant that looking to the left from the southward running hole, it was 188 yards to the front of the green when he lined up the first chimney on the hotel with the second telephone pole running along the road. The green was thirty-three yards deep.

At the tee of the fourth hole, Argea wrote: CONCRETE MARK RT. 151-27. Nicklaus would know, then, that from the bit of concrete Argea had noticed poking through the ground, it was 151 yards to the front of the green and 178 yards to the back of the green.

At the eighth hole, Argea noted: END TRAP RT. 175-38 and then in smaller writing: 20 TO TOP. Here Nicklaus would know that from the fairway bunker on the right, it was 175 yards to the front of the green, plus twenty yards to get to the top of its slope.

On Bruce's Castle, Argea noted: CORNER WALL L HOUSE 176. Thus the approach yardage was determined in relation to the corner wall of the lighthouse.

Argea finished his work at the eighteenth hole by making a note in the fairway: END 1st TRAP 158-30. On the very bottom of the scorecard he penciled: #18 228 TO 260 OVER. This meant that from the new championship tee, it was 228 yards to the front of the first of the two bunkers on the left hand side and that Nicklaus would need a carry of 260 yards for his ball to safely fly over the same bunker.

Argea knew that his boss would double-check all these yardages for himself, but it was essential for the caddie to get them right. "All Jack ever needed was the right yardage," said Argea years later. "Once he knew that, he was good to go."

The R&A took notice of the lengths gone to by the caddies of the top players to cover every inch of Ailsa, and on Sunday, July 3, the R&A issued instructions to on-course stewards to tell caddies they were forbidden from pacing yardages on the greens. This order was given after Keith Mackenzie had seen Argea pacing out the eighteenth green. "If we have caddies pacing the green like that they'll wear a trench in it," said Mackenzie. "The Royal and Ancient rules clearly state that the caddies should take the distance of the greens from side to side by staying beside the putting surface."

One caddie interviewed after the ban was ordered said that "while we know the rules, sometimes the only way to get it right is to walk each hole. Anyway, most caddies will be out so early tomorrow that they'll be following the chap as the holes are actually cut. I doubt whether we'll see any stewards at that time." The speaker was Alfie Fyles. In the two years since he had helped Watson at Carnoustie, the two had made amends, urged on by Linda Watson, who saw Fyles as a good luck charm. Watson arrived at Turnberry from Spain on Sunday, the same day the caddies were warned off the greens. But by then, Fyles had all the information he needed to help his Mister.

ON MONDAY, July 4, the temperature at Turnberry soared into the high seventies and the skies were blue. The 6,369 spectators who turned up were cooled by a slight sea breeze, but that did not stop one newspaper from running the headline: "A blistering sun greets Open golfers."

One of the golfers greeted by the blistering sun was seventy-year-old Henry Cotton. The R&A had asked Cotton to play to mark the fiftieth anniversary of his first appearance in the Open, a debut in which he finished ninth behind Bobby Jones. Cotton had flown up from Sotogrande, Spain, where he lived, and had been recovering from abdominal surgery; his doctor ordered him to limit his practice rounds to twelve holes. Still, when he played on Monday with Tony Jacklin, the sixty-five he scored in winning the Open in 1934 still stood as the tournament's single-round scoring record. Cotton was a living link to the Open's early heydays, and on Sunday he dedicated a memorial stone at Prestwick in honor of the first Open Championship.

The British press was particularly interested in the presence of defending champion Johnny Miller. Known for his streaky play and straight talk, Miller's recent good finish on the American tour had the British writers anticipating a strong defense of his title. "Miller ready to come roaring back" screamed one headline on July 4, and writer Norman Mair's column in *The Scotsman* on the same day was headlined "Miller's appetite back." According to Mair, Miller attributed his poor play early in the season to "staleness," saying "I've been playing for twenty-five years, but I know I've still got game even if there are idiots who say I don't." Even at that, Miller had to admit that Tom Watson was the man to beat. "I knew years ago that Tom was destined to be kingpin at some time. He's always struck me as a little Arnold Palmer. Not that Tom is all that little, but you could see it in his eyes."

If Watson felt differently, he wasn't showing it. "Winning breeds winning warns on-form Watson," said one July 4 headline in the *Glasgow Herald*. Watson had said that very thing to the writer Raymond Jacobs before heading out with Fyles for his first look at Ailsa on Sunday, and years later, Watson recalled his first impressions of the course. "Because I was playing so well," said Watson, "I got a good feel for Turnberry and I knew I could play the golf course. Another thing I remember is that the fairways were mown as narrow as any fairways I'd ever seen. The third fairway was only eleven yards wide. I guess the R&A figured that if there wasn't much heavy rough, they'd make us suffer a little bit with the wispy stuff that was still left. Then Nicklaus got hold of them and said, 'This is ridiculous, it's unfair.' After that, they went out and widened the fairways by two passes of the mowers before the tournament started. I remember I was driving the ball very, very well at the time. And I was putting with a putter that I had used for only a few months, a Wilson 8813 that I had borrowed from a kid at the club back in Kansas City. It was not the same putter I had used at the Masters that year."

Lee Trevino was one of the last players to arrive at Turnberry, having played at the PGA Tour event in Milwaukee that finished on July 3. Once he got a look at the narrow fairways on Ailsa, Trevino cracked, "The guy driving that mower must have had one eye. I'm supposed to be the straightest driver of the ball in the world, and I can't hit these fairways."

Greg Norman, playing in his first major championship, thought the veteran players were making too much of the narrow fairways and "that they are talking themselves into feeling scared of the tee shots at the ninth and tenth holes. I look forward to playing the tee shot at the ninth. The only thing that will take my breath away there is the view." Newspaper headlines referred to a possible "Norman Conquest" of Turnberry, and the would-be conqueror was escorted during his practice rounds by countryman and five-time Open champion Peter Thomson. One directive Thomson gave Norman was to intentionally hit his tee shot in the thin rough left of the third fairway in order to have a better angle for the approach shot to the green. Thomson did not struggle for superlatives to describe his young protégé: "As a natural swinger of the golf club, Greg Norman is in the same class as Weiskopf and Miller. As a competitor, he has the same brand of spirit as [Dennis] Lillee or [Greg] Chappell [legendary Aussie cricket players]." Norman himself thought the course was playing so easy that "if the weather holds, someone will kill this course and shoot something like sixty-two or sixty-three."

A man of few words, Mark Hayes probably felt those comments a bit rash, because he realized there was danger in missing the fairways. Years later Hayes recalled that "back then before irons had square grooves on them, you'd get a flier lie in that light rough and end up hitting a seven-iron 220 yards. And you're trying to get it to stop on some little ledge on a green with no spin on the ball, and that just wasn't going to happen."

That aspect of playing out of the wispy rough was magnified by Ailsa's greens. "The greens at Ailsa do not receive running shots all that well," said Bradley Klein. "In many cases they have raised edges, and you have to carry the ball into them. Once a ball goes skidding off of one of those greens, there's not a lot of containment. The ball rolls out onto some very difficult areas above the greens that make for some awkward recoveries. There aren't any recovery areas that are floated out [flat], and a lot of heavy seaside bents and fescues [grasses] come into play."

A shot played from the fairway, however, would find safe haven on the greens. The rest of the golf course was brown, but the greens were emerald and receptive to incoming shots. Bob Charles, the New Zealander who had beaten out Nicklaus and Phil Rodgers for the title back in 1963, thought the greens were *too* soft. "The pace of the greens is pathetically slow," said Charles. "If they cut them down now, they'll have trouble with stubble." But there wasn't much support for Charles's sentiment, and years later George Brown, Turnberry's current-day greenskeeper, said it wouldn't have been surprising if the players thought the course in questionable condition. "I have a record in my office," said Brown, "that says that the golf course was not in great shape before the '77 Open. That's hardly surprising. British

Rail [the owner of Turnberry] spent most of their money on Gleneagles [another golf hotel it owned]. Turnberry had all the hand-me-down machinery from Gleaneagles. Turnberry probably only had one or two tractors and maybe three mowers."

As the Wednesday start of the Open approached, the R&A announced the groupings and the tee times for the first two rounds. John Schroeder was dismayed to discover that his first round starting time wasn't until almost 5 PM, but since the sun would stay up until nearly midnight, Schroeder would be able to finish his round. The reason he was glum about the starting time was that it indicated he was not a marquee player—the fans would have left for home or the pubs by the time he played the back nine—and that he would be putting over a minefield of cleat marks left by nearly the entire field that preceded him. "Still," said Schroeder, "I was pretty fired up about playing. On Tuesday when I went to the first tee for practice, and Tom Weiskopf and Nicklaus were standing there. I said, 'Do you guys mind if I join you?' They said that would be fine with them, and we started playing. Pretty early on I mentioned my lousy starting time to Jack. He said, 'John, don't worry about it. The first time I played in the Open [1962] I was the reigning U.S. Open champion. They sent me out last and I had to play with a marker [a noncompetitor who plays with a single competitor to establish a normal pace of play].' After that, I felt a lot better. I probably drove those two guys crazy. I asked them a million questions trying to pick their brains about the course."

As Nicklaus played his practice round, he was watched by Peter McEvoy, a twenty-four-year-old amateur golfer who was playing in the Open by dint of his victory in the Amateur Championship the previous month at Ganton in England. "It was my second Open," said McEvoy. "I had played the year before at Birkdale and missed the thirty-six-hole cut. I didn't do spectacularly badly however." McEvoy was born in London, but had lived twenty miles north of Turnberry for much of his youth. "We moved back to London when I was eleven years old," said McEvoy twenty-five years later. "I didn't play much golf as a youngster relative to most of my peers, but when I was about nineteen I got quite keen on it. My father was a member at Turnberry, so I had played quite a lot of golf there. I'd seen Nicklaus in the practice rounds at the '72 Open at Muirfield, and that was the first year I tried to qualify. The first time I saw him I remember thinking he was much smaller than I expected, and I couldn't believe how slow his swing was. I can still picture his swing on the practice ground at Muirfield. It almost seemed as if it was in slow motion. At Turnberry when I went out to watch players practice, he was the one I wanted to see."

One player McEvoy did not see out on the course that Tuesday was Brian Barnes. As one of only fifteen Scots in the field, Barnes had delighted the locals by wearing tartan shorts in Monday's practice round. He was considered the Scot with the best chance of winning, but he alarmed the fans who would be cheering for him by skipping Tuesday's practice round to go fishing. "I feel my game is as good as it will ever be," said Barnes to writer Ian Paul before heading to a nearby loch. "The day before the Open is pretty hectic, and I think it would be more productive for me to have a relaxing day away from it all."

The groupings for the first two rounds of the Open were decided by placing the names of twenty leading Americans in one hat, twenty leading British players in another hat, and twenty leading players from other countries in a third. When the names were drawn, the first name out of the hatful of British players was McEvoy's. "I was somewhere near the clubhouse when Keith Mackenzie told me my name had been the first drawn," said McEvoy. "He joked that he'd thought about putting my name back after he drew the next two. That's when he told me I'd be playing with Nicklaus and Gary Player in the first two rounds. Initially I thought it was a great thing, but as the moment drew closer it started to become a bit intimidating. I recall being excited, and then the excitement turning into fear."

McEvoy wasn't the only one growing fearful. The famous bookmakers, Ladbroke's, who set the odds on Watson at 7 to 1, with Nicklaus the favorite at 6 to 1, grew increasingly nervous as the heaviest action came in on the Masters champion. A headline in Wednesday's *Scotsman* declared: "The punters [bettors] go for Tom Watson," and the story reported that "big money was rolling in to the bookmakers last night on America's Tom Watson. Ladbroke's reported a £500 each way bet; Corals [another betting shop] took the same. Playboy had £500 [on Watson] to win and Hills took one bet of £400 and two bets of £200. With many smaller bets being placed on the Masters champion, Watson is the big loser for the bookmakers. Strangely, the bookmakers, for the first time they can remember, wouldn't mind Jack Nicklaus winning." Meanwhile, the odds on Weiskopf were 10 to 1, Hubert Green and Miller were 14 to 1 and Hale Irwin was 16 to 1.

IN THE YEARS AFTER 1977, Peter McEvoy would play in three Masters Tournaments and seven more Open Championships as an amateur, and in the process grow more comfortable playing with famous professional golfers. On July 6, 1977, however, he was on tenterhooks the likes of which he had never known. "My parents owned a holiday cottage about twelve miles away from Turnberry and I was staying there," said McEvoy years later. "On that Wednesday I was up at first light because I was nervous as nervous could be." His tee time was 9:25 AM, but McEvoy said "I got to the course *very* early. I hadn't met Jack Nicklaus or Gary Player at that stage. I had seen them around in the clubhouse and on the practice green, but I hadn't the nerve to introduce myself. So I didn't meet them until we were on the first tee that morning. I was a little bit more wary of meeting Player because he had a reputation of being maybe not quite so easy to play with as Nicklaus. And he [Player] struck me as a bit stern. In fact, he was fantastic toward me. They both were. To be honest, when we were introduced I was in a bit of a trance.

"At the time I was in the law. I was doing what in England we call articles. It's the same as what Americans call an internship. My boss was caddying for me, and as we walked down the first fairway Nicklaus came up beside me and said, 'Peter, I've heard you're studying to be an attorney.' I was so impressed that he would know that. Clearly he had gone out of his way to find out something about me to put me at ease. My boss was pretty impressed that Jack Nicklaus knew *I* was studying law.

"I remember thinking at the time that Nicklaus had the reputation of being the strongest hitter in the world even though he was in his late thirties. On the first few holes, I drove the ball right out there with him, and I was slightly surprised at that, only for him to really let one go at the seventh, which is a par five. He drove it about fifty yards past me there.

"Looking back now and having played in other major championships with Nicklaus and Tom Watson, I realize that when you get in an intimidating situation like that it either goes *really* badly or you end up playing better than you ever thought you could. On that day, it was very much the former. On the first nine holes, I was out in over forty strokes and Nicklaus played the same holes in thirty-one. So it was really embarrassing because I was doing *really* badly and he was doing particularly well. Player was playing just so-so. When we got to the tenth tee, Nicklaus hit another enormous drive right down the center of the fairway and Player hit a good drive. Then I hit a really quick hook onto the beach. There weren't any crowds on the left side of that hole, so the only people on this beach filled with little white sea shells were the caddies, Gary Player, Jack Nicklaus, and myself. And we were looking for *my* golf ball amongst white shells, and I remember thinking, 'Whatever happens in the remainder of my golf career, there will never be a moment as bad as this again. I didn't dare look at them. It was such a humiliating moment, but as it turned out it was a turning point for me. We found the ball, I knocked it up onto the green and holed the putt. The rest of the round I managed to recover from the dreadful front nine." With an eagle three at the seventeenth, McEvoy had scored seventy-eight for the day. Nicklaus and Player shot sixty-eight and seventy-one respectively.

Not that McEvoy would have noticed, but it was hot at Turnberry that Wednesday. A front-page headline in the *Glasgow Herald* declared: "80 in the shade at the Open." Since there were no trees on the Ailsa links, there was no shade for the golfers or spectators once they set foot outside, and the cooling sea breeze was absent after the noon hour. The fans were so unaccustomed to the heat that more than seventy of the 16,539 spectators were forced to visit first-aid tents; many more sought shelter and beer in the courtesy tents. But the heat was only a problem if a spectator could *get* to Turnberry. The streets of tiny Maybole were packed with stalled traffic, and at one point more than 1,900 vehicles *per hour* were reported on the road from Glasgow to Kilmarnock, a town on the main road about halfway between Glasgow and Turnberry. Those with fat wads of pounds could be delivered to the front lawn of the hotel via helicopter from any point in central Scotland. The cost was £125.

One person who couldn't be bothered with it all was John Philip, the former caddie who was sixth alternate. "I stayed to watch a friend play a few holes, then I went back to St. Andrews," said Philip. "I watched the Open on television."

THE EARLY PACESETTER on the first day of the 1977 Open was Severiano Ballesteros. Off early at 8:10 AM with Hale Irwin and England's Neil Coles, he turned in a score of sixty-nine. Twenty minutes behind Ballesteros came Faldo and Crenshaw, each with seventy-one. Thirty-five minutes after those two, Greg Norman came limping in with seventy-eight. Just a few groups later than Norman were McEvoy, Player, and Nicklaus. When Nicklaus posted sixty-eight, it was the best score of the morning rounds.

In the early afternoon came Brian Barnes, fresh off his day of fishing. Barnes took seventy-nine blows on the day, his worst tournament round in five years. His scorecard had eight fives and one six on it. "It looks as though I will have a couple of extra unexpected days with the family," said Barnes after his round.

Tom Watson came in with a scrappy sixty-eight around tea time. At the first hole, Watson's approach pitch had bounded over the green, and at the second he put his approach into a bunker. Both times he made par. At the long seventh hole, he reached the green in two shots, playing his driver both times. At the eighteenth, he pulled a five-iron shot into the grandstands to the left of the green.

Throughout the day, good scores continued to trickle in. The weather conditions were ideal, but Ailsa was not being "killed" as the eight-over-par Norman had suggested it might be a few days earlier. The reason was the hole positions on the greens. After signing for his score, Watson said that "the pins were on the tops of marbles out there today." Johnny Miller called the hole positions "Sunday settings," saying also that "the course was playing so easily that it needed those difficult pin positions. It took some brains to get around today." Miller scored sixty-nine; despite noting that the course boasted "the eighteen hardest hole positions I've ever seen. On one hole I looked at the line of my putt and felt like I was negotiating Everest."

The hole positions exacted a toll on much of the field: Tom Weiskopf had seventy-four, as did Jerry Pate, Manuel Pinero, and Peter Thomson. Jack Newton shot seventy-five, Antonio Garrido shot seventy-seven, and Seve Ballesteros's brother Manuel shot eighty.

After his round, Nicklaus talked about the greens. "The greens here are slick but not fast," said Nicklaus. "They are good by British standards. I don't mean to be rude by that, the mixture of the grasses here just doesn't allow for greens as smooth as we have in America. They all have a different rate of growth." Pointing to the table at which he was seated, Nicklaus said, "The greens at Muirfield Village are as smooth as the green cloth covering this table—or as smooth as this cloth will be once I brush the crumbs off it."

By day's end, only eight players broke the par of seventy. The first six to do so were Watson, Nicklaus, and Lee Trevino (sixty-eight), Ballesteros, Miller, and quite unexpectedly, Gaylord Burrows (sixty-nine). The pack of six players matching level par included Tommy Horton, George Burns, and Hale Irwin. At one over par along with Player, Crenshaw, and Faldo was Roger Maltbie.

The two most nostalgic rounds of the day were played by Arnold Palmer, who shot seventy-three, and Cotton, who playing along with Palmer and the legendary Irishman Christy O'Connor, shot ninety-three. "I hope no one was too ashamed of me," said Cotton. When the crowd rose as one to greet Cotton at Ailsa Home's green, he knew that no one was.

When Brian Barnes flubbed his round, it left the hopes of a British champion resting with Horton and Faldo, or so it seemed. No one expected that a twenty-five-year-old player from Yorkshire named Martin Foster would zoom into the lead at the Open Championship. After shooting a score of sixty-seven, however, Foster was suddenly thrust into the role of championship leader. In the electric sporting atmosphere created by Virginia Wade's win at Wimbledon the previous weekend, the British fans thought they were on a roll with Foster. He eagled the seventeenth hole and after his round posed for photos holding up three fingers in the manner of a Boy Scout salute to signify that he was three under par.

The British press clacked away madly at their typewriters writing the story of the new hero and then retired to the Turnberry Hotel for dinner. Writer Ian Paul's newspaper column about Foster the following morning would be headlined: "We can still swing with the best."

While everyone was toasting Foster, John Schroeder was still making his way around the course. After playing the front nine in thirty-five strokes, Schroeder got his game humming on the home nine. That he was able to do so was remarkable, because as he recalled years later, "it was chaos out there. When we got to the fourteenth hole it was around eight o'clock in the evening," said Schroeder. "All the stewards and spotters had left for the day, and I had to back off of my tee shot at fourteen three times because of all the horns honking as they left the parking lots. When I finally swung, I pulled the ball about forty yards left of the fairway, and since there were no spotters, I couldn't find the ball. We had to let the group behind us play through while we searched for it. I have to say I was pretty steamed. Somehow I managed to pull it together and birdie the final two holes." With those two birdies, Schroeder had an inward half of thirty-one and a total of sixty-six. It was 9:15 PM when he finished.

The first thing he did after exiting the eighteenth green was complain to the first R&A official he saw. "I think the players out last should be given the same attention as early players," said Schroeder. "I know that spectators had seen all the stars, but everyone should be treated equally." The dining writers were forced to head back down to the golf course to interview Schroeder, but he was mostly interested in complaining, and they were mostly interested in the fact that he was the son of Ted Schroeder, who had won the Wimbledon singles title in 1949.

Schroeder cooled his heels in his room at the hotel while he put on a jacket and tie for dinner. He made his way to the dining room at the far right side of the hotel as it faces the golf courses. When he entered, Schroeder was in a room of kings. Eight chandeliers hung from the ceiling. Six giant windows, each nine feet across, created a visual sandwich between the white frames at the top and bottom: The top layer was the warm orange sky, below that the sea and Ailsa Craig, then the turf of the links. It is a view more perfect than any painting. Four white pillars stood out in the dining room amid the plush red chairs, carpet, and table coverings. Around

Schroeder, an army of servers in black tuxedos swarmed the dining room floor. "Dinner was a show," said Hubert Laforge, who was then a young Frenchman in his second week on the job in the Turnberry dining room. "Everyone dressed up and looked their best. It was an occasion. Everyone looked smart; it was like a parade of models coming through that door." On the plates of the guests was everything from *caviar sur glace* (£27.50 per ounce) to *la tortue vert au xeres* (Clear Turtle Soup with Sherry, £2.50). Specialties of the house included *caneton roti bigarrade* for two; a dish of roast Norfolk baby duck in an orange and Drambuie sauce, which took sixty minutes to prepare and cost £14.50. For the authentic taste of Scotland, one could order haggis with "champit tatties an' 'neeps" (mashed potatoes and mashed turnips) for £3.

"I went into that room," recalled Schroeder twenty-five years later, "and I looked around at all the British swells in their jackets and ties. And when I sat down, I looked over and there was Tom Weiskopf holding court at his table. Tom was the man on the scene at the Open, and you could just tell he loved it so much. I looked out those windows and around the room again, and then it hit me. I was the leader of the Open Championship."

# EIGHT

✦

Notable scores after one round of the 106th Open Championship:

    John Schroeder, U.S., 66
    Martin Foster, England, 67
    Jack Nicklaus, U.S., 68
    Tom Watson, U.S., 68
    Lee Trevino, U.S., 68
    Johnny Miller, U.S., 69
    Severiano Ballesteros, Spain, 69
    Gaylord Burrows, citizen-in-waiting, U.S., 69
    Raymond Floyd, U.S., 70
    Tommy Horton, England, 70
    Hale Irwin, U.S., 70
    George Burns, U.S., 70
    Nick Faldo, England, 71
    Ben Crenshaw, U.S., 71
    Roger Maltbie, U.S., 71
    Hubert Green, U.S., 72
    Arnold Palmer, U.S., 73
    Mark Hayes, U.S., 76

Second round, July 7, 1977. Temperature: 86 degrees at midday. Wind: Nearly absent. Attendance: 17,948

When Ted Schroeder heard that his son was leading the Open Championship, his sly response was, "Gosh, I hope he makes the cut." But the bliss of leading the championship was short lived for Schroeder. He shot seventy-four on day two, and his fall from grace was accentuated by the misspelling of his name on the giant scoreboard by the eighteenth green.

149

In the years since Henry Cotton's single-round Open record of sixty-five, seven players had matched his score. (They were Eric Brown, Leopoldi Ruiz, Peter Butler, Christy O'Connor, Neil Coles, Jack Nicklaus, and Jack Newton.) Early in the day on July 7, the record score was matched again, this time by *el Abuelo,* Angel Gallardo, who had the first starting time and played his round in just more than two hours.

Even with only an occasional baby's breath of wind, however, the course avoided complete decimation until Mark Hayes teed off two hours behind Gallardo and delivered the hammer blow to Ailsa's pride that had been expected. Hayes was a polite, quiet man from Edmond, Oklahoma, and aside from his handful of victories on the American tour, the most notable thing about him was that he was one of a gaggle of tour players who wore a bucket hat emblazoned with the logo of the Amana home appliance company. The Amana hats were an icon of professional golf in the 1970s, and the corporation was among the first nongolf companies to pay players to sport its logo. They paid their endorsers $50 per tournament, and if they won they received a free appliance—most asked for refrigerators. Some players were also covered by the company's life and health insurance policies. The Amana Bridge was made up almost entirely of players who were devoid of charisma, including Bob Goalby, Don January, George Archer, Dave Stockton, and as the world was about to find out, Mark Hayes.

As it turned out, few golfers in history would have remained as unfazed as Mark Hayes after what was about to happen to him. Years later, Hayes recalled that "even though Turnberry was my first Open Championship, I had won three tournaments in the States during the previous year. My first round at Turnberry was pretty shaky, and I felt pretty shaky early in the second round, too." The discomfort Hayes was feeling about his game centered around his putting. On the practice green at the Western Open two weeks prior to the Open Championship, Hayes had listened to fellow tour player Bruce Lietzke explain the virtues of using a cross-handed grip while putting (i.e., placing the left hand below the right hand on the shaft of the club and more commonly referred to by British golfers as "cackhanded"), and he decided to give it a try. "To be honest," said Hayes later, "it didn't seem to be working all that great. I didn't putt too well in the first round at Turnberry. Between that and the struggle to figure out what kind of approach shot to hit on every hole, I felt kind of lost out there."

In the second round, the cackhanded putting began producing staggering results for Hayes. He putted only twenty-three times during his round, and there were thirteen holes where he used his bronze Bulls-Eye putter only once. If Hayes had made par at the eighteenth hole, he would have recorded the lowest single round in major championship history. As it was, he bogeyed the hole after his tee shot took what he described as "a wicked bounce" into one of the two fairway bunkers. When the numbers were added up, Hayes had scored sixty-three and bettered Cotton's record by two shots.

Everyone but Hayes seemed to be agog at what he had done. "I knew I had played a good round," he said, "but I couldn't believe it when they told me I'd broken the all-time record. I guess I just assumed the record had to be lower than sixty-five. I *was* amazed, but only by what a big deal everyone made of it. The R&A gave me a sterling scorecard to commemorate the round, which was a nice gesture."

Writing in *Sports Illustrated*, Dan Jenkins was beside himself at Hayes's lack of reaction to his accomplishment. "Surrounded by a mere 900 million members of the press," wrote Jenkins, "Mark Hayes was asked what his reaction was to his monumental feat. He sat there. He looked down. He thought. Finally, he said, 'I have a lot of trouble figuring out the distances over here.'

"That was it," continued Jenkins, "The Eagle has landed. If I have but one life to give . . . Lafayette, we are somewhere . . . Mark Hayes had shattered Britain with a sixty-three, and Amana had not sent a poet with him to Turnberry."

In the twenty-five years that passed since that day, Hayes did not become any more expressive about the round that to this day remains a record. "The funny thing is," said Hayes, "I never felt comfortable putting cross-handed. It just never felt right. I quit doing it about a week after that round."


AS THE BRAND SPANKING NEW U.S. Open Champion, Hubert Green knew he had to play better on Thursday than he had on Wednesday. "Winning the U.S. Open didn't mean I was the best player in America," said Green years later, "but it did mean I had the privilege and the honor to be the American champion for a year and to represent the country. Being a good ol' American boy, redneck and all, it was a great honor. I was thrilled to go to Scotland as the American flag holder. I loved it. And I was playing good and was cocky as heck at the time."

If ever a course was there for the taking, thought Green, this was the day. "These seaside courses are designed for a lot of wind," he thought at the time. "If it was blowing, this course would be ten shots harder. But now it's just a turkey shoot. I know the people who run the Royal and Ancient are powerful. They may even be two shots better than the queen. But they're not ahead of the Man upstairs. There is nothing they can do."

Green started playing like he was blessed at the fourth hole on Thursday. On that par three, he hit in his words "my worst shot of the day," a six-iron pushed dead right of the green. The ball deflected off the hillside next to the green and ran across the putting surface and into the hole—for an ace. Green giggled when he heard the crowd roar. "I thought about telling the spectators that's how I played it," said Green. "But they knew better."

After a bogey four at the sixth, Green put the pedal to the floor starting at the ninth hole, where he began a streak of five consecutive birdies. He was hitting the ball very close to the hole; the longest putt among the five birdies was eighteen feet, and two were just more than a foot. "It was right around then," said Green years later, "that I thought I was going to shoot so low that I was going to be the next superstar in the world. I was thinking I could shoot sixty. My name was near the top of the leaderboard and things were looking pretty good for Hubert Green. I had my speech ready and everything. And then, bam!, I took it right in the face." The "bam!" came in the form of three putts at the fourteenth and sixteenth holes, and at the seventeenth, another "kapow!" hit Green in the kisser when he played a poor bunker shot that went sailing over the green, leading to a double bogey. When the round was over, Green signed for a score of sixty-six. Afterward he posed for photos hoisting a jeroboam of Bollinger's champagne he received to mark his hole-in-one.

After his Thursday round of seventy-four, Johnny Miller sounded like a man who wished someone would hit him over the head with a jeroboam. "I just blew my chances," he said at the time. "The way I'm playing it's a sin to shoot seventy-four. I just threw away the tournament." With twenty-five years to reflect, Miller saw things differently. "After I won the Open in 1976," said Miller, "I was done emotionally. I was burnt out. I had no interest in playing golf. I had just bought a ranch in Napa [California], and working in the vineyards I had packed on about twenty pounds of muscle. I looked good—I was buff—but I couldn't swing the club. My heart wasn't totally in it, and I couldn't swing the club with the little dropping movement I had at one time. On top of that, we were dragging three kids around with us by that time."

THE WAR THAT NEARLY SPELLED the end of Turnberry during the 1940s was indirectly responsible for the presence in 1977 of the Open's leader after two rounds, twenty-six-year-old Californian Roger Maltbie. The golfer's father, Archie (nicknamed Lin), was a fighter pilot during the war, and he flew the American-made fighter plane known as the Republic P-47 Thunderbolt. The P-47 did not possess the purring engine of the American P-51 Mustang, the "Cadillac of the sky," nor the elegant lines of the British Spitfire. Rather, the P-47 was something of a tank with wings. It was the most heavily armored Allied fighter to see action in World War II, and it could take a tremendous beating and remain in the air. The pilots such as Lin Maltbie who flew the P-47 knew that its bulk made it slow in climbing but were also confident that when nosed into a dive not a plane extant could keep pace with it. The Thunderbolt had tremendous range and was the first plane able to escort bombers for the length of a mission into Germany. P-47 pilots would fly above 30,000 feet until they spotted Nazi fighter patrols; then the young airmen would tilt the Thunderbolts into a screaming descent toward the enemy. The unlucky *Luftwaffe* pilots below would see the blur of the enormous (twelve feet in diameter) four-bladed propeller's painted tips as the Thunderbolts came hurtling toward them and then the flash of the eight .50 caliber machine guns mounted in the wings.

It was in just such a moment that Lin Maltbie squeezed the trigger on a Messerschmitt 109 over France. In fact, Lin Maltbie did his job *too* well: His Thunderbolt was so close to the German plane as the .50 caliber bullets ripped into it that he flew directly through the resulting explosion. The American pilot instantly realized his plane was damaged beyond saving and bailed out. Once on the ground, Lin Maltbie could hear the dogs of a *Wehrmacht* patrol, and they were looking for him. He made his way to a nearby farmhouse, and the family there hid him until they could make contact with the French underground. With the help of the resistance fighters, the young pilot eventually made his way back across the English Channel. There he met a young girl named Joan, who was from the village of Kirkintilloch, just a few miles north of Glasgow. (Longtime readers of the *Saturday Evening Post* may recall stories of the ship's engineer whose favorite drink was Duggan's Dew from Kirkintilloch.)

In 1977, Roger Maltbie was one of the most talented young American golfers, and when he decided to play in his first Open Championship, he brought his parents, Lin and Joan, along with him. Their son had been playing golf since he and his brother started sneaking into the San Jose Country Club as young boys. When Lin Maltbie noticed his sons' interest in the game, he joined that club, and the boys no longer had to be stealthy about their golf. The fighter pilot's son was a bit of a hellraiser: When he won the

1976 Memorial Tournament, the partying afterward reached such heights that Maltbie lost his winner's check. He didn't lose it in a card game or at a casino; he lost it as in he could not locate it.

Like Mark Hayes, Roger Maltbie had never played links golf before the 1977 Open Championship. With his long hair and eyeglasses with lenses as big as dinner plates, the only thing that gave Maltbie away as a professional golfer was the polyester slick slacks he wore. But when he shot sixty-six in the second round, he was all alone in the lead at three under par for the tournament. Twenty-five years later he recalled a range of feelings regarding the round. "Initially at Turnberry I had trouble trusting my alignment before I swung the club," said Maltbie. "I had never played a golf course without trees on it, so I felt like I was just aiming out into a void. I also had the distinct impression that I was being cheated from a real Open experience. It was really bluebird weather. I had watched the tournament for so many years on television when the wind was blowing stuff all over the place. I had packed cashmere sweaters and rain suits and all that. I wanted to be forced to play some low, running shots just to learn how to do it. I wanted to be able to go home and tell my buddies, 'Man, I stood there and the rain was going sideways and I hit a three-iron from one-twenty!' Those are the kinds of stories I had always heard, and instead I was getting California weather. It was strange, but I'm sure that helped me. I hadn't played links golf in *any* weather before. If the weather had been rough I probably would have had trouble dealing with it. As it turned out, it wasn't much different from playing at home. I was just firing the ball right at the green."

After having failed to pry anything quotable out of the reluctant Hayes, the famished press corps bore down on Maltbie, and he made their day. When British writers found out his mother was from Scotland, he said, "It's okay with me if you write that I'm top Scot in the Open." And when a writer asked if it was his first trip to Scotland, Maltbie said, "Hell, I've never been east of New York before, unless you count Boston."

That Maltbie was in a jovial mood said a lot about what a good round can do for the spirits of a professional golfer, though he had every right to be a bit edgy. One of the nice touches of staying at the Turnberry Hotel is that the giant windows in the guest rooms all open outward. On a lovely, breezy day, this gives a visitor gusts of fresh air while he reads the newspaper or nurses a drink with his feet up. The chirping of birds that nest under the eaves lends a melody to the relaxation. For Maltbie, the open windows provided something completely unexpected. "It was so hot," said Maltbie, "that everyone left the windows in the rooms wide open all day and night. While I was out of the room on Wednesday evening, someone got in there—

through the windows I guess—and stole all my traveler's checks and some other stuff. It wasn't the end of the world for me, but it was kind of shocking. In the end, I just decided to chalk it up as part of the neat adventure I was on."

Maltbie and Green were in first and second place respectively at the end of play on Thursday. On Friday they would be the final twosome to head out onto Ailsa. Normally this meant they could expect to be followed by a huge gallery, and there was no reason to think otherwise. "I was young and aggressive enough that I couldn't see any reason why I couldn't win," said Maltbie years later. But like the seafaring Gaels who had sailed past Ailsa Craig nearly 1,000 years before, it was impossible for Maltbie or anyone else at Turnberry to comprehend what it would be like to witness the effect when an irresistible force meets an immovable object. They were about to find out.

IF ROGER MALTBIE was going to win the Open, he was going to have to go through Jack Nicklaus to do it. As Maltbie and every other tour player knew, "when you saw Nicklaus's name on the leaderboard, you knew one thing. It wasn't going backwards."

At the end of the second round, Jack Nicklaus was in what for him was the perfect position. After a round of seventy, he was two shots off the lead, and his name was most definitely on the big board by the eighteenth green ("J. Nicklaus," next to a red numeral "2"). Meanwhile, he played his round with the fatherly pride that went along with the news he received at 2 AM the previous morning that his son Jackie had finished second at Muirfield Village in the qualifying for the U.S. Junior Championship.

In truth, young Jackie may have been putting better than his father at the time. Peter McEvoy remembers thinking after the second round that "I felt as if I could hit any shot Gary Player hit, but Nicklaus's long game was peerless. The thing that stood out was Nicklaus's really poor putting."

Nicklaus agreed. "I was actually kind of fortunate to shoot seventy," said Nicklaus after the round. "With putting like that—I mean nothing would go in." It didn't appear that it would be that way when Nicklaus made the turn in thirty-three strokes, but he three-putted at the tenth hole, missed a five-footer at the fourteenth, and missed from eight feet for eagle on the seventeenth. He finished the round with a sloppy drive at the eighteenth and made a bogey.

Still, Nicklaus had not gone backward and managed to do something only the very best golfers can do: play a solid round when their game is not especially sound from top to bottom. Twenty-five years later, Nicklaus said,

"The course wasn't playing particularly difficult as far as I was concerned. I just needed some putts to start falling."

Nicklaus was one of four players with a two-round total of 138; the others were Green, Lee Trevino, and Tom Watson. Trevino, who was one of the last players to arrive at Turnberry, was delighted with his 4 PM tee time for the day. When asked if he was tired, Trevino said, "Nope, I'm feeling great. I slept for twelve hours last night, woke up, tuned the television in to a cricket match, and that put me right back to sleep. Besides, my golf clubs don't know where they are. They don't know what day it is. It makes no difference to them."

Tom Watson's score of seventy meant that for the second day in a row his number matched that of Nicklaus, and he was not overly confident with his putter either. "I drove the ball well again today," said Watson after finishing a round that began at 3:20 PM. "I kept it in play all day. My iron play has not been solid for two rounds, and the putter didn't feel too good in my hands. I'm surprised that with the championship already half over, only seven players are under par in view of the conditions we have had so far." The following afternoon, Watson and Nicklaus would be paired together and play directly in front of Maltbie and Green.

After his round, Jack Nicklaus went to the practice tee for a short session accompanied by Angelo Argea. "Jack never hit many balls after a round," said Argea. "He'd hit just enough to stay tuned up. After a round, he'd hit a couple of nine-irons, a couple of six-irons, a couple of three-irons, and then a few balls with the driver. Since he hadn't putted well that day, after he hit the balls we went to the practice green. I squatted down near the hole and tossed the balls back to him after they stopped moving or went in the hole. Whatever the problem was, it seemed like he got it worked out there."

When Nicklaus got into his low crouch over the ball on the putting green, his body was bent at almost a right angle. He was one of the few great players who left the leather glove on his left hand when he putted. Early in his career the glove was sometimes black, but by 1977 it was almost always white. Argea recalled watching Nicklaus hit the practice putts that Thursday evening and thinking everything was going to be all right. "Jack was concentrating on those putts like they were the real thing," Argea said.

As Nicklaus practiced, he was preparing for a run at the Open Championship for the fifteenth time. He had not missed a single Open since he first played at Troon in 1962, and his record over that time span was awesome. Aside from his victories in 1966 and 1970, Nicklaus finished second five times, third three times, and only once since 1963—when he finished twelfth in 1965 at Birkdale—had he been out of the top six.

If everyone else had an inkling that something colossal was about to happen, Johnny Miller *knew* it. "That was a different era," said Miller twenty-five years later. "It was the era of the superguns. Some guys you never heard of might have been leading a tournament after the second round, but by the end of the third round that wasn't going to be the case. These days, every third major or so, you'll have a final-round leader no one has ever heard of, at least until Tiger Woods got rolling in 2000. That just didn't happen back then. You just knew that by the end of the third day, everyone else would trail off and the superguns—Nicklaus, Watson, Trevino, Floyd, Irwin, Weiskopf—would be in control."

# NINE

★

Notable scores after two rounds of the 106th Open Championship:

Roger Maltbie, U.S., 71-66=137
Hubert Green, U.S., 72-66=138
Jack Nicklaus, U.S., 68-70=138
Tom Watson, U.S., 68-70=138
Lee Trevino, U.S., 68-70=138
Mark Hayes, U.S., 76-63=139
Peter Butler, England, 72-68=140
Chi Sun Hsu, Taiwan, 70-70=140
John Schroeder, U.S., 66-74=140
Severiano Ballesteros, Spain, 69-71=140
Ben Crenshaw, U.S., 71-69=140
George Burns, U.S., 70-70=140
Gaylord Burrows, U.S., 69-72=141
Martin Foster, England, 67-74=141
Johnny Miller, U.S., 69-74=143
Tommy Horton, England, 70-74=144
Arnold Palmer, U.S., 73-73=146
Nick Faldo, England, 71-76=147
Greg Norman, Australia, 78-72=150

Third round, July 8, 1977. Early day temperatures in the high 70s. Possibility of electrical storms in the afternoon, temperature cooling. Attendance: 18,881

Third-round tee times:

2:25 PM—Gaylord Burrows, George Burns
2:35 PM—Ben Crenshaw, Severiano Ballesteros

2:45 PM—John Schroeder, Howard Clark (England)
2:55 PM—Chi Sun Hsu, Peter Butler
3:05 PM—Mark Hayes, Lee Trevino
3:15 PM—Tom Watson, Jack Nicklaus
3:25 PM—Hubert Green, Roger Maltbie

Despite some fine individual rounds, after two rounds of Open competition Ailsa was holding her own against the field. The thirty-six-hole cutoff came at ten over par (150). Of the eighty-five players who were at that number or lower, fifty-five of them were between five and ten over par. In the annals of the game, it is unfailingly noted that Ailsa was playing easy that week in July 1977. If that was the case, then the bulk of the field must have been playing exceedingly poor golf. By the time play was completed on Saturday, Ailsa would have repelled the best efforts of all but two players: Jack Nicklaus and Tom Watson. The fact that no other player was able to tear into Ailsa strongly suggests it is nonsense to think it was playing easier than any other course on the championship rota. Rather, over the Friday and Saturday rounds, Nicklaus and Watson would take the game to such a dizzying summit that they would have shot low scores on *any* golf course under the same conditions.

The scintillating golf played by Nicklaus and Watson over those last two rounds also created another popular but errant perception regarding the 106th Open Championship: that as of Friday's round the tournament evolved into a "match play" contest strictly between Nicklaus and Watson. By early in the day on Saturday, it would become clear that the contest was a man-to-man battle between the two, but as of Friday morning the tournament was still very much up in the air, and in the early going on Saturday it was not inconceivable that other players would contend down to the wire. For certain, Saturday's sun-drenched duel would have the *feel* of match play about it, but it was still stroke play. A single disastrous hole by either Nicklaus or Watson would have cost him the championship, whereas in genuine match play the effects of a botched hole are limited. In addition, it's not uncommon in tournament golf for two players who have separated themselves from the pack to focus so intently upon each other that another player who feels he has nothing to lose can suddenly get hot and steal the show. That was admittedly unlikely in the case of Nicklaus and Watson, but it wasn't as if the other players decided to hide in their rooms at the Turnberry Hotel. As of Friday morning, players as far back as seven shots off the lead still felt like they were in the fight.

One of the players who had not given up was thirty-six-year-old Tommy

Horton of England. As a young boy, Horton lived on Jersey, the largest of the Channel Islands and home of the Royal Jersey Golf Club and of Harry Vardon, the man who won more Open Championships (six) than any player in history. Though Vardon died in March 1937, four years before Horton was born, he was still revered on Jersey. "From my earliest days," said Horton when he was sixty years old, "I knew that Harry Vardon had lived on the edge of the golf course, no more than 200 yards from where our home was. In that part of the island, all people talked about was Vardon. I had a couple of golf clubs and would go out and knock the ball around on a spare piece of ground at the club. I started caddying at Royal Jersey when I was eight years old. I remember caddying for the Honourable Michael Scott, who won the Amateur Championship when he was fifty years old. He told me that he had competed in the Open and that it was the ultimate championship. From that moment on, winning the Open became my goal.

"Since the Open is always played on links courses, I spent all my time practicing low shots, you know, hitting those knockdown shots. To be a links champion meant to keep the ball under the wind. I used to pretend I was Harry Vardon hitting those shots."

Horton had finished as the low British professional in the 1976 Open at Birkdale. "If I couldn't win the Open," said Horton, "that was the next best thing. In 1977, I was playing well, and as leading British player from the year prior, I thought the only thing left to do was win it. The truth was in those days we felt outnumbered by the American players. We were playing second fiddle in the Ryder Cup, and we had only three or four good worldwide players. The rest, like myself, didn't tour the world as much. So it's safe to say that we felt overly awed by players like Jack Nicklaus and Arnold Palmer. We watched them on television winning the Masters and the U.S. Open, and when they actually appeared at the Open, they were looked upon as the best players in the field. Some of us, however, chose not to be frightened by their presence and instead looked at it as an opportunity to make a name for ourselves. I had played in my first Ryder Cup in 1975, and in a single day of singles play I halved Hale Irwin in the morning and beat Lou Graham in the afternoon. Those two had won the two previous U.S. Opens, so after that I felt like I could compete against anyone."

That Friday morning as Horton prepared for his round, he thought to himself, "This is a links golf course and you know how to play links golf. You have a chance. There's only one chance of winning the Open each year. You're on form, now all you need is a bit of luck."

Tommy Horton got his bit of luck and then some. On the eighteenth green on Friday he holed a long birdie putt, and when the ball went into the hole he dropped to his hands and knees. His score was sixty-five, and after opening rounds of seventy and seventy-four, Tommy Horton was back in the fight.

GAYLORD BURROWS was never one to practice a lot. "I know it sounds crazy," said Burrows years later, "but if you played field hockey like I had, your hand-eye coordination was pretty good. Golf came pretty easy to me." After the first two rounds, Burrows was considered the standard "no-name" player who hangs around the lead early in major championships, and it was probable that he would wither when confronted by the "superguns." It was the first time Burrows had played in a major championship, and according to him, "I was confident and playing good, but to be realistic about it I had never been in a big tournament before. I'd won in Japan, but that didn't mean a hell of a lot at the Open."

Burrows might not have practiced much, but he did warm up before a round like any other player. Since his tee time on Friday was just fifty minutes ahead of Nicklaus and Watson, he was finishing up his preround warm-up on the practice tee when Nicklaus and Angelo Argea arrived to begin theirs. "I was standing there watching Jack a little," said Burrows, "and someone in the crowd asked me who I thought was going to win. I said probably Nicklaus or Watson.

"The guy said, 'Why, you're hitting the ball as good as they are. Why don't you think you can win?'

"And that got me to thinking that maybe I could play with these guys," said Burrows with a Louisiana mumble that would make it impossible to guess he'd ever lived in India or Africa. Burrows was further inspired when he arrived at the first tee for his 2:25 PM starting time. He was paired that day with American George Burns, a talented player who carried himself with a patrician air on the golf course. In comparison, Burrows was a hipster; his olive skin and bushy sideburns almost unnoticeable due to the wildly colorful outfits he wore. "I didn't know Burns at the time," said Burrows, "but he gave me incentive to play well because he was a cold customer, pretty cool and distant. I walked over to my buddy Johnny Mize and I told him, 'I'm going to beat this guy's butt.'

"Burns was a pretty long hitter of the ball back then, but I outdrove him and outplayed him and he shot seventy-two and I came in at sixty-eight. That was pretty satisfying." When Burrows finished his round, he was at one under par for the week. He went into the clubhouse and had a drink. "I was pretty relaxed," said Burrows. "I never thought I was going to do that well, and then it just happened fairly easily."

In the meantime, the press concluded that it was time to get writing about Gaylord Burrows. "The first thing they asked me was where I was from," said Burrows. "As soon as I said Louisiana, they started talking about how the Mississippi riverboats used to go down to Louisiana, and since they didn't know anything else, they just assumed I was some sort of riverboat gambler. That's how they described me the next day in the papers. Before I knew it, the whole world thought I was a riverboat gambler."

After finishing his postround drink, Burrows decided to hit some practice balls. "I was working on a new grip at the time," he said. "Johnny Mize had convinced me that I needed to weaken my grip [place the left thumb more toward the top of the shaft] if I was going to get better. It had been working pretty good, so I thought I'd go hit some balls and groove my swing." Burrows was still on the practice tee when Nicklaus arrived for his own postround practice.


SHORTLY BEFORE 3:15 PM ON FRIDAY, July 8, Jack Nicklaus and Tom Watson arrived at the tee of Ailsa's first hole. Jack Nicklaus was thirty-seven years old and had the unmistakable look and presence of a successful *man* in the prime of his life. Gone were the boyish, chubby face and the hint of freckles that dotted his face when he beat Palmer at Oakmont in 1962. His frame was now as lean as possible for a person of his body type, his face smooth and deeply tanned. His famous mane was a mix of light shades of blond, a fact that could not be missed because he had long ago ceased wearing a hat on a regular basis.

Jack Nicklaus at thirty-seven was the premier thinker the game had ever known. It was that quality as much as his physical talent that allowed him to stay on top for fifteen years during the most competitive era in the game's history. The superguns had been blazing away at Nicklaus for as long as anyone could remember—Palmer, Billy Casper, Gary Player, Lee Trevino, Johnny Miller, Hale Irwin, Raymond Floyd—and still he remained standing. He could do so because the mistakes of overly aggressive play in his youth had created within him the mind-set of an ancient king facing an upstart challenge: *Let them come to me.* "Immaturity and inexperience drove me away from aggressive play to the opposite end of the competitive spectrum," said Nicklaus. "By the middle years of my career, I was analytic, careful, and conservative, particularly in the major championships. I had learned by then that far more golf tournaments are lost than are won, especially the most important among them, where the pressure squeezes the hardest." There was no question that Nicklaus could still play attacking golf, but he would only do so when there was no clear alternative. "To play like Jack did required an enormous amount of patience," said Tom Weiskopf. "Most players just couldn't do it—they'd get too antsy and feel as if they must force the issue. Nicklaus had more patience than anyone I ever saw play."

Nicklaus, for all his greatness, played the game at an agonizingly slow pace. This was due in part to the meticulous manner in which he double-checked the yardage for each shot and because of his level of concentration. "He could block out *everything* when he was playing," said Angelo Argea. "Everyone used to complain that he played slow. He was concentrating, man! The other guys just didn't know what it was to concentrate that hard." Argea recalled an occasion when he was caddying for Nicklaus on a golf course they hadn't been to in years. When they got to a certain hole, Nicklaus paused for a moment and looked around. "There should be a tree right here," said Nicklaus. "My yardage was from a tree that was right here." Argea looked at his man blankly, then asked another caddie in the group who was a local. "He was right," said Argea. "The guy said there was a tree there, but they had taken it out a long time ago."

Once Nicklaus was settled on his yardage, he did not rush with his club selection. "When he picked a club," said Argea, "he'd ask me if I agreed. I always agreed because I didn't want to get in the way of his confidence."

The self-confidence Nicklaus possessed was neither arrogant nor brash. To his uncertain opponents, however, the obvious sureness with which Nicklaus went about his work was a source of intimidation. "Coming down the stretch in my best years," said Nicklaus, "I knew exactly how intimidating I was. That gave me a huge edge. I knew that if I could keep the pressure on and didn't do anything stupid, I would often win. It wasn't arrogance. I knew that many of my opponents had physical skills equal to or even superior to my own. But I also knew that few of them had the mental or emotional capability to use them as effectively as I generally could mine." The intimidation factor was bolstered by a hitman's stare that gave grown men the shivers. "When things got tight," said Argea, "no one looked at Jack."

Peter McEvoy's reaction upon meeting Nicklaus—that he was much smaller than McEvoy expected—was not uncommon. Nicklaus stalked the golf course with his shoulders back and posture that must have made his mother, Helen, very proud. Nicklaus did not slouch like Lee Trevino or walk like a duck as Raymond Floyd did. When he appeared on television screens it was often in the role of victor and often with no one else in the picture. He filled the television screen, and his erect, unhurried stride was viewed by golf fans with the same awe the Romans accorded Caesar. Nicklaus was a figurative giant; golf fans loved Palmer, but by 1977 they revered Nicklaus.

As Nicklaus stood on the first tee with Watson, he had gone six consecutive major championships without a victory. It was the second longest such stretch of his career, topped only by the twelve that passed between his wins at the 1967 U.S. Open and the 1970 Open Championship. Other than those two exceptions, since 1962 Nicklaus hadn't let more than five major championships go by without a victory.

Despite the fact that Nicklaus was averaging well under twenty tournaments a year and was by then distracted by a business empire, his excellence remained undiminished. Though he no longer shattered the face inserts on drivers (in fact, he wasn't even the hands-down longest driver on the tour), he could still summon power when he needed it, and the acquired knowledge of his fifteen-year competitive career more than made up for the slight decline in physical skills. Nicklaus would not lose when he was on top of his game; he would have to be beaten.

For a golfer to remain unbowed in the presence of Nicklaus required an extraordinary mind. The Tom Watson who shared the first tee at Turnberry was no longer the raw talent who had played with Nicklaus in the final round of the 1975 Masters. Watson had trumped Nicklaus at Augusta National just three months prior to this moment, and now he was looking for something. "I was playing my best golf ever about that time," said Watson years later. "I haven't played much better in my career than I did then. I was at peace with myself. I'd had a hard time learning how to win, but I won the Masters when I had to. I knew that if I won at Turnberry it would be a confirmation of what happened at the Masters. Now I had the chance to see if I could take my career to the next level, to see if I really belonged."

Watson was ten years younger than Nicklaus, but he was not a typical twenty-seven-year-old, and his early exposure to the pressure of major championships had taught him something about focusing his energy under pressure that stood in stark contrast to the nearly hallucinatory experience Weiskopf described having at the 1975 Masters. "Let me put it this way," said Watson. "When you're at peace with yourself and with your golf swing, you feel more comfortable about the way you're swinging the golf club. The environment around you is more serene. It's not so electric. You're at the perfect level of consciousness, but you're never in a total tunnel where you don't know what's going on outside of yourself. In the heat of battle, you must be able to respond to those things that are happening around you in a logical way."

One factor Watson would have to be cognizant of was the difference in his own pace of play from that of Nicklaus. Watson moved around the golf course like a man perpetually late for a bus. Over the next two days, when Nicklaus was second to play from the tee, Watson would stand off to the side with his arms crossed. As soon as Nicklaus made contact with the ball, Watson was off to chase down his own ball. Nicklaus had barely completed his follow-through when Watson started walking.

As he stood on the tee in 1977, Watson's appearance had not aged one bit from his early years on tour. His hair might have been a tad shorter, but it was still long in the style of the day. His skin was on the pasty side, refusing to bronze like that of Nicklaus. His most outstanding physical feature was his meaty forearms, which had by then drawn comparison to those of the cartoon character Popeye. Watson's forearms were not massive, but they were bigger than average and one could easily picture them on a dockworker or a man who swung a sledgehammer all day. By his own account, and that of Nicklaus, he was driving the ball longer and straighter than anyone else at the time. "I played a practice round that week with Tom," said Nicklaus years later, "and he was doing everything beautifully."

Of special interest was Watson's bold play with the driver off the fairway at the seventh hole in Wednesday's opening round. For the modern professional, and to some extent even the modestly talented weekend player, hitting a driver off the fairway is a very simple matter. Modern metal driving clubs, with severely rounded soles, have removed much of the challenge in executing such a shot. In 1977, however, every player in the field of the Open Championship was using a driver made from the wood of persimmon trees. The clubheads were bulky and had essentially flat bottoms. To execute the shot Watson had played required strength and no small amount of verve. It was *not* a shot routinely played by professionals at the time, and the baked fairways of Ailsa made it even more difficult. If the clubhead hit the ground just a fraction behind the ball it would be akin to a club striking a paved surface at the bottom of a swing—the head would instantly deflect upward and the ball would be caught with a glancing blow. (Readers who recall the persimmon era will also recall that some players carried a number two wood, but even that club was useful only in the hands of a talented player.)

The day was clear and warm as Nicklaus and Watson began their rounds. Spectators, sunburned from the previous two days, were scattered about the links as one might expect with so many contending players already out on the course. The classic wool caps had been left at home in favor of floppy, cotton bucket hats, and a large number of the men in the gallery opted to go shirtless, which was not an appealing sight. The half-naked lobstermen of Scotland were countered by the conservative dress of Nicklaus and Watson. The senior man wore blue plaid trousers and a white shirt; Watson wore dark blue trousers, a white shirt, and black shoes. Some spectators found a comfortable hillside spot and dozed off, others shielded themselves from the sun with umbrellas. The importance of the championship did not supersede the naturally drowsy pace of a warm day, not even as Ivor Robson told Nicklaus and Watson it was time to play away.

At the first hole, Nicklaus hit a short iron shot approach to within three feet of the hole and buried his first birdie of the day. It was the opening volley in the most torrid stretch of scoring by two players in major championship history.

ALREADY WELL INTO HIS ROUND ON AILSA, Arnold Palmer had grown frustrated with his indifferent putting. Palmer was just a few months shy of his forty-eighth birthday and had not won a major championship in thirteen years. Palmer's love for the game was as strong as ever, and his desire to win had not waned, and after missing short putts at the second, fourth, fifth, and sixth holes, Palmer decided it was time to shake things up. Everyone in the field, including Palmer, knew that Mark Hayes had used a cross-handed putting stroke in setting the Open scoring record the day before. Such a stroke was considered unorthodox—for many years it was referred to as the "give-up grip"—but Palmer did not care. "No one was laughing at Hayes yesterday," said Palmer. Putting cross-handed at the seventh he made a testing putt of the same distance as one he had missed on the previous holes and decided to stick with the grip for the rest of the round. "There was so much difference in my putting I couldn't believe it," said Palmer. On the back side, Palmer poured birdies into the hole like it was 1960 all over again. At the eighteenth he used his putter from off the green and knocked the ball into the hole. The turnaround had been glorious; after a front nine of thirty-seven, Palmer had come charging home in thirty strokes. His glory years were long past, but once again people were talking about Arnold Palmer. They were also talking about five-time Open Champion Peter Thomson, who at age forty-eight also shot a round of sixty-seven. "It was a good day for the old guys," said Thomson.

ON THE FIRST HOLE of his Friday round, Hubert Green showed that no matter how convenient it is to view a stroke-play contest in match-play terms, the two are nothing alike. Out last with the leader, Maltbie, Green pushed his drive to the right off the first tee. His second shot went into the second of two bunkers to the left of the first green. The ball settled in a spot that forced Green to take an unusually awkward stance; he took a mighty swing at the ball, and a cloud of sand and dust rose up in front of him. The ball stayed put. On his fourth swing, Green sent the ball sailing across the green. He got it on the green with his fifth shot and took two putts to get down. On Ailsa's easiest hole, Green had taken a triple bogey seven. In match play, the debacle would have merely cost him the hole, but in stroke play, all the work of the previous two days was wiped out, and going forward the march would be entirely uphill. Hubert Green's chances of winning the Open Championship drifted away with the cloud of dust he created with his third swing on the first hole, and he played the next seventeen in one over par for seventy-four on the day. "At the time I wasn't worried about Nicklaus and Watson," said Green years later. "I was just worried about Hubert Green. Of course, I should have worried more about him because he fell apart."

Maltbie did not suffer any single implosion as severe as Green's first-hole nightmare, but the fans soon caught on to the fact that it would be a rather pedestrian round for the overnight leader. In the end, Maltbie would score seventy-two. "By the time Roger and me got to the fifth hole," said Green, "there was no gallery following us at all. I mean nobody. I think even our wives went off to watch Jack and Tom play."

The reason for the vanishing gallery was that up ahead Jack Nicklaus was in full flight. The putting woes he had the previous two days were absent as he birdied the fourth hole from twelve feet and the long par-three sixth from the same distance. With a birdie at the par-five seventh, Nicklaus was already four under par for his round, and his name had shot to the top of the leaderboard. All of the reverberations that went along with the posting of J. NICKLAUS atop the big board were felt by the entire field, with the exception of Tom Watson. With birdies of his own at the third from eight feet and the fourth from no more than eighteen inches, Watson was keeping up with the early pace set by Nicklaus. At the sixth however, Watson had a hiccup that resulted in Nicklaus pulling ahead by two shots. There Watson pulled his tee shot into a bunker left of the green. He played a solid recovery shot to within five feet of the hole, but the putt did not fall.

About the time that Watson was making his bogey at the sixth hole, the sky began to rumble. A fast-moving storm was forming over Arran, and within thirty minutes it would be on top of Ailsa. Both Nicklaus and Watson made birdie fours at the seventh hole, and it was just after Watson struck his six-iron approach shot to the eighth green that lightning flashed across the golf course. The strike occurred while Watson's ball was still in the air. The two men were not at the absolute farthest point from the clubhouse, but very nearly so; there was literally nowhere to hide. Watson felt it prudent to immediately stop play and seek some sort of shelter, while Nicklaus wanted to finish the hole first because he faced a delicate chip off of loose sand next to the green. After both men made their par fours, they climbed down the seaside ledge and sought shelter amid the rocks. Years later, Nicklaus, Watson, and Argea could not remember any of the conversation that took place down on the rocks but they did recall talking. When asked after the round if there had been any conversation during the interruption in play, Watson said, "Of course there was. We're not zombies."

As potentially dangerous as the moment was, it led to some of the most famous photographs in golf history. To be a good photographer requires a touch of lunacy, and as the storm escalated overhead, snap-happy chaps oblivious to the lightning clicked away at the four men sitting on the rocks. At one point, Watson removed his shoe while Nicklaus, legs crossed, looked on with a bemused expression. Alfie Fyles sat next to Watson puffing on a cigarette, his yellow caddie bib emblazoned in black with the word WATSON. Argea settled in with a cigarette as well. The four men appear absurdly calm considering that the storm was powerful enough to knock out electricity in the hotel, the clubhouse, and the press tent. The only known thought among the four men sitting on the rocks by the water occurred as Fyles exhaled a puff of smoke and said, "Water is a fine conductor of electricity, isn't it?" The four looked at each other with wide eyes and scrambled back up the rocks. They were in luck. A nearby BBC vehicle had enough room for all of them.

Not so lucky was Lee Trevino. As the storm approached, he had quipped to the crowd, "If this thing gets any closer, you can find me in a pub in Glasgow." Trevino had reason to be nervous: Two years previously he was struck by lightning at the Western Open. "I heard that thunder," said Trevino, "and I thought 'I'm going to Boston right now.' I've been hit by lightning and I know what it's like. It's something I'm scared of. When I'm at home and I hear thunder, I turn the volume on the television up real loud so I can't hear the bangs. Hell, if you get hit by a train you become scared of trains, right?"

When the storm hit, Trevino wasn't keeping pace with Nicklaus and Watson, but he was playing well enough that a rally was not out of the question. He remembered reading after his encounter with lightning in Chicago that the best thing to do when lacking shelter is to find a low spot in the ground. So Trevino and his caddie found a depression in the dunes and hunkered down. Oddly, Trevino sat with an umbrella over his head, an act akin to holding a lightning rod. He survived physically unscathed, but emotionally the damage had been done. He had double-bogeyed the eighth hole as the storm approached and then bogeyed the ninth. He was out in thirty-nine, and even with his incoming thirty-three, he was out of the championship.

ONE OF THE PLAYERS who just made the thirty-six-hole cutoff at one-fifty was South African Hugh Baiocchi. This was a good thing for Philip Jonas, who had stayed around to watch the tournament and depended on Baiocchi for a ride back to Troon each evening. "They gave you tickets to the tournament when you played in qualifying," said Jonas years later. "I arrived at Turnberry each day about nine o'clock. The daughter of the woman whose home I was staying in would drop me off. There was a guy named George Blumberg who was Mr. Golf in South Africa. He took me up to lunch in the hotel, and I remember sitting there one day and Nicklaus was sitting at the next table over. I met Crenshaw and Johnny Miller, and I watched Miller play with one of his sons on the little par-three course in front of the hotel. For me it was unbelievable.

"I loved going to the practice range. Graham Marsh's caddie was shagging balls with a baseball glove, and I'd never seen a baseball glove before. I'd sit in the stands at the range and watch the Americans. They were all so flamboyant and wore these flashy, hip pants. I was totally amazed by the tented village. George Blumberg had promised me a cashmere sweater if I qualified, and I didn't even know what cashmere was. I just remember looking at the Pringle sweaters with the big lion on the chest and thinking, 'I want one of *those*.'

"The food was awful in the concessions on the course. I remember eating a little round pork pie. It was cold, and I had a warm drink with it. God, it was terrible. But no one complained about it. The best part of all, though, was that George Blumberg got me a ticket for the front row of the grandstand at the eighteenth hole for the final round."

THE POINT OF DEMARCATION between the beginning of the 1977 Open Championship and its end came when the lightning and thunder subsided after thirty minutes on Friday. Although it would still not be a clear Nicklaus–Watson runaway by the end of the round, it started to take the shape of a man-to-man battle when they resumed play at Bruce's Castle. The little spit of land with the boxing-ring feel was a fitting place for the battle to commence in earnest. While the thunder and lightning had left, iso-lated showers of warm rain would appear for a moment over a given hole and then leave just as quickly as they had begun. The temperature had cooled enough so that Nicklaus and Watson both took sweaters from their oversized tour-player golf bags. Nicklaus donned a deep navy blue affair. Watson pulled on a gray sweater that appeared at least a size too large for him. The wind was gusting as they stood on Ailsa's ninth tee. It was not the kind of wind that nearly blew Jack Newton over the guardrail at the rear of the tee during the 1973 John Player Classic, but it was strong enough to blow about Nicklaus's poker-straight hair as he lashed into his drive. Watson's thicker and sturdier hair was less affected by the breeze as he tore into his own drive. The light was softer now, and the rains had subdued the dust that had been starting to kick up from the 80,000 or so spectators who had been tramping across the dried out grass all week.

With a par at the ninth, Nicklaus was out in thirty-one to Watson's thirty-three. At the tenth, where two days prior Nicklaus helped Peter McEvoy look for his ball on the beach, both Nicklaus and Watson made siz-able birdie putts. They matched each other shot for shot over the next three holes, which were played in level par. Nicklaus made his first and only bogey of the round at the fourteenth hole. With his putting under control, Nick-laus was now struggling with his driver. At the fourteenth, he pulled his drive into the rough on the left hand side of the green, and on the subse-quent shot, the effect of the light rough could be fully seen. Nicklaus played a seven-iron shot that bounded onto the green, but the ball had no spin on it. The ball actually brushed the flagstick as it barreled past the hole, but by the time it stopped moving it was on the back edge of the green, forty feet from home. Nicklaus played his first putt aggressively and ran it five feet be-yond the hole. He missed the five-footer.

At the fifteenth hole, Ca' Canny, Watson knifed a three-iron from the tee and the ball settled twenty feet from the cup. He gutted the hole with the putt, and for the first time since the sixth hole, Watson had drawn even with Nicklaus.


WHILE WATSON AND NICKLAUS were on their collective tear, the Next Nicklaus from Texas, Ben Crenshaw, was sneaking into contention. Sneaking, that is, because few spectators on the course were watching him play. Crenshaw would one day become known as the professional golfer with the greatest love for the game's history, and early in the week his ap-preciation for the game's roots had led him to forgo a Sunday practice round at Ailsa and instead drive to Prestwick for a round at the club where the Open was born. Now on Friday afternoon, he was looking to make some history of his own.

"I was always plagued with inconsistent play throughout my career," said Crenshaw years later, "but that afternoon I was holding enough of my game together to be a contender. My experience at Augusta National that spring had helped me be a little more comfortable as a contender."

The chink in Crenshaw's game was that his long, sweeping swing required immaculate timing. When he had it, he was a stunning player; when he did not, he never knew where the ball might end up. Even at that, he was such a superb putter that oftentimes he could still hold his game intact. "In those days," said his caddie, Bobbie Millen, "Ben got up and down so many times it just wasn't true. He was such a deadeye putter that anything close to the hole was as good as in."

After making the turn on Friday, Crenshaw was working on a round that was something of a rarity for him: He had not made a single bogey on the front nine. With birdies at the tenth, eleventh, and seventeenth holes, Crenshaw realized he was still very much in the game. "We were playing with Seve [Ballesteros] that day," said Millen, "and he kept referring to Ben as 'One Putt.' " After playing a perfect tee shot into the fairway at the eighteenth, it started to rain. "It was a warm rain," said Crenshaw, and playing in just his shirtsleeves he seemed oblivious to the downpour. "Walking down the fairway," said Millen, "we said we wanted par for sixty-seven. Then he hit a gorgeous six-iron with the rain pelting down on him. The ball stopped about ten feet from the hole, and Ben turned to me and said, 'Bobbie, I'll just brush this one in and that will be a good day's work.' I knew then he'd make it."

Crenshaw did make the putt and was around in sixty-six for a three-round total of 206—four under par. He was in sole possession of third place behind Nicklaus and Watson, who by now both had aggregates of six under par. "When we posted that sixty-six," said Millen years later, "I felt we had a really good chance." So did his man. "I like my position," Crenshaw told the press after his round. "I just don't know how many more birdies Jack is going to make." At the Masters in April, Nicklaus had spoken of Crenshaw as a contender to the exclusion of Watson. Here, Crenshaw spoke of Nicklaus as if Watson were again an afterthought.

AT THE PAR-FIVE SEVENTEENTH HOLE, Jack Nicklaus hit a majestic shot. The long whack called for in the hole's name, Lang Whang, was blasted with a two-iron. Always considered a peerless long-iron player, Nicklaus here reinforced that reputation. The ball bounced just short of the green and grabbed just two feet from the hole. Watson followed that with a three-iron to within fifteen feet, and as soon as he struck the shot, he walked quickly down the fairway stalking the ball while it still hung in the air. Watson was first to putt on the green, but left his eagle try short and left. Despite the easy birdie, it seemed likely that Watson would cede the lead once Nicklaus holed his short eagle putt. Almost unbelievably, Nicklaus hit a miserable putt that never touched the hole, shoving it to the right. Commenting on the BBC, Peter Alliss could say only that "Nicklaus looks almost embarrassed about that." Years later Nicklaus said he had no recollection of the putt.

At the eighteenth hole, Watson played a one-iron to the fairway, and Nicklaus followed with a one-iron pushed to the right. Nicklaus's ball came to a halt in light rough, and once again he had a problem with distance control on the approach. His ball landed hole high but bounced through the back of the green. He chipped down surely, and made his par. Watson two-putted for par after bouncing his approach onto the green.

For the third consecutive day, Watson and Nicklaus had identical scores; this time it was sixty-five. Their totals were 203, seven under par. After signing their scorecards, they made their way to the press tent. Most of the spectators on the premises followed them and headed for the parking lots. Ten minutes later, when Maltbie (seventy-two on the day) and Green (seventy-four) finished their rounds, they shook hands in front of a nearly empty grandstand. The next day a photograph of the moment would run in the newspaper. The photo was three by four inches in the paper. There were 156 seats visible in the bleachers—only twenty were occupied. The message of the empty seats was clear: Maltbie was six strokes back of Nicklaus and Watson, Green was nine back.

In the press tent, Nicklaus and Watson talked with the writers. Watson said, "We had a great battle out there today. But there was too much golf left to play to think it was just between the two of us. Being so close, you don't want to take any unnecessary risks, which you can do if you have some strokes to spare. I'll go against Jack tomorrow with respect, as I would with any other player. I will be trying a little bit harder. I have never played in the same pairing with him down the home stretch. It is going to be interesting to say the least. That was really something out there today, to come to a different country and experience something like that. I felt like I was playing in the World Series." After a few confused looks from the non-American writers, Watson added, "That's baseball." Alliss noted that while both men had shot sixty-five, Watson was intent on making it clear that his sixty-five had been the better one. "Watson mentioned that some of Nicklaus's driving had been wayward," said Alliss, "and that he [Nicklaus] had been lucky with the lies he found in the rough. Watson said he felt his own ballstriking had been a little bit better." Watson was already in the process of convincing himself he could handle the coming storm.

Then it was Nicklaus's turn. He acknowledged that he had struggled with the driver, and that the light rough let him get away with some poor tee shots. With fourteen major championships to his credit, he still had to face the inevitable question: How did it feel to once again be the target of the newest hot gun in the game. Nicklaus shook his head. "I've had these same challenges for fifteen years," said Nicklaus. "From Arnold, Gary [Player], Trevino, and Miller. I enjoy it. It's all about putting more notches in your belt."

With that said, Nicklaus made his way out to the practice tee to work with his driver. Angelo Argea was waiting on the tee for his man, and he had placed Nicklaus's bag in the spot next to Gaylord Burrows's. In the press tent, Nicklaus had seen a name on the leaderboard he didn't recognize; after hitting a few balls, Nicklaus looked over at Argea and said, "Who's this Burrows guy?"

"I heard him," said Burrows years later, "so I said, 'That would be me, Jack.' "

Nicklaus turned around and looked at Burrows. "Hi," said Nicklaus, extending his hand to shake. "Tell me, Gaylord, where do you play?"

"I play a lot in Asia and on the municipal course in Monroe, Louisiana," said Burrows. "Jack got a laugh out of that. I just sat there with Angelo and watched Nicklaus hit balls for about an hour. Angelo didn't shag the balls, he had someone else do it for him. He just sat on the end of Jack's bag and smoked. It struck me that Jack wasn't driving the ball too well."


WITH NICKLAUS AND WATSON departed from the press area, the room was filled with the chatter of typewriters. (That sound gave a press room a frantic air that disappeared when computers became the tool of the writer's trade.) In front of his typewriter, Pat Ward-Thomas of Manchester's *The Guardian* wrote: "After one of the finest contests imaginable, which both obviously enjoyed, between Nicklaus and Watson, the Emperor and his likely successor, the Open Championship at Turnberry could not be in a more enthralling state. . . . The golfing world and thousands in the west of Scotland await what could be an epic contest between the two supreme players of the moment."

Ted Green, from the *Los Angeles Times,* wrote to his West Coast readers: "Now the weather, the low scores, Mark Hayes' record 63, Lee Trevino's comeback and the little-known players who had their moments are nothing more than conversation in the pubs around here.

"Now 13 of the 14 players who had Jack Nicklaus and Tom Watson in sight after the second round are so far behind they couldn't see them with a telescope.

"Now the British Open, unless Ben Crenshaw has another big day today, is apparently a two-man golf tournament."

In his story for the *New York Times,* John Radosta wrote that the third round was "reminiscent of some of the close matches Nicklaus has played in other years, but more immediately it called to mind this year's Masters, when Watson beat him by two shots.

"There was a difference. In the Masters they were playing in separate pairings, keeping an eye on each other's every move. Today they were in the same pairing, pitted like combatants in a cockfight, matching blow for blow . . ."

One writer who did not have a deadline that day was Dan Jenkins of *Sports Illustrated.* Jenkins was the best golf writer in the world and a source of amazement to his peers because of the ease with which he appeared to do his work. Jenkins invited Watson and his wife, Linda, to dinner at the nearby house being rented by the *Sports Illustrated* contingent. They accepted, and to the amazement of all present, Watson (by his own account) proceeded to "eat at least fifteen profiteroles."

While Watson ate, the writers made their way to dinner or the bar. They had primed their readers for a closing drama that would lay waste to every legend in major championship history. The only hitch was that no one could be certain it would actually happen.

# TEN

★

Notable scores after three rounds of the 106th Open Championship:

Jack Nicklaus, U.S., 68-70-65=203
Tom Watson, U.S., 68-70-65=203
Ben Crenshaw, U.S., 71-69-66=206
Tommy Horton, England, 70-74-65=209
Roger Maltbie, U.S., 71-66-72=209
Gaylord Burrows, U.S., 69-72-68=209
Hubert Green, U.S., 72-66-74=212
Arnold Palmer, U.S., 73-73-67=213
Severiano Ballesteros, Spain, 69-71-73=213
Nick Faldo, England, 71-76-74=221
Greg Norman, Australia, 78-72-74=224 (Did not qualify for final round)

Fourth round, July 9, 1977. Clear skies, temperature in the mid-80s. Slight but steady breeze off the Firth of Clyde. Attendance: 17,909

Fourth-round tee times:

1:10 PM: Roger Maltbie, Gaylord Burrows
1:20 PM: Tommy Horton, Ben Crenshaw
1:30 PM: Jack Nicklaus, Tom Watson

After fifty-four holes of the 1977 Open Championship another scoring guillotine dropped and again reduced the size of the field. The fifty-four-hole cutoff was used at the Open Championship until 1985. At Turnberry in 1977, only players at 221 (eleven over par) and lower would play in the final round. Those who missed out on the final day included Isao Aoki of Japan, Simon Owen of New Zealand, and Greg Norman, the man who had given

175

newspaper headline writers a gift before the start of the Open; there would be no Norman Conquest. Those who failed to survive the thirty-six-hole cutoff went home with empty pockets. Norman, Aoki, and the rest of the players who made it to the third round but failed to make the final day were each given £150. Sixty-four players would participate in the last round, with the first pair, Vincente Fernandez and Nick Faldo, teeing off at 8:05 AM.

Ivor Robson awoke in his room at the Turnberry Hotel three hours before the first tee time on Saturday. Even though his commute to work would only involve walking down the steps in front of the hotel and crossing the street, there was no sleeping in for Robson. He was accustomed to rising early from his youth, when his father trained racehorses. Robson buttoned up a fresh white shirt, cinched his French cuffs with cuff links, and tied his official Open Championship tie in a full Windsor knot. A backup tie was hanging in the closet. His black leather Foot-Joy golf shoes were "absolutely sparkling and shining." There was no morning coffee or tea for Robson nor any breakfast. He had not consumed *anything*—not even a glass of water—since early the prior evening, and would not eat or drink anything until after he'd sent Nicklaus and Watson on their way, nearly nine hours after he got out of bed. Once his work began, there was no time to visit the loo.

By 7:05 AM, Robson had arrived at the first tee after visiting the temporary R&A office on the grounds. There he had collected scorecards and checked on whether any new local rules would be in effect for the day. Once at his station, he looked around to make sure there was no litter on the ground, checked to make sure the tee markers were aligned properly, and confirmed that he had enough pencils for all of the players and their caddies. Finally, Robson checked to make sure his microphone was functioning. Throughout the day, he would stay alert for shifts in the strength and direction of the wind so his voice would not inadvertently carry to a nearby green or tee where players were in action. His first appointment, with Fernandez and Faldo, was still an hour away. He would accept nothing but promptness from every player. "If a man is late with me," said Robson, "he is late. They get four calls for their tee time. If they hear the words 'fourth and final call,' they know I mean business."

While Robson waited on the first tee, Gaylord Burrows was just waking up in the farmhouse he was staying at twenty-five miles from Turnberry. It was the biggest day of his golf career—"Hell, I was in the top four at the Open, that doesn't happen every day," said Burrows—and he didn't want to be late. Traffic approaching Turnberry had been snarled all week, so Burrows and Johnny Mize decided they'd head out for the course right after breakfast. The farmer who was renting rooms to them agreed to drive them to the course, and almost as soon as they hit the road, they encountered gridlock. Anticipating a Nicklaus–Watson showdown, *everyone* had decided to get to the course early. Sitting in the car, Burrows stewed. Finally, he said out loud what he was thinking. "I'm going to miss my tee time."

The farmer behind the wheel took action, waving down a policeman on a passing motorcycle.

"Look here," said the farmer, "I've got Gaylord Burrows in the car. He's level fourth in the Open, and we've got to get him to Turnberry."

"Aye," said the officer, "the riverboat gambler. Right. Follow me." He flipped the switch on his siren, and the line of cars pulled off to the side of the single lane road to let the farmer's vehicle pass. "I got there an hour earlier than I wanted to," said Burrows.

In his room at the Turnberry Hotel and safe from traffic worries, Tom Watson looked through the clothes he packed for his trip to Europe. He had a contract that required him to wear Jantzen sportswear in competition, and that Portland, Oregon–based company had provided him with a selection from a line known as the 3 Under Collection. (The company, which today manufactures only swimwear, was founded by two brothers from Missouri, Watson's home state.) Watson, Hale Irwin, and Dave Marr were the three primary endorsers of the 3 Under Collection, and the advertisements featuring Watson were accompanied by the copy: *The classic look of an untraditional golfer. When Tom Watson, this year's Masters winner, plays golf, millions watch. So he wants to look as good as he plays. That's why Tom wears Jantzen's golf classic from our 3 Under Collection. Because some golfing traditions never go out of style.*

In an era of outlandish clothing styles for men, the 3 Under Collection was wild, baby. From his closet, Watson took out Jantzen style number 1M516, the Falkirk Slacks. They were one hundred percent polyester double-knit, machine washable and dryable, and they featured two front half-top pockets and two Reece back pockets. 1M516 was modeled in the Jantzen catalog by Marr, and even he, the hip pro of Fifty-second Street, looked absurd in them. The slacks had a white base crisscrossed by thick overlapping stripes of bright green and light gold, which appeared orange from a distance. To complete his look for the day, the man who would be king selected a bright lime green shirt, emblazoned with the Jantzen "J" logo on the left breast pocket. He held it all together with a thick white belt and white golf shoes with kilties over the laces. Twenty-five years later Watson laughed and said, "Anybody who played back then wore ridiculous clothes like that. I had a contractual relationship with Jantzen. They paid me to wear the clothes, and I wore 'em." So it was that Watson went off to fulfill his destiny dressed like the court jester. It could have been worse: Watson had been featured on the cover of the

3 Under Collection catalog wearing a pink shirt and pants with pink and light blue paisleys swimming around on them like drunken amoebae.


JACK NICKLAUS ALWAYS SAID he had a comfortable level of nervousness before big rounds, but he was never overwhelmed by the jitters. He loved to sleep, and would often do so for up to ten hours no matter what the next day held. Before the final round of the 1975 Masters, he had been so relaxed talking with writers in the locker room before his warm-up session that only upon arriving at the practice tee did Nicklaus notice he was still wearing his street shoes. "All the other players would get to the course about ninety minutes or two hours before their tee times," said Argea. "I'd usually arrive about two hours before our starting time and get things ready. I'd check to make sure there were only fourteen clubs in the bag, and we would check again at the first tee—driver, three-wood, one-iron through nine-iron, pitching wedge, sand wedge, putter. Then I'd mark the balls he was going to use. Not too many guys were playing the [MacGregor] Tourney back then, but I'd put a little pencil mark next to the number just to be sure it was ours if he hit a wild one. We'd use six balls, three on the front, then I'd put them in the bag and we'd use three new ones on the back. We'd rotate them so the ball we used on the first hole only got used again on the fourth and the seventh holes." By 1977, Nicklaus no longer endorsed Slazenger equipment overseas. He was paid to play MacGregor equipment. The bigger "American" ball—1.68 inches in diameter—was made mandatory in Open play in 1974. The MacGregor Tourney ball used by Nicklaus was considered by the equipment testers at the USGA to be a horrible golf ball, even by the standards of the mid-'70s. Frank Thomas, who was the USGA's technical director at the time, thought it was so bad that Nicklaus would have won several more major championships if he had played another brand of ball. That, of course, must be weighed against the fact that Nicklaus knew more about how to play the game than any person alive and would therefore be unlikely to play a low-quality golf ball.

"Jack would show up about forty minutes before we were set to start," said Argea. "He didn't like to stand around a lot. He would do his stretching and then he'd hit balls. He always started with the woods, the three-wood and then the driver. Then he'd hit some eight-irons, then some five-irons, then some two-irons. Next he'd hit a couple of sand wedges off the ground. Then we'd go to the putting green and he'd putt for a few minutes. I would toss the balls back to him wherever he was standing. And that was about it, that was his routine. Somewhere along the line he'd make sure he had three pennies in his pocket to mark his ball on the greens. The reason for that was he wanted two in case he lost one and an extra in case someone else needed one. Then we'd head to the first tee."

At about 1:25 PM on Saturday, July 9, 1977, Nicklaus, Watson, and their caddies arrived at the first tee. Nicklaus was wearing dark blue trousers and a yellow sweater over a striped shirt with a white collar. "Nicklaus was dressed a lot more staid than I was," laughed Watson years later. The group was greeted by Robson, who said to one and all, "Well played yesterday."

At 1:28 PM, Robson addressed the two players. "Have we counted our clubs gentlemen, have we?" said Robson. "Right, here are your scorecards and the local rules. We've got two minutes to go. Jack, you're up first."

During those two minutes, Argea and Fyles could both be almost certain that no matter what lay ahead, neither would be called upon to read the line of a putt for his man. "Back in the mid-'60s we were playing in a tournament at a course we played before," said Argea, "and they'd put a new green in at one of the holes. Since Jack didn't know the green, he asked me to take a look at the line of his putt and I told him it would break just slightly to the left. He pulled the putt and missed it way left. He turned to me and said, 'That broke pretty hard.'

"I said, 'It shouldn't have.'

"So Jack kind of grinned and said, 'That's the last putt you're ever reading for me.'

"I said, 'Fine, then I won't get blamed when you miss one.' The truth is I wish he would have asked me sometimes. I was pretty good at reading greens."

Years later, Watson would recall that despite his fondness for Fyles, "I never, ever had Alf read a putt for me. I never required much help from a caddie. Just be on time, know the yardage, and at times help me with club selection. Like Trevino always said, if those guys can pick the clubs and read the lines, they ought to be playing the tour instead of us."

At 1:29 PM, Argea removed the knit headcover with an enormous green and white pom-pom from Nicklaus's MacGregor driver and handed it to his man.

At 1:30 PM, Robson spoke into his microphone.

"Now on the tee, Jack Nicklaus."

After Nicklaus smashed his drive down the first fairway, it was Watson's turn.

"Now on the tee, Tom Watson."

Watson striped his drive down the fairway, his ball finishing forty yards past Nicklaus's.

As Nicklaus and Argea started down the fairway, Argea completed the pair's final ritual. "Oh, by the way," said Argea, "Good luck." Years before he had forgotten to say those words once, and Nicklaus had to remind him on the second hole. After that, Argea never forgot to wish his man luck walking down the first fairway.

Robson's job was finished at that point. "At a regular tour event, I would immediately leave for the next tournament. But at the Open back then I had to stay around in case there was a playoff the next day. After I teed off the final game, I cleaned up the tee area and reported to the R&A office that everything was off on time." After nearly twenty hours without one, Ivor Robson could have a glass of water.

TWO GROUPS AHEAD of Nicklaus and Watson, Gaylord Burrows was playing with his pal Roger Maltbie. "We were good friends," said Burrows years later. "I had played with Roger on the mini-tours and stuff, and we got talking and it was more distracting than playing with someone I didn't know. Burns had given me incentive, but I may have gone too far in the other direction with Roger. On the first hole I stuck my approach in there to about a foot and a half. About then I was thinking maybe I could shoot another sixty-eight. Funny things go through your mind when you're in that position. As I drew the putter back, I said to myself, 'Don't miss it high.' And I totally quit on the stroke and missed it low. I pretty much knew right then my chances were done. The rest of the day the putter felt like a snake in my hands."

Ben Crenshaw and Tommy Horton were playing immediately in front of Nicklaus and Watson, and it was Crenshaw's caddie, Bobbie Millen, who was the first to notice something that would become a problem for the small group of players with an outside chance of catching the leaders. "The pace of play was quite slow up front," said Millen years later. "When we were lining up putts on the green, Nicklaus and Watson were back in the fairway with their arms folded, waiting to play. Professional that Ben is, I knew it was on his mind that those guys were waiting on every hole. So maybe some of the putts that might have dropped didn't. I always thought Ben might have won a few more tournaments if he was a little meaner. It was very difficult, though, because the crowd with that last match was running ahead and arriving at the green while we were putting out." With just sixty-four players on the course and only a handful in contention, every spectator among the nearly 18,000 present was chasing Nicklaus and Watson. The thick lines of people moving along the course brought to mind endless columns of infantrymen moving toward the front. The youthful and often shirtless ones among them frequently broke into a full sprint to get into position to see the next shot. The level of energy and anticipation rapidly built toward a boiling point.

While the main event was getting underway, the living connections to the days when the Open struggled to keep its nose above the waterline were finishing off the championship in style. Roberto De Vicenzo, who was born in 1923 and had once traveled seventeen days by ship to get to the Open, holed out a chip shot at the final green to cap his round of seventy-eight. As the ball went into the hole, the fifty-four-year-old Argentine spun his club around like a baton, and the crowd gave him a moving ovation. He had out-played more than half of the original field, most of whom were twenty to thirty years younger than him.

There was a time when it had taken Peter Thomson three days of air travel to get to the Open. Thomson first played in the Open in 1951, and now as the crowd stood to cheer him home, he was still playing better than all but twelve players in the field. His final round of seventy-five put him in a tie for thirteenth place with young Englishman Howard Clark.

The fuzziest feeling of all was generated by the name of Arnold Palmer, whose name was creeping up the big board as he made his way around Ailsa. He had finished in the top ten in six major championships during the 1970s, the most recent being a tie for ninth in the 1975 U.S. Open. Using the cackhanded putting style for his entire final round, Palmer shot sixty-nine on Saturday for a total of 282, just two over par for the week. He finished in sole possession of seventh place. It was his last ever top ten finish in a major championship.


AS WATSON HAD TOLD the writers on Friday evening, the Saturday round was the first time he had been grouped with Nicklaus in the final pairing of the final round of a major championship. Watson's game was at its absolute peak, solid through and through. Nicklaus was playing well, too, but in a very different manner. All through the week, some element of his game had let him down; first it was his putter, then his driver. Still, he had long ago, in the words of Bobby Locke, "learned to play badly well." This was the telltale sign of a great champion, and it was a stage that Watson, by his own admission, had yet to reach. Yet the inconsistent play presented a problem for Nicklaus, and he knew before the round that he would have to operate outside of his comfort zone. Rather than letting the Open title come to him, he must go out and attack Ailsa. "With somebody other than Tom Watson against me," said Nicklaus, "maybe I would have felt like they'd lose it. Against Watson, I knew I was going to have to *win* it."

In years past, Nicklaus had been able to strike fear into his opponents with his mighty blasts from the tee, but one of the few players who could outdrive the Golden Bear circa 1977 was Tom Watson. (All things being equal, it's unlikely that Watson at twenty-seven could have outdriven Nicklaus at the same age. This is, of course, irrelevant to the story, but nonetheless worth noting.) As Peter McEvoy had seen firsthand, Nicklaus could still generate the thunder ball when he chose to, but as he set out against Watson, his attack would be that of a savvy veteran rather than a youthful, raging bull.

At the second hole, Mak Siccar, Nicklaus drew first blood. The younger man played a sloppy approach shot on the par four and followed it with an ordinary chip shot. When Watson missed the putt and Nicklaus rolled in his birdie three, it opened up a two-stroke lead for Nicklaus at eight under par. Though early in the round, the turn of events was potentially fatal for Watson. Things got worse for him just two holes later when Nicklaus smoothed in a birdie two from twenty feet at Woe-Be-Tide. Watson played a fine shot from the tee on that hole, but it was too strong and left him with a six-foot downhill putt that even he could not prudently charge at the hole. Watson missed the putt. Spotting Jack Nicklaus a three-shot lead was never a good idea, but to do so in the final round of the Open Championship in Scotland was especially dangerous because of the momentum the crowd could give him. "Of all the places I played golf," said Nicklaus, "Scotland is my favorite. Not just because the game evolved there, or because of the marvelous old links courses. The primary reason I love Scotland is the people. They are the most knowledgeable golf fans in the world, and accordingly, the most sparing with applause. The final day at Muirfield in 1972, there was a wildness about the spectators that was out of character. Even with the third leg of the Grand Slam on the line, the ovations that greeted me as I moved more and more into contention were stunning. When I hit that seven-iron so close to the hole on the eleventh hole there and all the people would not stop cheering and applauding, I was on the brink of tears."

Nicklaus had won the Open Championship twice in Scotland, and now that he was bearing down on a third, the hue and cry of 18,000 sunburned Scots was letting him know they were pulling for him, the best ever player of their national game. Ahead of Nicklaus and Watson, Ben Crenshaw could feel the atmosphere becoming charged. "The crowds were very vocal," said Crenshaw years later. "They knew they were seeing something rare, something beyond anything they had ever seen before."

Fifteen-year-old Philip Jonas was caught up in what was now a tidal wave of spectators following Nicklaus and Watson. Twenty-five years later Jonas said, "You could tell most of the people were pulling for Nicklaus. They were cheering louder for him. I know that *I* really wanted him to win. He was a big fascination for me."

Three things—the lack of prolonged rain, the stressed and dried-out grass, and the simultaneous mashing that grass was taking under 30,000 or so feet—combined to kick up a cloud of dust surrounding the length of any hole Nicklaus and Watson played *and* the hole immediately in front of the one they were on as the runners in the crowd vied for viewing positions. "The crowd was absolutely chockablock," said Bobbie Millen. "Considering how isolated Turnberry is, that was a lot of people. The dust was flying everywhere, and several times Ben [Crenshaw] had to pause for a moment and attempt to get the dust out of his eyes. I had to do the same myself a few times." Crenshaw's nerves were frayed at the Masters by the heat of a Nicklaus charge, and once again his propensity for allowing his emotions to get in the way of his performance was showing itself, only this time there was the additional issue of the overly energized crowd.

For the moment, the swelling body of spectators had the most distracting effect on the players in front of Nicklaus and Watson. "I realized what was happening behind us," said Roger Maltbie twenty-five years later. "It was wild. There was all kinds of noise, and it was so dry that this cloud of dust was around the people. They were so excited they were almost stampeding. It was not the genteel, well-behaved galleries you always hear about at the Open. Up until that time, I had never heard noise that loud on a golf course. The people were storming up behind us as we were playing, just completely enamored by what they were seeing out of Jack and Tom. I didn't have enough experience . . . I just couldn't deal with what was going on. I understood why the people were acting that way, but, boy, it was a scary situation. At least it got to be." Maltbie and Gaylord Burrows went into full collapse mode, each shooting eighty for the day.

Bobbie Millen thought he saw an early sign that fate was against his man. "A very early omen might have been at the short fourth hole," recalled Millen. "Just as Ben's tee ball reached the apex of its flight, it nearly hit a seagull. The ball dropped down about thirteen feet behind the hole and it was lightning fast coming back down to it. Normally that suits a stroke like Ben's, but we missed it. Had we made it that would have gotten us back in line with the other two. There was no almighty disaster, but we couldn't get it going." Crenshaw tried to hang on as long as he could, feverishly chewing on gum in an attempt to remain calm. He made an eight-foot birdie putt at the sixth hole to get to five under par for the tournament. The moment that putt fell, he was four strokes behind Nicklaus and just a single stroke behind Watson.

Crenshaw recalled it was about the time he neared the turn that he realized he was out of contention. "I had trouble with the ninth hole all week," said Crenshaw. "I couldn't get the ball in the fairway off the tee to save my life." Crenshaw left his second shot forty yards short of the green, then inexplicably played an out-of-control third shot through the green and finished the hole with a bogey five. "That was about it," said Crenshaw. "It's a feeling every golfer goes through at some point. It's a feeling of futility and the knowledge that you didn't hold your game together. You just have to wait for another time. Tommy [Horton] seemed to hold it together nicely, though." Despite this recollection, Horton was playing no better than Crenshaw. Both would finish with seventy-five for the day, but Horton was still on a quest to finish low British player.

JUST ABOUT THE TIME CRENSHAW was making his birdie at the sixth hole, Tom Watson was starting to claw his way back from the three-stroke chasm he found himself in after four holes. At the fifth hole, Fin Me Oot (Find Me Out), Watson played a five-iron onto the green for his second shot, and made a sixteen-foot putt for birdie. He was back within two shots of Nicklaus now, but at the long par-three sixth, Tappie Toorie, there was the possibility of another stumble. Watson played a three-wood from the tee and pulled it left into a greenside bunker. Watson's short game was already considered among the best ever, but it had let him down at the second hole. He played a bunker shot that was neither fantastic nor horrible, the ball stopping six feet from the hole. The most fearless putter in the game at the time, Watson now faced a putt that Peter Alliss described to BBC viewers as one to "get the heart a-thumpin'." Watson paced the green, trying to get a line on the putt. He did not look uncertain (because he never did); his face was a blank, a look his caddie on the American tour, Bruce Edwards, had once seen as Watson's ball went sailing over the cliffs into Carmel Bay at Pebble Beach. Watson followed the ball's entire flight until he could no longer see it. "Why didn't you react?" Edwards asked of his man on that occasion.

"Because that's my punishment," said Watson.

Watson surely realized the gravity of the moment as he looked over the six-foot putt on the green of Tappie Toorie. For the only time in their association, Watson turned to Alf Fyles and asked him to take a look at the line. Fyles stood behind the ball and bent his knees slightly, his hands resting just above his kneecaps. His cap sat cockeyed on his head. "It will move to the left just at the last," said Fyles. Watson nodded his head and settled over the ball, taking his brisk practice strokes. He played the ball on the line Fyles called for and the ball tumbled in, saving his par. As the two walked from the green, Watson said, "Good line," and that was the end of Alf Fyles's green-reading experience with Tom Watson.

As they worked their way through the crowd to the seventh tee, the swarm of people parted just wide enough to allow the players and caddies safe passage. The bodies were strung out around the two players for as far as the eye could see now, and those within sight of Watson were about to see him play one of the most brilliantly executed shots in major championship history.

The hole was Roon the Ben, the same hole where Peter McEvoy learned that Nicklaus could still summon forth tremendous power seemingly at will. Watson was the first off the tee based on his birdie at the fifth and played a solid ball down the fairway. Now Nicklaus swung the club like the Nicklaus who had driven his ball *through* the eighteenth green in the playoff at St. Andrews in 1970, and the ball landed far beyond Watson's. On the 528-yard hole, Nicklaus was in position to reach the green in two shots.

By now Watson was fully aware that for one of the rare times in stroke-play golf, he had only one player other than himself to worry about. He was two strokes behind Nicklaus and could not afford to let him make a birdie or possibly even an eagle without doing the same. Over the course of two days he had matched Nicklaus shot for shot, but now he *must* keep in stride with Nicklaus. If Watson did not, he would quickly run out of holes. Watson had reached the green at Roon the Ben with two drivers on Thursday, and now he prepared to copy that feat. With the ground as hard as the runways across the way next to the Arran course, it was a risky shot. If he hit slightly behind the ball, the clubhead would ricochet off the ground, and he would catch the center of the ball with the lead edge of the club. If that happened, the ball could go anywhere. If he caught the ball too much on the upswing in attempting to lift it, he could hit a wicked hook or a wild slice. He thought through the shot carefully. "I had something like 240 [yards] to the green, and I was pretty good with the driver off the deck," said Watson years later. "Wooden drivers had a high center of gravity, and it was tough to get them airborne off the ground unless you had a swing like Sam Snead's. I thought it was the best shot I could play. If I hit it a little thin, it would still run down the fairway. Also, if I pushed it right or pulled it left, the lower trajectory of the ball would keep it from ballooning up and over the dunes. So I felt like I could keep the ball in play even if I hit it off line."

Fyles handed Watson the driver. It was a Tony Pena model favored by many tour players at the time. Watson's persimmon driver had a cherry stain as opposed to the more common brown or blond, and featured a bright red face insert. "It was not a deep-faced driver like some persimmon woods," said Watson. "It was just a normal face for back then, which today would look tiny." The Ben Hogan Apex ball sat on the tightest of lies— almost hardpan—with no cushion beneath it. Watson made a confident strike at the ball, and its trajectory was that of a bazooka shell. The ball drifted almost imperceptibly from left to right and bounded up onto the back of the green. "It was my best shot of the day," said Watson. Nicklaus would say afterward that he "admired that shot."

In the previous three rounds, Nicklaus had laid back with an iron on his second shot at the seventh hole. Even with Watson's ball on the green, Nicklaus saw no reason to change his strategy. He held the lead and there was no reason to attack, so he played an iron short of the green and, after playing a wedge, took two putts for par. Watson holed his ball in two putts for a birdie, and was now only one back of Nicklaus.

At the eighth hole, Goat Fell, Watson drew even with a twenty-foot birdie putt that in later years would be considered vintage Watson. He smashed the ball toward the hole, and it went fully in the center of the cup. "That was a lucky putt," said Watson. "It had the line, but not the touch. If it wasn't dead center, it would have gone six or seven feet by the hole." It was lost on all but the most astute in the crowd that Nicklaus could have left the green at Goat Fell actually trailing by a stroke. After Watson holed his putt, a good bit of the crowd scampered away toward Bruce's Castle, but Nicklaus still had a full six feet remaining for par. He gave it his most work-manlike effort, and there was never any doubt that it would go in the hole.

The two men made their way to the tee of Bruce's Castle. They were alone now. Alone together, together alone, just fifty yards or so from a roiling cauldron of humanity on the brink of pandemonium.

"All spectators at Golf Matches are requested to be silent and to stand still while the Parties are striking or are about to strike."
—*John Mansfield, Captain, Honourable Company of Edinburgh Golfers, 1839*

THE REPUTATION of Scottish golf fans as people who fully understand the game ("They know it through and through," said Ben Crenshaw) is a well-deserved one. So, too, is their reputation for refusing to demonstrate the boorish behavior that has undermined other sports and, to some extent, even professional golf as we know it today. On the rare occasions when a championship is genuinely exciting, however, it is difficult for golf fans to simply sit on their hands and keep their mouths shut. This is not unbecoming to the game or to the spectators, and to a certain degree it serves as a reminder that a closely played golf competition *can* be thrilling. And since the thrills are few and far between for golf fans, it's no more rational to expect spectators to behave like mannequins than it is to expect absolute silence from people on a roller-coaster, and golf fans in the Ayrshire region of Scotland had a history of getting overexcited long before the 1977 Open Championship.

The last Open before World War I was played at Prestwick in 1914, and it featured two of the Great Triumvirate: Harry Vardon and John H. Taylor. Going into the final day of thirty-six holes, Vardon, at 150, held a two-stroke lead over Taylor. Bernard Darwin was on the championship committee that year and later wrote, "I was present when the draw was made for the last day's play and can testify to our emotions when the names of Taylor and Vardon came out of the hat together. With the knowledge of what a Prestwick crowd could be, how big, how unruly, how difficult to control as they swirled around the Cardinal [the third hole with an infamous bunker with railroad sleepers facing it] and the famous loop [the part of the course that swings back toward the clubhouse], how inevitably they would all follow this one couple, there was an immediate and universally felt temptation to put the names back and take another dip into the lucky bag. It could not be done; much agony would have been saved if it could have been."

The "agony" was due in large part to the fact that the fans could walk right alongside the players down the fairways and crowd around them as they played a shot. Modern-day fans catch a glimpse of this in miniature when a player hits a wayward tee shot that ends up on the opposite side of the gallery ropes, but Vardon and Taylor would play *every* shot with the crowd pressing in around them. The jostling for viewing positions during the showdown was so intense that when an appeal was made to make room for the players to move about more freely, a local miner in the crowd was heard to say, "Players be damned! I've come to see!"

When Jock Hutchison won the Open in 1921 at St. Andrews, he was potentially denied back-to-back holes-in-one when a spectator rushed onto the green at the ninth hole and yanked the flagstick out of the cup as his ball was approaching it. In the last Open played at Prestwick (1925), the swarming crowds who showed up to root for Macdonald Smith, from Carnoustie, may have cost him the championship. Henry Longhurst wrote of the day, "If

Mary Tudor had the word Calais engraved upon her heart, so assuredly must Macdonald Smith . . . have had Prestwick. Colossal crowds turned out . . . to see the Scotsman win. In their combined determination to see the play at all costs (or, in the case of those who did not pay to come in, no cost) and to cheer their hero home, they lost him the ambition of a lifetime and, as I shall always feel, set permanently in the top of the second-class a golfer to whom no heights might have been unattainable." Long Jim Barnes, a Cornishman living in America, won; Mac Smith needed seventy-eight to win, seventy-nine to tie, and, wrote Longhurst, "the hordes trampled poor Macdonald Smith into an eighty-two."

As a result of the mob scene at Prestwick in 1925, the R&A instituted admission fees the following year at Royal Lytham with the sole purpose of restricting the number of spectators. A writer in *The Times* of London decried this as a "bombshell," but the R&A defended its decision as the only practical response given "the great number of people who sweep across the links in uncontrollable swirls and eddies, that no number of stewards, ropes, rosettes, megaphones and police can prevent them from interfering with play."

In 1933, *The Times* reported that a newly formed R&A committee "worked for months devising a system for shepherding crowds" during that year's Open Championship at St. Andrews. The idea settled upon by the committee called for local fishermen to follow each group of players with their fishing nets. The fishermen would stop ten yards behind where a player's ball rested and stretch out the nets to hold back the crowd.

By 1946 at St. Andrews, stewards were using walkie-talkie radios in an attempt to keep each other apprised of problems with the gallery, but this did not prevent spectators from crisscrossing the Old Course at random in search of a favorite player. The helter-skelter nature of the proceedings led Darwin to suggest in *The Times* that the time had arrived for "permanent and comprehensive roping off" of the playing areas of the golf course. It wasn't until eighteen years later, in 1963, that the R&A heeded Darwin's suggestion. That year at Lytham, the area of play from tee to green was roped off to spectators. From that point forward, the only players who would have to worry about being engulfed by the crowd were the two players in the lead pairing of the final round. In that round, the crowd was permitted onto the eighteenth fairway behind the players after they were in position to play their approach shots to the home green. The spectators were held at bay with a rope strung across the fairway by stewards until the second of the two approach shots was played toward the green. Then the rope was dropped, and the spectators dashed down the fairway swallowing up the players and their caddies as they walked along. Some referred to this as the

Open "charge," and it was an inevitability Jack Nicklaus and Tom Watson knew awaited them at Ailsa Home. But as they stood on the tee of Bruce's Castle, tied for the lead in the championship, the Open charge was the farthest thing from their minds.

THE NINTH HOLE of Turnberry's Ailsa course is the point where the coastline turns from running north by northwest and begins to head northeast. There is no sand dune for the next three coastal holes, and since the ninth, tenth, and eleventh holes literally hug the shoreline, there is no room for spectators on the left side of those holes in the direction of play. There had been room on the preceding holes despite their route up the coast, because the giant sand dune provided good viewing and was removed from the fairway. Once the mass of spectators turned away from the green at Goat Fell, they would be penned in like so many cattle as they followed Nicklaus and Watson for the next three holes. It would not be until the twelfth hole, Monument, that the spectators could again get to both sides of a fairway.

With the breeze in their faces, Watson and then Nicklaus played their tee shots on the difficult ninth hole. It was soon after they set out toward the fairway that the dam burst. The ropes holding back the spectators gave way to the surge, and in an instant frenzied fans were running down the fairway past Nicklaus and Watson. "It was a stampede," said Argea. "The people were going wild. I thought for sure Jack was going to get trampled."

At first, Nicklaus was unaware of what happened. "We were so wrapped up in our games that it took a second to realize what was going on," said Nicklaus years later. "Nothing like that had ever happened to me at a golf tournament before." Not only had it not happened to Nicklaus before, it had never happened in the entire modern era of championship golf since fairways began being roped off. Once he grasped the situation, Nicklaus collared nearby stewards and police officers and asked Watson to join them. While continually waving his right hand parallel to the ground in the universal sign that enough is enough, Nicklaus laid down the law. "This is getting out of hand," said Nicklaus. "You've got to get control of the situation. We can't play with the people running down the fairways. We'll wait until they are under control."

"Once Jack said what he was thinking, we all agreed," said Watson, though the younger golfer was not filled with the same concern that Argea felt. "I was never afraid," said Watson. "I'd been in enough football plays to know how to dodge a crowd. I was a pretty good running quarterback in high school. I couldn't pass, but I could run."

Nicklaus sat on the edge of his golf bag as it lay in the fairway and waited, while Watson stood nearby. "The stewards made their way down the length of the hole," recalled Watson, "and said with typical Scottish manners, 'Please abide by the ropes here.' And after about fifteen minutes of waiting we resumed playing."

Although neither player would later blame the interruption, their play was initially spotty after the crowd was brought under control. This was due in part to the fact that Bruce's Castle is among the most difficult holes in the world; the delay, however, must have caused some tightening of their muscles. Play was slow early in their round, but now they had come to a dead stop. Watson's second shot was played with a one-iron, and he yanked it across the width of the fairway into the rough to the left of the green. He needed three more strokes to hole out. Nicklaus managed to make a par at the ninth only after making a downhill twelve-foot putt. Nicklaus went out in thirty-three strokes compared to Watson's thirty-four.

The scorecards after nine holes looked like this:

Par: 4-4-4-3-4-3-5-4-4 = 35
Nicklaus: 4-3-4-2-4-3-5-4-4 = 33
Watson: 4-5-4-3-3-3-4-3-5 = 34

Both players made par at the tenth and eleventh holes. At the short eleventh, Maidens, Watson bunkered his six-iron tee shot and got up and in from the sand for his par. Now the golf course reversed itself toward the southwest, and for the first time all day the two were playing a hole with the entire glory of Ailsa's setting in view. There, through the rising dust and hazy sea air, was Ailsa Craig, just to the right of the lighthouse. Dead ahead was the war monument. Both players mashed solid drives and were left with only wedge shots to the green, but it was Nicklaus who got his putt to go down, from twenty-two feet. With the monument to the dead airmen looming above him, the man who was the best ever player of the world's most maddening game was two strokes clear of his pursuer. Looking on, Herbert Warren Wind said, "Many of us felt at that moment we had perhaps watched the decisive blow of the struggle. Only six holes were left, and how often does a golfer of Nicklaus' stature fail to hold on to a two-stroke lead as he drives down the stretch."

At that moment, Watson said, "I had the blinders on." His ability to maintain, in his own words, "the perfect level of consciousness" was what now allowed Watson to mount a furious comeback. Nicklaus's modus operandi in such situations was to avoid mistakes and outlast his pursuers.

Right on cue, he churned out par fours at the thirteenth and fourteenth holes. Watson pressed the attack at the thirteenth with a wedge shot that put on the brakes twelve feet from the hole. As Watson looked over his putt, Angelo Argea, feeling comfortable for the first time all day, stood off to the side of the green with an unlit cigarette dangling from his lips. Argea had a match poised in his hand, ready to strike it as soon as Watson's putter made contact with the ball. The putt was on line all the way, however, and Argea held back from lighting the match while he watched the ball plop into the hole. With a single shake of his head as if to say, "Doesn't this guy ever give up," Argea lit his cigarette. Both players made par fours at the fourteenth hole and made their way to the fifteenth hole, Ca' Canny—Take Care.

Watson was one stroke back now, and when he arrived at the par-three fifteenth tee he saw what he already knew would be the case: The hole was cut on the far right side, bringing into play the steep drop-off just to the right side of the green. He played a four-iron from the tee intending it for the safe left side of the green. The ball was pulled however, and after barely avoiding one of two bunkers on the left of the green, it settled in patchy, short rough beyond the fringe. His ball was six paces from the edge of the putting surface proper and sixty feet from the hole. He would do well to make a three.

For Nicklaus, playing second had turned into an advantage. Realizing that Watson was looking at par or possibly even a bogey, the opportunity was at hand to put him away for good. Nicklaus took his ball on a courageous line, directly at the flag. It was a brilliant shot. "Jack's ball was twelve feet from the hole at most," said Argea years later. "I thought we had it won right there. I was expecting we'd pick up at least another stroke there, maybe two. And then . . ."

Watson played his second stroke. Despite the scruffy lie and the bumpy ground between his ball and the green, he used the putter he borrowed off the kid back in Kansas City. As soon as the ball left the clubface, it popped up into the air. In almost every case when a ball struck with a putter leaves the ground, it is thrown off its intended line. After its brief hop, however, Watson's Hogan Apex landed exactly on the line he had started it on, and it was speeding across the green, certainly too fast for the distance. And then it was in the hole, smack in the center of the cup, rattling the flagstick as it fell, and Watson had made a two.

"That was an arrow through the heart," said Argea. "God, from all the way across the green . . . that hurt."

Throughout the game's history, the best players have always prepared themselves to expect the unexpected. This, however, was more than any rational person could have anticipated. Nicklaus had a blank look on his face and could not coax in his birdie putt. As soon as Nicklaus's putt rolled past the hole, Philip Jonas broke from the crowd and dashed to his assigned seat in the grandstand by the eighteenth green.

At the sixteenth tee, all tied once again and with the sun casting a cozy light on the scene, Watson looked out and saw what twenty-five years later he called "an exceptional sight. It was so warm, and people had their shirts off. They were fried like lobsters and red-skinned and running everywhere. The people had just finished crossing over the fairway, and a cloud of dust hung in the air. It was a little like [the book] *Golf in the Kingdom*. I just really felt that I had always wanted to compete against the best, and here I was doing it. And not doing too badly."

It was then that he turned to Nicklaus and said, "This is what it's all about, isn't it?"

Nicklaus, the northern light giving his hair its most golden hue, smiled. "You bet it is," said Nicklaus.

"It just came from the heart," said Watson years later.


UP AHEAD, Tommy Horton was finishing his round. He and Crenshaw had played on while Nicklaus and Watson sat in the ninth fairway. Horton's day started poorly and he never recovered, saying, "My tee shot on the first hole went into a bunker, and that was a big blow because I thought of that hole as a birdie chance and instead I made five. It was a struggle from then on. I hit two more fairway bunkers that day, and that ruined any chance I may have had. British bunkers are not the same as American bunkers. They're not shallow. Once you get in a fairway bunker, you cannot get on the green with your next shot."

Horton had to get down in two putts to be the leading British player in the championship, and with his mallet-headed putter he struck the first from twenty feet. With its last gasping turn, the ball fell into the hole. Horton thrust his putter into the air, and for just a moment he was the golf version of the Statue of Liberty. A relieved smile spread over his face. For the second year in a row, he was the leading British player. "Whether people realize it or not, that's a lot of pressure," said Horton. "To finish leading home player two years running was the biggest thrill of my career." Horton removed his hat before shaking hands with the disappointed Crenshaw. Then the low home player tossed his ball into the crowd and walked off the green to sign his scorecard. Later in the day he would get a pleasant surprise. "The manager of the Turnberry Hotel was quite a golf follower," said Horton, "and he had quite a large bet on me to finish leading British player. So there was a case of champagne waiting for me from him." But that reward was still a few hours off. For the moment, Horton and Crenshaw would stick around as spectators for the most riveting finish anyone would ever see in a golf tournament.

BOTH NICKLAUS AND WATSON took four uneventful shots at the sixteenth hole. The Open was down to the final two holes—the seventeenth, a straightaway par five reachable on the second shot with a long iron, and the eighteenth with its awkward tee shot. Watson drove first at the seventeenth and sent his ball down the center of the fairway. Nicklaus hit a longer drive but shoved the ball slightly to the right, and it came to rest in light rough. Watson played the first approach shot, a three-iron that produced a flag-seeking missile. The ball bounced just short of the green and leapt onto the putting surface and past the flag. Just beyond the hole, Watson's ball hit an uphill slope and curled back toward the cup. When the ball stopped rolling, it was twelve feet from the hole.

Nicklaus could tell from the reaction of the crowd that Watson's ball was very close. The pressure was fully on Nicklaus now. His ball was sitting nicely in the rough, and since he could count on it to bounce forward like Watson's, Nicklaus chose a four-iron for the shot. Nicklaus was such a pure long-iron player that it was almost a certainty he'd put the ball on the green. As soon as he struck the ball, however, his body language announced that he pushed the shot. He caught too much of the ground with the club, and the weak shot drifted short and right of the green. For a moment as the ball was in flight, Nicklaus leaned away from the green with the four-iron in the position of a fisherman pulling in the big one. Then he looked ruefully at the ground where the ball had been only seconds before.

By the time Nicklaus reached his ball, he had put the heavy four-iron out of his mind. He knew it was far from certain that Watson would make his putt, and that he still had an excellent chance to make his own birdie. To get it, he would have to play a deft running chip shot over two ridges in the green; playing a soft, high shot was out of the question. The ground was too hard to slip the club underneath the ball, and if he failed to carry the second ridge the ball would stop almost immediately, leaving him too far from the hole for a reasonable chance at birdie. Over the years, when critics tried to identify a weak spot in Nicklaus's game it was inevitably stated that his short game was only average for a player of his eminence. Surely, that aspect of his game was weaker than the other elements—and nowhere near in the same league as Watson's short game—but it was not horrid, and at the seventeenth he played a clever little shot that demonstrated he could play *any* shot a situation demanded. With a middle-iron, Nicklaus bumped the ball low along the ground. It was airborne for only a second, and then trickled up one ridge and then the next and, finally, stopped three feet from the hole.

Watson had rolled the ball confidently all day on the greens, but he did not make an aggressive try at the eagle; the ball wandered down in the vicinity of the hole, but never threatened to fall. Watson cleaned up what was left and was in with a birdie four.

Nicklaus felt his three-foot putt would move just a shade to the right as it neared the hole, but he was wrong. The putt stayed out to the left, never even grazing the edge. For the second day in a row, Nicklaus missed a rather simple putt at the seventeenth green without even scaring the hole. For the first time in four days, Tom Watson held the outright lead in the Open Championship.

It was an enormous advantage for Watson to have the honor of playing first at the final hole. If he could just keep his ball in play and out of trouble, he was assured of a playoff at the very least. Angelo Argea had noticed there wasn't much conversation in the group all day. "Jack and I didn't talk much," said Argea, "and neither did Watson and Alfie. It was pretty much all business out there." As they made their way to the tee of Ailsa Home, Fyles spoke a single sentence to his Mister. "Go for the jugular," said Fyles. Watson nodded the slightest of nods in agreement, and tore the heart out of a one-iron from the tee that found the fairway.

Watson's shot forced Nicklaus's hand; the strategy that won Nicklaus so many major championships—that of letting things come to him—did not apply now. Nicklaus could leave nothing in reserve, and he asked Argea for the driver. "We had hit the one-iron there all week," said Argea. "But Jack felt like if he could bust a long one over the corner of the bunkers, he would only have a short shot in. He was playing for birdie."

Argea took his notes from his pocket: #18 228 to 260 OVER.

"Two-sixty to clear 'em," said Argea as he handed the club to Nicklaus.

The fact that he was the longest, straightest driver in the game's history could not hide the fact that Nicklaus's big club had betrayed him over the past two days. "He was not driving the ball well," said Watson. "At the beginning of the round, he'd hit his tee shot on the second hole into the third fairway. He was trying to hit a fade and hit a double-cross. Of course, he birdied the hole."

Nicklaus blocked his final tee shot far to the right.

"It was a wild shot," said Watson, and according to Argea, "It was going right as soon as it left the clubface."

Nicklaus instantly knew it was a poor strike. He looked up for only a second, the turned his back to the ball and looked off into the distance across the now empty course. He then turned back toward the ball and stood on the tee looking at the ground. By the time he started walking, Watson was halfway to his own ball. Years later, Nicklaus said he didn't recall much about the shot.

The bad swing wasn't the half of Nicklaus's problems. The ball had made a beeline for the gorse on the right side of the fairway. When Argea arrived at the ball, he was shaken. "That gorse had horns on it," said Argea. "His ball wasn't in the gorse, but it was in the thickest rough on the whole course." The gorse was a factor, however; a renegade branch stuck out behind Nicklaus's ball, directly in the path of his backswing. (George Brown, the current-day greens superintendent at Turnberry, explained why the patch where Nicklaus's ball landed was so deep in comparison to the burned-out rough in other places on the course: "His ball was on the edge of the north-facing gorse bushes," said Brown. "That spot was less exposed to the sun and drying winds.")

Watson played first, but years later recalled that "I walked over to where Nicklaus's ball was because I wanted to see what his position was over there. At first I thought he might be in the gorse, but his ball had stopped about two inches short of it in some heavy rough. The first thing I thought to myself was, 'He's not dead yet.' It wouldn't have affected my shot if he had been in the gorse, but I wanted to know what my options were. When I walked over to my ball, I still felt like he had a shot."

The mass of spectators had moved in behind Watson and Nicklaus now, a wall of bodies clear across the fairway restrained by a waist-high rope held by two stewards. Fyles reminded Watson to consider the adrenaline pumping through the golfer's body as he made his club selection. Watson chose a seven-iron. "I had 178 to the hole," said Watson.

It was a surreal scene that embraced Watson as he prepared to play. The sun was at his back, the white hotel with its cinnamon-colored roof sprawled across the ridge as a backdrop to the green. The grandstands to both sides were packed with 8,000 bodies. To the back left, the arm of a giant hydraulic crane was bent at a severe angle, a BBC camera perched at its tip appearing to be directly over the green. Seagulls hovered overhead, and the yellow flag blew gently over the hole. "I hit the ball as solid as I could," said Watson. A blast of dust rose from the ground at the impact of the club, just as it had for players all week. "The ball started a little left of the hole and just kind of stayed straight," said Watson. "When it hit on the green and rolled up by the hole the people cheered loudly, but I didn't know how close it was. I thought it was maybe five feet from the hole, but it was hard to tell because it was so bright out. It was one of those shots you love, though, because the closer I got to the green, the closer the ball got to the hole."

The ball stopped just two feet from the hole. "I was standing behind the green," said Ben Crenshaw. "I remember that Tom made such an authoritative swing at that ball in the fairway, and the reaction of the crowd was fabulous."

If the situation looked grim for Nicklaus after the tee shots, it was now dire. Like Watson, who lived by the credo that if you quit once there's always a chance you might do it again, there was not a trace of surrender on Nicklaus's face. He made several slow practice takeaways to be certain that his club could get underneath the overhanging branch. Behind the green in an R&A tent, Tommy Horton watched on a television monitor along with some other players. (He cannot recall who they were.) "I saw his ball at the edge of that bush," said Horton, "and I thought, 'Well, as long as he can swing beneath the lowest branch of that gorse bush, he can get this very near the green. He might have to take a slightly flatter swing, but I felt if anyone could fashion the needed swing, it was him. He had the best golfing brain ever. Other guys had golf swings that were pretty, but Nicklaus was able to focus on the only thing that mattered at a given moment: playing the best shot he possibly could."

Nicklaus had a yardage of just more than 160 yards to the hole, and he had an eight-iron in his hands. He needed the loft to get the ball free of the tangled grass, but he would have to make a mighty swing. All was quiet as he steadied himself to play the shot. Then there was the cocking of the head away from the ball. On a normal swing with an eight-iron, a professional golfer takes the club back to about a point where the shaft of the club is perpendicular to the ground or just a tad beyond. Nicklaus drew the club back to fully parallel—the length of a swing with the driver—and lashed into the ball. From his BBC position near the green, Peter Alliss called the swing "animalistic." The lead edge of Nicklaus's club acted like a scythe, and it disinterred a large clump of grass at the roots. The now dead grass clung to the club until he completed his follow-through, only then falling to the ground.

"I was watching from across the fairway," said Watson. "And sure enough, the ball came out of that stuff like a normal shot, like only Jack could do it. He was the best rough player who ever played the game, no question about it."

Nicklaus could not see the ball finish its flight. The instant he struck the shot, the stewards behind him dropped the ropes and the crowd rushed in. "They were running full tilt the second he hit the shot," said Watson. Nicklaus could only listen, and in a moment the greenside arena exploded with noise. Somehow, someway, Nicklaus had muscled the ball onto the front right edge of the green, thirty-five feet from the hole set on the back of the green.

"At that moment," said Horton, "I looked at the other players around me and said, 'How does he do it?' But they couldn't hear me. I could barely hear the words coming out of my mouth as I spoke."

IT IS CUSTOMARY in Britain for a bridegroom to fill a pocket with coins before the wedding ceremony. Just before the newly married couple pull away from the church in their shiny car, the groom tosses the coins into the crowd of cheering friends and family. It is a symbol of good luck. (It's an old custom; fans of the 1995 movie *Sense and Sensibility* will remember that in the final scene, the new groom tosses gold pieces into the air while seated in a horse-drawn carriage.)

Among the British people, the Scots are the most frugal, and the joke goes that the wedding coin toss is the only time you'll see a Scotsman throw money away. But as the crowd of Scots surged toward the green after Jack Nicklaus played his approach, some lingered staring in awe at the gash Nicklaus left behind in the ground. First one coin was dropped into the gash, then others followed until a small pile of coins lay in the divot in the hope they might coax a miracle from the Fates.

It was bedlam now, the golfers and their caddies having been engulfed in the Open charge. "They ran over Alfie," said Watson. "He put out his arm to break his fall, and he sprained his wrist and broke his watch."

In the grandstands, fifteen-year-old Philip Jonas watched wide-eyed. "You couldn't see the players at all through the crowd," said Jonas. "And then suddenly, Watson popped out into view, and then his caddie, and then a few seconds later, Nicklaus and his caddie. I wanted desperately for Nicklaus to make that putt." Somewhere in the same crowd was a teenager named Brian Gunson, who would one day become the head golf professional at Turnberry. "I can't really put into words what it felt like to be there and see it all happen," said Gunson years later. "It felt like electricity was running through my body."

Fyles, recovered for the moment, looked his man in the eye as they approached the green. "Well, sir, you've got him now," said Fyles to Watson.

Watson replied, "Alf, no I don't."

Years later, Watson recalled that Fyles "looked at me almost cross-eyed. And then I said, 'We have to expect him to make this putt.' He looked at me again like I was crazy."

Watson slid a coin under his ball to mark its position near the hole and backed away as Nicklaus prepared to play. Angelo Argea moved in to tend the flag. "I got a sick feeling when I saw how close Watson's marker was," said Argea years later. "I kept looking at that coin, and it looked like it was moving closer and closer to the hole. I think I was hallucinating."

Looking on, Tommy Horton recalled that he once played with Nicklaus and Hale Irwin in an exhibition match and watched in amazement as the great man holed a forty-foot putt at the final green for an eagle. It was not so much the putt that amazed Horton as it was that before he struck it, Nicklaus bet Irwin that he would make it. "Afterwards," said Horton, "I asked Jack, 'How do you *do* that?' "

"Sometimes," said Nicklaus to Horton, "you get a feeling and you can condition yourself to remember that feeling from the last time you had it."

"I had that feeling," said Nicklaus about his putt at the final hole of the 1977 Open. "The putt was thirty-five feet across the green with some break in it, and I just knocked it in the hole." As the ball slid down, Nicklaus jabbed the air with his putter in his trademark style.

Horton remembers those around him averring that it had been a lucky stroke. "There was no luck about it," said Horton.

"Sure enough," said Watson years later, "Jack sinks that putt and the crowd goes ape. The roar was deafening. As I remarked my ball, the crowd was still going wild. As I lined up my putt, the crowd was *still* going wild. Then Jack put his hands up to quiet the crowd."

It has been suggested in the ensuing years that when Nicklaus's ball went in the hole it suddenly made Watson's remaining two-footer look like a mile. On the final green at St. Andrews in 1970, Doug Sanders had shown that even the shortest of putts could be missed when the Open Championship hung in the balance. On that day, seven summers previous, the pressure had a visible physical effect on Sanders. Facing that short putt, he looked like a man about to vomit. The queasiness was almost assuredly heightened for Sanders because his putt was not just to win the Open, but to beat Jack Nicklaus as well. Perhaps if Watson had not come through at the Masters against Nicklaus just a few months earlier, he too would have had the seasick look that overtakes someone who suddenly realizes a defining moment in their lives is upon them. Instead, said Watson, "I just took a couple of quick practice strokes and knocked it in the hole." Watson raised both arms into the air in triumph as the noise rained down upon him. After a quick congratulatory hug from Fyles, Watson was face-to-face with Nicklaus. Together, the two had taken the old championship to a place never before imagined and never equaled since. Nicklaus threw his arm around Watson's shoulder and in doing so revealed his true nature to anyone watching. He did not pout nor have the slightest look of dejection. With the soft light giving his blond hair and yellow sweater an almost heavenly shine, Nicklaus walked arm and arm with Watson to the scoring tent.

"I can't remember exactly what I said," recalled Nicklaus twenty-five years later, "but it was something like, 'Well done, you little S.O.B.' Or something affectionate like that, because I like Tom and he had beaten me. He smiled back and said, 'I got you this time.' I think that's what is great about the game of golf. Guys beat on each other's heads all day and then walk off the eighteenth green arm in arm."

Looking on, Barbara Nicklaus knew to expect nothing less from her man. "It takes a special person to lose graciously," she said twenty-five years later. "Jack has always been a gracious loser. His father told him at age eleven to 'Keep your head up, look the person in the eye, and say congratulations—and mean it.' For his entire career, Jack has been gracious in defeat. Also, there is a difference between losing a tournament and someone winning a tournament. Tom Watson won that tournament. You can prepare for an event and then play your best, but sometimes someone simply plays better. That's what happened at Turnberry."

The final scorecards looked like this:

$$\text{Par: } 4\text{-}4\text{-}4\text{-}3\text{-}4\text{-}3\text{-}5\text{-}4\text{-}4 = 35 \quad 4\text{-}3\text{-}4\text{-}4\text{-}4\text{-}3\text{-}4\text{-}5\text{-}4 = 35 = 70$$
$$\text{Nicklaus: } 4\text{-}3\text{-}4\text{-}2\text{-}4\text{-}3\text{-}5\text{-}4\text{-}4 = 33 \quad 4\text{-}3\text{-}3\text{-}4\text{-}4\text{-}3\text{-}4\text{-}5\text{-}3 = 33 = 66$$
$$\text{Watson: } 4\text{-}5\text{-}4\text{-}3\text{-}3\text{-}3\text{-}4\text{-}3\text{-}5 = 34 \quad 4\text{-}3\text{-}4\text{-}3\text{-}4\text{-}2\text{-}4\text{-}4\text{-}3 = 31 = 65$$

IF A VISITOR TO TURNBERRY needed any reminder that he was at a very special place, it would strike him late in the day when the haunting strains of a lone bagpipe drift across the links and through the open windows of the hotel. With the championship won, Tom Watson was changing for dinner at the hotel when he heard the music. "I remember," said Watson years later, "hearing that lone piper crank up his octopus. And I looked out the window and he was walking across the terrace in front of the hotel. It was a wonderful sight to see. The stands, now emptied, the early evening sun . . . to see that happen with a glass of champagne in hand and understanding that you had just won against the best player who had ever played the game . . . that was a great feeling. That was when I fell in love with golf. I'd always loved it, but from that point forward it was a stronger love."

After the press interviews and other postround commitments were completed, Jack Nicklaus was approached by his friend and business colleague Ken Bowden. The Nicklauses planned on having dinner at the hotel with Bowden and his wife, Jean, but now Bowden suggested that perhaps Jack would like to cancel dinner in favor of a quiet evening with Barbara.

"What's the matter, Ken?" said Nicklaus. "Don't you want to eat?"

"I was just thinking of your feelings right now," said Bowden.

"You'd better go get cleaned up for dinner," said Nicklaus. "After all, Kenny, it's only a game."

As it turned out, the applause was not yet finished for Nicklaus and Watson. They arrived separately to the Turnberry Hotel dining room, and for each the people in the room rose as one to applaud them. Looking back wistfully, waiter Hubert Laforge recalled the moment in his French-flavored English. "It was a magical evening," said Laforge, "when those two arrived the whole room burst into cheers. They were both dressed impeccably."

The first to congratulate Watson and Nicklaus at their respective tables was Ben Crenshaw. "I just wanted to tell them what a thrill it had been to watch that magnificent battle," said Crenshaw, "and to tell them it was a shame somebody had to lose."

"Those were different days," said Laforge. "Olden days. And it is always sad to see the olden days go, no?"


DOWN THE ROAD a few miles from Turnberry in Girvan, Angelo Argea was having a drink at the Swee Inn. The pub was overflowing with spectators from Turnberry and others who watched on the BBC. Argea, with his distinctive gray Afro and mustache, could not go unnoticed. One of the pint-drinkers finally screwed up the nerve to ask Argea a question.

"Did you help Jack with the line for that putt at the seventeenth?" asked the man.

"I never read putts," said Argea. "And just remember, Jack's made his share of those."

Twenty-five years later, Argea shook his head and said, "I'm still a good reader of greens. I really wish Jack would have asked me sometimes."

# AFTERWORD

★

Final scores and prize money, 106th Open Championship, Turnberry Hotel, Ailsa Course

| | |
|---|---|
| Tom Watson, U.S., 68-70-65-65—268 | £10,000 |
| Jack Nicklaus, U.S., 68-70-65-66—269 | £8,000 |
| Hubert Green, U.S., 72-66-74-67—279 | £6,000 |
| Lee Trevino, U.S., 68-70-72-70—280 | £5,000 |
| Ben Crenshaw, U.S., 71-69-66-75—281 | £4,250 |
| George Burns, U.S., 70-70-72-69—281 | £4,250 |
| Arnold Palmer, U.S., 73-73-67-69—282 | £3,750 |
| Raymond Floyd, U.S., 70-73-68-72—283 | £3,500 |
| Tommy Horton, Eng., 70-74-65-75—284 | £2,875 |
| Johnny Miller, U.S., 69-74-67-74—284 | £2,875 |
| John Schroeder, U.S., 66-74-73-71—284 | £2,875 |
| Mark Hayes, U.S., 76-63-72-73—284 | £2,875 |
| Peter Thomson, Aus., 74-72-67-73—286 | £2,200 |
| Howard Clark, Eng., 72-68-72-74—286 | £2,200 |
| Guy Hunt, Eng., 73-71-71-72—287 | £1,350 |
| Bobby Cole, S. Afr., 72-71-71-73—287 | £1,350 |
| Peter Butler, Eng., 71-68-75-73—287 | £1,350 |
| Jerry Pate, U.S., 74-70-70-73—287 | £1,350 |
| S. Ballesteros, Spain, 69-71-73-74—287 | £1,350 |
| Graham Marsh, Aus., 73-69-71-74—287 | £1,350 |
| Bob Shearer, Aus., 72-69-72-74—287 | £1,350 |
| Tom Weiskopf, U.S., 74-71-71-72—288 | £687 |
| Gary Player, S. Afr., 71-74-74-69—288 | £687 |
| Peter Dawson, Eng., 74-68-73-73—288 | £687 |
| John Fourie, S. Afr. 74-69-70-75—288 | £687 |

Gaylord Burrows, U.S., 69-72-68-80—289          £448
Roger Maltbie, U.S., 71-66-72-80—289          £448
Rik Massengale, U.S., 73-71-74-71—289          £448
David Ingram, U.K., 73-74-70-72—289          £448
Martin Foster, Eng., 67-74-75-73—289          £448
Angel Gallardo, Spain, 78-65-72-74—289          £448
John O'Leary, Ireland, 74-73-68-74—289          £448
Noiro Suzuki, Japan, 74-71-69-75—289          £448
Eamonn Darcy, Ireland, 74-71-74-71—290          £380
Ken Brown, Scot., 74-73-71-72—290          £380
Brian Barnes, Scot., 79-69-69-74—291          £345
Hsieh Min-Nan, Taiwan, 72-73-73-73—291          £345
Manuel Pinero, Spain, 74-75-71-71—291          £345
Baldovino Dassu, Italy, 72-74-72-73—291          £345
J.D. Morgan, U.K., 72-71-71-77—291          £345
Neil Coles, Eng., 74-74-71-73—292          £310
David Vaughan, U.K., 78-72-71-72—292          £310
Jamie Gonzalez, U.S., 78-72-71-72—293          £285
Tony Jacklin, Eng., 72-70-74-77—293          £285
Bob Charles, N.Z., 73-72-70-78—293          £285
Stewart Ginn, Aus., 75-72-72-75—294          £272
Hale Irwin, U.S., 70-71-73-80—294          £272
Roberto De Vicenzo, Arg., 76-71-70-78—295          £257
Vincente Fernandez, Arg., 75-73-73-74—295          £257
Brian Huggett, Eng., 72-77-72-74—295          £257
Michael King, U.K., 73-75-72-75—295          £257
Christy O'Connor, Jr., Ireland, 75-73-71-77—296          £250
James Farmer, U.K., 72-74-72-78—296          £250
Rodger Davis, Aus., 77-70-70-79—296          £250
Brian Waites, U.K., 78-70-69-79—296          £250
Maurice Bembridge, Eng., 76-69-75-77—297          £250
Vincent Tshabalala, S. Afr., 71-73-72-81—297          £250
Ian Mosey, U.K., 75-73-73-77—298          £250
David Jones, U.K., 73-74-73-78—298          £250
Hsu Chi-San, Taiwan, 70-70-77-81—298          £250
Gary Jacobsen, U.S., 74-73-70-81—298          £250
Nick Faldo, Eng., 71-76-74-78—299          £250
Silvano Locatelli, Italy, 72-72-76-79—299          £250
Vin Baker, S. Afr., 77-70-73-79—299          £250

JUST AFTER THE 1977 Open at Turnberry, Herbert Warren Wind wrote the following in *The New Yorker:* "Everything being equal, the British Open should be back at Turnberry in about seven years. By that time, we should have a much better idea whether Tom Watson is just a very talented golfer or a great golfer. While he is different from Bobby Jones in many ways, there is in him more than just a touch of Jones. In seven years, Jack Nicklaus will be forty-four, and yet I wouldn't be at all surprised if at that distant date this prodigious athlete still loomed as a serious contender for the championship."

Wind was the most straightforward reporter of golf in the second half of the twentieth century, and the bit of clairvoyance at the end of that paragraph is out of character in his writing. It is also accurate to the point of being eerie.

There is no suggestion in this book that his defeat at Turnberry marked the end of the major-championship line for Jack Nicklaus. It did mark the end of his reign as the most consistently dominant individual in the game, but there were still many weeks to come when the name NICKLAUS would appear on a leaderboard and bring to mind what Winston Churchill had said of Hindenburg: "The name itself is massive."

When the Open was played at St. Andrews in 1978, it was Jack Nicklaus who strode up the eighteenth fairway the final day to claim the claret jug. It was a terrific moment in his career, with fans cheering him not only from the course but also from the windows of the buildings alongside the length of the eighteenth hole at the Old Course. There were so many such moments in Jack Nicklaus's career that no single one can be pointed to as the crowning moment. It is safe to say, however, that only a moment still eight years in the future surpassed the one he had marching up that fairway at St. Andrews.

Left behind Nicklaus on the scoreboard that week at St. Andrews were Ben Crenshaw, Raymond Floyd, Tom Kite, and New Zealander Simon Owen. For Crenshaw and Floyd, card-carrying members of the Next Nicklaus club, it was just one more reminder that there could only be one Nicklaus. The Scots surely knew this, and if the reason they hung out of windows was because they sensed that was to be the great man's final Open victory, they were correct. To twist latter-day sports parlance, that victory completed a "three-peat" of the professional major championships for Nicklaus. He won them each at least three times. No other player in history had won each of the big four even twice.

In 1979, Jack Nicklaus had the worst year of his professional career up to that point. He played in only thirteen events in the U.S., and the only serious challenge he mounted in the majors was at the Open Championship, where along with Crenshaw he finished three shots behind the winner, Ballesteros. For the first time in his career, Jack Nicklaus finished out of the top ten on the American money list. From 1962 to 1978 he had finished lower than third on that list only twice: He was ninth in 1970 and fourth in 1978. In 1979 he ranked seventy-first in earnings. Suggestions abounded that finally, after seventeen years as a professional, Nicklaus was washed up. That was all Nicklaus needed to hear. In 1980 he roared back, winning the U.S. Open in a duel with Isao Aoki of Japan (who just missed the fifty-four-hole cutoff at the 1977 Open). Later in the summer, Nicklaus lapped the field in winning his fifth PGA Championship.

In the ensuing years, Nicklaus gave way to the younger generation, but still he was not through in the major championships. On a sunny April Sunday in 1986, at the age of forty-six, Nicklaus covered the back nine at Augusta National in thirty strokes and won the Masters for the sixth time. It was a scintillating charge that stood the crowd on its collective ear. It was too much for Ballesteros, Norman, and Tom Kite, who crumbled under the pressure.

In 2000 Nicklaus played in all four of the major championships in the same season for the final time. His record in those tournaments over forty years was one of the finest in twentieth-century sports: eighteen victories, nineteen runner-up finishes, and twelve third-place finishes. Few figures in the history of sport are clearly and inarguably the best ever at their chosen pursuit. Pele, Michael Jordan, Wayne Gretzky, and Nicklaus are four who come closest to that status. Without question, Nicklaus remains the top golfer in history. Many believe Tiger Woods will eventually supplant Nicklaus in that position, but if that indeed does occur, it is still many years in the future.

Two of the eighteen runner-up finishes Nicklaus had in major championships came after 1980, at the '81 Masters and the '82 U.S. Open. The winner on both occasions was Tom Watson.


IF NICKLAUS was the Ailsa Craig of the major championships—immovable and unassailable—Tom Watson was the celestial fireball that collided with the rock. His victory at Turnberry marked the moment Watson knew, in his own words, "that I belonged." From 1977 through the next seven years, Watson ruled the professional game. He was the U.S. PGA Player of the Year in 1977, '78, '79, '80, '82, and '84, and during that run he won twenty-nine tournaments, including four Open Championships, one U.S.

Open, and two Masters. His win at the '82 U.S. Open, which was clinched by a dramatic pitch-in for birdie at the seventy-first hole, thwarted Nicklaus's chance at a record-setting fifth U.S. Open title.

Just two years later, Watson pursued a record-tying victory of his own. After winning the 1980, '82, and '83 Open Championships, Watson was looking for a third straight Open title in 1984 at St. Andrews; had he won it would have tied him for the most Open titles with Harry Vardon. On the seventy-first hole of that championship at the Old Course's confounding Road Hole, Watson played an aggressive long-iron shot toward the narrow green. He was chasing Ballesteros, who was playing just ahead of him. As Watson's ball landed, he held his hands out to the side, palms facing up. He couldn't tell what had happened to the ball, and his body language was asking the crowd to hint at his fate. The spectators were quiet. By now Watson had become a hero in his own right to the Scottish fans, and they were disappointed that his ball had bounded over the green, across the footpath that gives the hole its name, and up against a stone wall. Up ahead, Ballesteros was holing a short birdie putt at the final green. In that moment, the fireball flamed out.

Watson won three American tour events in 1984 and then went winless until the final tournament of the season in 1987. He did not win a tournament again until 1996, when he was forty-six years old. Fittingly, that drought-ending victory came at the event Nicklaus founded, the Memorial Tournament.

Watson's career record in the major championships over the ten years from 1975 to 1984 included eight victories, five runner-up finishes, and a single third-place finish. One of the runner-up finishes was in the 1978 PGA Championship at Oakmont, which he lost in a playoff to John Mahaffey. (Jerry Pate was also in the playoff.) It was Watson's best ever finish in that tournament, the only professional major championship that eluded him. The Open Championship was the base of Watson's superb record over his ten-year prime, and his eight major professional championship victories are exceeded, as of this writing, by only Nicklaus, Walter Hagen (eleven), and Ben Hogan and Gary Player (nine each). When Watson finished in the top ten in the 2000 PGA Championship at age fifty, it was the forty-fifth such finish for him in a major championship. Only Sam Snead (forty-six) and Nicklaus (seventy-three) finished in the top ten in the majors more often.


THE BIG YELLOW SCOREBOARD next to the green at Ailsa Home told not only the story of the 106th Open Championship, but of a game in transition as well. Regarding the championship that had just concluded, the tale of the board was a whopper. Tom Watson set a new Open record with 268. The record Watson beat, 276, was established in 1962 by Arnold Palmer at Old Troon and tied by Tom Weiskopf in 1973 on the same course. Watson bettered that record by eight strokes, and Nicklaus had shaved it by seven himself. It is duly noted that par for four rounds at Ailsa was 280 as compared to 288 at Troon, but that does not dilute the record set by Watson when one considers that the player in third place, U.S. Open champion Hubert Green, was at 279, *eleven* strokes behind Watson and *ten* behind Nicklaus. Excluding Watson and Nicklaus, the sixty-two players who made the cut required a grand total of exactly 18,000 strokes to play four rounds over Ailsa. That works out to an average score of slightly more than 290, or ten over par.

Two logical questions arise in light of the numbers posted by Watson and Nicklaus: Why were they able to distance themselves so far from the field? And how was it that only one other player managed to break par over four days? When asked the first question, every person interviewed for this book proposed a similar answer, specifically that Watson and Nicklaus fed off each other's emotions and level of play in a self-perpetuating manner that excluded the rest of the field simply because the two were playing together over the last two days. It was this phenomenon that moved Green to say the day after the championship, "I won the golf tournament. I don't know what game those two guys were playing."

And what about the second question: Why did only one other player, Green, manage to break par? The answer that makes the most sense is that Ailsa played difficult even without significant wind. The dry conditions made the ball difficult to control, and the lack of control was a severe strain on the patience of most players. "When you look at the two guys who played so well," said Tom Weiskopf years later, "you're looking at two enormously patient men. Easily the two most patient players I've ever seen."

The revelations of the big yellow board did not end with the obvious point that Watson and Nicklaus were the two best players in the world and that they had just concluded an incomparable duel. It was seventeen years since Arnold Palmer made his journey to St. Andrews as the lone American competitor of consequence, but the impact of that long ago trip was evident on the scoreboard, where the top eight finishers were all Americans, as were eleven of the first twelve. Only Tommy Horton's performance prevented an American sweep of the top ten. It was a high-water mark for American participation in the old championship. A total of nineteen American players survived both cuts and completed the championship. Only two Americans missed the cuts: Mark Lye was out after thirty-six holes, and Deray Simon was cut after fifty-four.

On the evening of July 9, 1977, it could be said that the Open Championship had fully reemerged as the game's world championship. A close look at the top seven names on the big board showed a definitive chain of champions who had led the Open back to the top of the major championship mountain. In seventh place, Palmer, who energized the Opens of the early 1960s with his charisma and popularity. In second place was Nicklaus, whose reputation as the greatest player ever owed much to the fact that his seminal moments as a champion were man-to-man struggles against Palmer. The short chain ended with Watson, who at age twenty-seven had earned his stripes as a player in head-to-head battle with Nicklaus. Palmer to Nicklaus to Watson, a succession of grit that invites the suggestion that Watson was the last great player to forge his legend while standing *in* the fire.

ONE MONTH after the 1977 Open Championship, Lanny Wadkins won the PGA Championship at Pebble Beach, which was every bit as burned out as Ailsa. Wadkins's win meant that the year's four major championships were swept by players—Watson, Green, and Wadkins—who all began their professional careers in the 1970s. In the 1960s, it took until 1969 for the same type of youth movement to sweep the majors. It did not occur at all during the 1950s.

It is only in retrospect, of course, that it can be said an era came to an end in 1977. The era that ended was one of towering figures, the "superguns" of which Johnny Miller spoke. The most gruesome sign that an era had concluded was provided by a man who was not a professional golfer. His name was Clifford Roberts, and he founded the Augusta National Golf Club and the Masters along with Bobby Jones. Roberts was a polarizing figure in the game; some thought him the dictator of the Masters, and Peter Alliss went so far as to call him a racist. (Though Roberts must have had some redeeming qualities as a man to be as close a friend as he was to Bobby Jones.) When Jones died in 1971, it left Roberts as the living symbol of the fourth modern major championship. On September 30, 1977, Roberts, suffering from cancer, walked alone out onto the Augusta National course, put a pistol to his head, and pulled the trigger.

The emerging new era was represented at Turnberry by Watson, Seve

Ballesteros, Nick Faldo, and Greg Norman. In that age golf fans watched the dominance of the major championships center around Watson, and then slip away from him to be redistributed equally around the globe. It would stay that way until Tiger Woods emerged at the turn of the century as the first dominant player since Tom Watson. Ballesteros was the soul of the movement that saw all of the game's major championships morph into international events. When he won the Masters in 1980 at age twenty-three, Ballesteros was the youngest ever winner *and* the first European do so. By the end of the 1980s, the Masters had been won by a Spaniard (Ballesteros in '80 and '83), a German (Bernhard Langer, '85), a Scot (Sandy Lyle, '88), and an Englishman (Nick Faldo, '89). Ballesteros, Lyle, and Faldo would also win four of the Open Championships played in the 1980s, and a fifth was won by Greg Norman. The U.S. Open and PGA Championship remained in the hands of Americans throughout the 1980s with the exception of the 1981 U.S. Open won by Australian David Graham. (Graham had lived in the U.S. since the early 1970s, however).

The broadening of golf's competitive base was also influenced in great part by a shift in the makeup of the teams in the Ryder Cup. That event's influence on international golf went from being negligible to enormous when the scope of the team opposing the Americans was expanded beyond Great Britain and Ireland to include all of Europe. That meant including Ballesteros and his deep well of emotion and belief that if he must he would beat the Americans single-handedly. The last year that Great Britain and Ireland played and lost alone in the Ryder Cup was 1977. The Americans won comfortably against the combined golf strength of Europe in '79 and '81, but by 1983 it was left to Lanny Wadkins to win the last hole of the last match to secure a one-point victory for the U.S. In 1985, a solid American team captained by Lee Trevino went to the Ryder Cup at the Belfry in England. The Europeans, led by Ballesteros, not only beat the Americans, they massacred them.

SHORTLY AFTER THE 1977 OPEN, Seve Ballesteros was back in his air force uniform. He served out the time due his country and went on to win five major championships: the 1979, 1984, and 1988 Opens, and the 1980 and '83 Masters. He never reconciled within himself the feeling of being snubbed by the American tour, and turned that feeling into a fury that inspired European Ryder Cup teams throughout the 1980s and 1990s as both a player and captain. His record in that event as a player was nineteen matches won, ten lost, and five halved. In 1997, he was the nonplaying captain when the Ryder Cup was played in Spain. His team hammered the Americans.

Greg Norman went on to become the most enigmatic player of his time. He won the Open Championship twice. The first time was in 1986, when the tournament returned to Turnberry for the first time since 1977. Norman had a marvelous run in the majors in 1986, holding the lead going into the final round in all four. This "Saturday Slam" was fraught with bizarre occurrences for Norman. At the Masters, he succumbed to the Nicklaus charge. In the U.S. Open, at Shinnecock Hills on Long Island, New York, Norman let a heckler in the crowd get the better of him on the early holes and dropped to twelfth place. He won at Turnberry, and the following month was the victim of his own collapse and a miracle shot at the PGA Championship, when Bob Tway holed out from a bunker on the final hole to win. In the very next major championship, the 1987 Masters, Norman lost in a playoff when Larry Mize ran in an improbable chip from all the way across the green at the second playoff hole. (Ballesteros was also in the playoff, but bogeyed the first extra hole to drop out.) Norman eventually finished second in eight major championships. His only other major victory came at the 1993 Open Championship at Royal St. George's, where he broke Watson's Open record with a score of 267.

Nick Faldo was the third main character of the immediate post-Watson era, and unquestionably the best of the three players. Faldo did not win a major championship until 1987, when he won the Open Championship at Muirfield; by then he was thirty years old. In the years between the 1977 Open and his win at Muirfield, Faldo overhauled his golf swing and worked feverishly at producing a solid and consistent game. The effort paid off handsomely, and Faldo was the closest thing to Ben Hogan modern golf fans had ever seen. He won the Open Championship again in 1990 and 1992, and won the Masters in 1989, '90, and '96. The last Masters victory for Faldo came as a result of yet another final-round collapse by Norman. During the early years of his career, Faldo was hounded by the British press for not living up to his potential and was the subject of a vicious newspaper headline that dubbed him *Nick Fold-o*. When he won the Open at Muirfield in 1992, Faldo said, "I have to thank the press from the bottom of my, well, from my bottom." It was the single cheekiest and most appropriate remark ever uttered by an Open champion.


ARNOLD PALMER, the man who went to the Open while his contemporaries stayed home because of financial worries, remains the most popular golfer in the game's history. At age seventy, he earned in the neighborhood of $18 million in product endorsement income.

THE WEEK AFTER THE 1977 OPEN, Lin and Joan Maltbie went to France to visit the family that saved Lin's life during World War II. The former fighter pilot wanted to give the family a gift, but they insisted that was unnecessary. In the end, he presented them with a clothes washer and dryer. He'd noticed the farmers didn't have those modern appliances in their house.

Roger Maltbie did not return to the Open in 1978; instead he played in the Quad Cities tournament on the American tour. That week, he met his future wife. The only time he returned to the Open was in 1986, when it was once again at Turnberry. In other years, he preferred to play at Quad Cities since it was his wife's hometown. After his playing career ended, he became one of the best analysts of the game on American television. He worked for the NBC network, which also employed Johnny Miller, whose straight-talking style made him the premier analyst of golf on television. Miller's 1976 Open title was his second and final major victory. It was one more than that of another Next Nicklaus, Tom Weiskopf: the 1973 Open at Troon was Weiskopf's sole major championship win. When he quit playing competitively, Weiskopf became one of the world's finest golf course architects.

In 1985, Hubert Green won the PGA Championship at Cherry Hills, the same course where Palmer won the U.S. Open. After completing his final round at Turnberry in 1977, he went up to the hotel to watch the finish on television. He played in the Open Championship "every year I was eligible, even though there was no money in it back then. It cost a fortune to go over there, and if you didn't finish in the top ten, you lost money." Years later he recalled that he thought the players "got shafted pretty well" in regard to the cost of staying at the Turnberry Hotel.

Mark Hayes never won again on the professional tour after 1977. He quit playing the tour full time in 1990. In later years, he designed golf courses and played on the Senior PGA Tour.

Ben Crenshaw never compiled the record that was expected of him, but he came to personify the gentlemanly nature of the game. He won the Masters in 1984 and 1995, and in 1999 captained the American Ryder Cup team to the most frantic comeback victory in that event's history. Crenshaw and Bobbie Millen became close friends, and Millen was a guest of Crenshaw's at the '99 Ryder Cup at The Country Club in Brookline, Massachusetts. When Crenshaw was named captain of that team, there was some suggestion in the British press that Crenshaw was soft, and that his team would be a pushover. "I tried to tell the writers," said Millen, "that there was a Texas grit about Ben that they weren't aware of."

Tommy Horton, Crenshaw's fellow competitor in the final round at Turnberry in 1977, never won a major championship. Horton considered his back-to-back finishes as low British player in 1976 and '77 to be the highlights of his playing career. In 2000 he was awarded the MBE, Order of the British Empire, for his services to golf.

THE 1977 OPEN CHAMPIONSHIP was the only major championship Gaylord Burrows ever played in. For years, a photo hung in the clubhouse bar at Turnberry with the images of Nicklaus, Watson, Lee Trevino, Gary Player, and Burrows. There was a standing bet for visitors that if they could name the five players in the photo, the first round of drinks was on the house. No one won the bet until 1980, when some friends of Burrows from Monroe, Louisiana, played a round at Turnberry. When offered the standard bet by the bartender, the players rattled off the five names without hesitation. The bartender looked at them in disbelief. "How in the world do you know Gaylord Burrows?" said the bartender.

"Hell, we play golf with him every Saturday," said one of them.

In 1995, Burrows was driving in Louisiana on what he described as a "bluebird morning" when an eighteen-wheeler smashed into his car. "I had thirty-seven broken bones and they were pretty certain I wouldn't live," said Burrows. Today, Burrows says that "when the temperature gets up around eighty-five degrees, my ribs don't hurt so much. I'll tell you, though, the fact that I didn't like to practice my golf sure shows now." Burrows and his wife run a service that helps care for senior citizens in the Monroe area.

Peter McEvoy had a revelation after being paired with Jack Nicklaus and Gary Player for the first two rounds at Turnberry. "It was the moment I decided I didn't want to turn professional," said McEvoy years later. "If I was going to be a pro, I didn't want to be a journeyman, I wanted to be like Nicklaus. After playing with Nicklaus, I started to understand that whatever it is that makes the really, really great player was missing in me. It wasn't something I wanted to accept, but there was just something there I knew I couldn't replicate." McEvoy continued playing as a successful amateur and today lives in England where his company, Sporting Concepts, specializes in golf course design and reconstruction. McEvoy has left his mark on "about twenty courses around Europe."

Philip Jonas turned professional in 1986 after attending Lamar University in the United States. Today he lives in Canada and plays on the Canadian professional tour and is the head professional at Vancouver Golf Club. He has won four events as a professional: the 1990 Goodyear Classic in South Africa, the 1996 and '97 Peru Opens, and the 2000 QuebecTel Open in Canada. He has never played in the Open Championship proper. "I tried to qualify for the 1986 Open at Turnberry," said Jonas years later, "but didn't make it. If I didn't live up to expectations, I'm still proud I persevered."

ALF FYLES NEVER RECOVERED from the wrist injury he suffered when he was trampled by the crowd on the eighteenth fairway at Turnberry. The stiffness in his wrist left him unable to play golf thereafter, but he worked the bag for Watson in all five of the player's Open Championship victories. His reputation as a great "eyeball" caddie and worthy assistant to his Mister was somewhat disputed in later years by one of his contemporaries who said, "Alfie couldn't club a caveman." Fyles died in March 1994.

Angelo Argea never caddied for Nicklaus again in the Open Championship. When Nicklaus won in 1978 at St. Andrews, Jimmy Dickinson was carrying the green-and-white MacGregor bag. Argea had his moments, however; he was with Nicklaus for both of the Golden Bear's major wins in 1980. "Those were the best," said Argea years later. Today he lives in West Palm Beach, Florida, where at seventy-one years old he "shoots between eighty-three and eighty-seven. When the money is up, I play pretty good," said Argea.

HUBERT LAFORGE NEVER LEFT TURNBERRY. Today he is the maitre d' in the dining room with the finest view of any in the world of golf. "I have made so many friends over the years," said Laforge. "Turnberry is the loveliest place. The sunsets alone have been worth it. If I can pass on the sense of continuity from myself to someone else, then I will have done my job."

After his first year as starter at the Open in 1975, Ivor Robson received a letter from Keith Mackenzie asking if he would remain in that position for the foreseeable future. He has been the starter for every Open since then. "It is the greatest honor in the world," said Robson. At Turnberry in 1977, he watched the climactic moments amid the crowd around the final green. Later that day, driving to his home in The Borders, Robson had to pull the car off the road and rest for a moment. He was emotionally drained from the week. Today, Robson is something of a celebrity on Europe's professional golf circuit, where he is the starter for all of the events. He is often approached by parents with their children seeking autographs. "The parents introduce me to the children as the 'man who starts the Open.' I sign every little scrap of paper they hand me. I have the greatest job in the world."


THE HEAT WAVE in that long ago July 1977 did not deter golf fans in the west of Scotland. The total attendance for the week at Turnberry's first Open was 86,167—the most people ever to watch an Open Championship in Scotland. On the Sunday following the championship, Norman Mair wrote in *The Scotsman* that "[86,167] is a figure which should go a long way in confirming Turnberry's place among the Open Championship venues." The Royal and Ancient agreed. In the ensuing years, Turnberry hosted the Open in 1986 (won by Norman with a score of 280) and in 1994 (won by Nick Price with 268).

In the 1986 Open, "we had rough like you've never seen before," said George Brown, who by then was working at Turnberry. "We had a very wet summer that year. It was just a freak of nature that it was so dry in 1977. We normally have a much damper climate here on the west coast than they do in, say, St. Andrews. Over there, they get about twenty inches of rain a year, which is about half of what we get. If there is one thing that is predictable on the west coast, it's that it's going to rain."

Mackenzie Ross died in 1974. He designed or rebuilt thirty or so courses in Europe, including work in the Azores, the Canary Islands, the Channel Islands, England, France, Northern Ireland, Portugal, Spain, and Wales. The only course of historic significance designed by Ross was Ailsa. Three years after his death, Ailsa was the site of a performance the wonderful English writer Peter Dobereiner reviewed as follows: "Tom Watson gets my prize for the best four consecutive rounds ever with his Open Championship victory at Turnberry in 1977, followed by the closest possible margin by Nicklaus, one stroke adrift in the same championship."

As of this writing, the Royal and Ancient has not decided when the Open will once again return to Turnberry.

# ACKNOWLEDGMENTS

★

THE AUTHOR IS INDEBTED TO THE FOLLOWING PEOPLE, all of whom graciously agreed to lend their insights to this story: Tom Watson, Jack Nicklaus, Barbara Nicklaus, Angelo Argea, Bobbie Millen, Arnold Palmer, Roberto De Vicenzo, Peter Thomson, Bob Toski, Tom Weiskopf, Ben Crenshaw, Tommy Horton, Mark Hayes, Johnny Miller, Hubert Green, Roger Maltbie, Gaylord Burrows, Philip Jonas, Peter Alliss, John Schroeder, John Philip, Vincente Fernandez, Nick Faldo, Peter McEvoy, Ivor Robson, Terry Jastrow, Hubert Laforge, Bradley Klein, George Brown, Sandy Tatum, and Brian Gunson.

THE IDEA FOR THIS BOOK came from my good friend Randy Voorhees, who always thought the 1977 Open was worthy of such a treatment. There is no way to accurately describe Randy's enthusiasm, encouragement, and inspiration during the time it took to write this book. I cannot thank him enough for his friendship.

Jeff Neuman, my editor at Simon & Schuster, was the person who took this book on faith. I thank Jeff for that and for his fine editing and that of his young colleague, Jonathan Malki. John Monteleone, my agent, and Mark Gola of Mountain Lion Inc., in Princeton, New Jersey, were exceedingly helpful and encouraging throughout the process.

The following people willingly helped with research for this book: Rand Jerris, Patty Moran, and Brett Avery, of the United States Golf Association; Elinor Clark, of the British Golf Museum; John Ledesma, Joseph Passov, Whitney Untiedt, Kristen Chanley, Guy Yocom, Geoff Russell, James "Scott" Burns, Jordan Matus, and Richard Donovan. Carol Alhadeff, the archivist at Janzen Swimwear, was also most helpful, as was Pat Donnelly, the bartender at the Harbour Bar in Girvan, Scotland. Greg McIsaac, a talented geologist, was happy to talk about giant rocks. Several uncommonly pleasant people at the National Library of Scotland in Edinburgh showed me how to find relevant information.

My travels to Scotland and Turnberry were made more enjoyable by the presence of my oldest pal, John Connelly, and two slightly newer pals, Tom Murphy and Tim Maloney. Debbie Phillips, of the Carnoustie Hotel, was helpful in our stay at that fabulous place.

The peerless staff of the Turnberry Hotel made staying there a feast for the soul. My special thanks to Ewen Bowman, Jennifer Rose Taylor, Euan Taylor, and especially to Brian Gunson, the golf professional, and his staff.

The following people all read and commented on parts or all of this manuscript: Joseph Passov, Ted Spiker, Eric Rinehimer, Bill Stump, Leslie Kirkpatrick, Tim Maloney, Randy Voorhees, Joe Bargmann, Jordan Matus, and John Monteleone. Alice Debus, a colleague from my days at *Men's Health* magazine, transcribed some of the interview tapes for me.

In Tom Watson's office, Kelly Fray endured endless contacts from me, and I thank her. In Jack Nicklaus's office, Scott Tolley and Kristen Diamond were very helpful.

AT THE TIME THAT Jack Nicklaus and Tom Watson were waging their duel in the Scottish sun at Turnberry, my brothers and I were caddies at Old York Road Country Club in Spring House, Pennsylvania. My brother Tim taught me how to caddie, and another of my four brothers, Jim, showed me how to play. Together, they taught me that golf was about more than striking the ball and carding the lowest possible score. Another of my brothers, Phil, used to take me to play on caddies' day and often let me use his clubs.

Finally, but not least: When I was a teenager, my uncle, Hank Fox, told me to take the wheel of his fishing boat while we were well out in the Atlantic Ocean. There was a problem with the engine, and he and my father and my cousin needed to deal with it. My response to my uncle's request was, "I can't do that."

He looked at me like I was crazy. "Don't ever say you can't do something," he said. Those words reinforced something my parents told me for as long as I can remember: "You can do anything." There is a subtle difference in those two phrases of encouragement. The words of my uncle stick with me to this day and remind me to never quit. The words of my parents make me believe all things are possible.

MICHAEL CORCORAN is a writer and editor whose multimedia experience includes magazines, books, radio, and video. He was editor-in-chief of *Golf Illustrated* and *Petersen's Golfing* and managing editor of ABC Sports/Jack Nicklaus Productions' *The Wide World of Golf* video series. Corcoran has written and edited for *Golf Digest* and *Men's Health*. He is author or coauthor of seven books, including *The PGA Tour Complete Book of Golf* (Henry Holt, 1999), and teaches magazine writing at Temple University in Philadelphia. He lives in Pennsylvania with his wife and three children.